# NAMIBIA'S RAINBOW PROJECT

# NAMIBIA'S RAINBOW PROJECT

Gay
Rights
in an
African
Nation

## ROBERT LORWAY

INDIANA UNIVERSITY PRESS
*Bloomington and Indianapolis*

This book is a publication of

Indiana University Press
Office of Scholarly Publishing
Herman B Wells Library 350
1320 East 10th Street
Bloomington, Indiana 47405 USA

iupress.indiana.edu

Telephone orders   800-842-6796
Fax orders   812-855-7931

© 2015 by Robert Lorway

Manufactured in the United States of America

Cataloging information is available from the Library of Congress.

ISBN 978-0-253-01514-3 (cloth)
ISBN 978-0-253-01520-4 (paperback)
ISBN 978-0-253-01527-3 (ebook)

1 2 3 4 5   20 19 18 17 16 15

*In loving memory of Sonia, Vincent, and Peter*

# Contents

# Acknowledgments

THIS PROJECT BEGAN with a series of questions about sexual health in southern Africa, questions that I was able to explore because of the generosity and mentorship of my dissertation adviser, Richard Borshay Lee. I will be forever grateful to him for providing me with the opportunity to study in Namibia. There are others at the University of Toronto to whom I owe a debt of gratitude. Sandra Bamford offered much intellectual guidance and encouragement throughout the early phase of my research. Her warmth and brilliance have left a lasting imprint on how I practice anthropology. I am also grateful to Bonnie McElhinny for challenging me both intellectually and politically as I formulated my study. I thank Michael Lambek for posing important theoretical questions that I explore in this book. Other fine minds at the University of Toronto shaped the way I conducted this research, including those of Hilary Cunningham, Hy Van Luong, Gavin Smith, and Holly Wardlow. I thank Stephen Brown, who is now at the University of Ottawa, for his always stimulating discussions with me on sexuality studies and social movements. My research in Namibia also gained much from sharing conversations, papers, and good-natured debates with Rinaldo Walcott. Studying with the social philosopher Brian Pronger was also an immense treat. His graduate seminar on the body and transcendence radically transformed the way I approached my research in Namibia.

In Toronto I had the good fortune of being surrounded by a circle of peers who were also completing their dissertations, including Marnie Bjornson, Saul Cohen, Irma Molina, Manuel Sevilla, Monir Moniruzzaman, Emma Varley, Jie Yang, and Jude Fokwang. I have learned much from hearing about their work and from the questions and ideas we discussed. A large debt of thanks is owed to my dear friend and intellectual comrade Maureen Murney, whose thoughtful comments at every stage of this project have been truly invaluable. I miss our regular excursions to the Toronto Women's Bookstore, which always left us broke but happy. Supervising anthropology and health science students in Namibia allowed me to learn from Ayaana Jean-Baptiste, Michael Callaghan, Melanie Campbell, Fotis Kanteres, Sandra Kendall, Ilona Kosova, Josh Lalour, Jing Jing Liu, Caitlin Mills, Nadia O'Brien, Jennifer Quinlan, Kate Rice, Nicole Rigillo, Alex Teleki, and Leonard Tooley.

Richard Parker, who kindly agreed to be my PhD examiner, invited me to Columbia University to present a significant portion of the work that appears in this book. My thinking greatly benefited from his feedback and the conversations

I had with other scholars working at the Mailman School of Public Health at that time, especially Mark Padilla, Theo Sandfort, and Robert Sember. My brief time spent at McGill University in Montreal for a postdoctorate degree gave me the chance to interact with a circle of thinkers who stimulated new questions about my research in Namibia. Immense gratitude is owed to my former postdoctoral adviser and dear friend, Vinh-Kim Nguyen. There aren't enough words to thank Vinh-Kim for sharing his insights, humor, bookshelves, and splendid meals with dynamic mixes of people. Through Vinh-Kim I made new intellectual companions whom I must thank: Emily Frank, Sean Brotherton, Kristin Peterson, and Jafari Allen. Emily's comments on earlier versions of this manuscript were particularly helpful in sharpening my thinking.

In 2008, thanks to the dean of the Faculty of Health Sciences, John O'Neil, I was fortunate to find an intellectual home for a short period at Simon Fraser University in Vancouver. There I benefited greatly from the generosity of faculty, especially Susan Erikson and Nicole Berry. Both gave tremendously insightful, detailed, and always constructive critical feedback on earlier drafts. At Simon Fraser I was also thrilled to have the chance to converse with Stacy Pigg and to learn from such an agile and creative mind. My current home at the University of Manitoba provides me with an exciting community of health researchers whose work both fascinates me and stimulates my intellectual interests in sexual health on a daily basis. I am particularly grateful for the intellectual camaraderie of Patricia Kaufert, Joe Kaufert, Sharon Bruce, Susan Frohlick, Stephen Moses, James Blanchard, and Deborah McPhail. I formed a particularly close intellectual friendship with Sushena Reza-Paul and Shamshad Khan. I am thankful to a number of graduate students at the Centre for Global Public Health, especially Claudyne Chevrier, Elsabé du Plessis, Anthony Huynh, Leigh McCarty, Souradet Shaw, and Laura Thompson, for their intellectual enthusiasm, inquisitiveness, and challenging questions.

I have been truly blessed to have had anonymous reviewers who provided close readings of earlier versions of my manuscript. They kindly identified themselves to me as Marc Epprecht, Karen M. Booth, and Paul Geschiere. Significant improvements from these earlier versions are the result of their extremely astute feedback. Any shortcomings in this book, however, lie solely with me. I was also very fortunate to have worked with the senior sponsoring editor at Indiana University Press, Dee Mortensen. Dee showed tremendous patience and wisdom in guiding me through the entire book production process. I am also grateful to the production staff, including Sarah Jacobi, Nancy Lightfoot, and Rhonda Van Der Dussen and copyeditor Jill R. Hughes, for their superb work in bringing this book to fruition.

I am of course most grateful to the Rainbow Youth and the staff of the NGOs (the Rainbow Project, Sister Namibia, the Legal Assistance Centre, and the Danish development organization known as IBIS) in Namibia who support the well-being of sexual minorities in Namibia and who facilitated many aspects of this project. Over the years I have conversed with and interviewed more than 240 members of the Rainbow Youth. I hope this book does justice to the time and energy they devoted in sharing their experiences and perspectives with me. Special thanks to the staff and volunteers of the Rainbow Project: Linda Baumann, Friedel Dausab, Florence ("Whoopi") Hanson, Madelene Isaacks, Carol Millward, Steve Scholtz, Ian Swartz, and the many others whose names I have omitted to protect their anonymity. For showing their supportive interest during my fieldwork, I am thankful to the following scholars: Dana-Ain Davis, Thomas Falk, Liz Frank, Kathe Hofne, Dianne Hubbard, Sckolastika Ippinge, Elizabeth Khaxas, Denise Moongo, Joshua Moses, Cheryl Mwaria, Annelie Odendaal, Michael Pröpper, Henriette Rispel, Mónica Ruiz-Casares, Ida Susser, Philippe Talavera, and Beatrice Zandelowski. During my stay in Walvis Bay, Stewart Langenhoven and Ricardo Amunjera were instrumental in helping me to conduct my research. Their friendship made the town feel like a second home to me. While in Keetmanshoop, Denise Moongo not only connected me to research participants but also helped me to think through the meanings of what I was observing in the town. Tangi Shiyuka facilitated almost every aspect of my study in Oshakati and Ongwediva. I also wish to thank Frank Fielding for assisting with my Afrikaans and Nama/Damara lessons and for lending a supportive ear during my research in Windhoek.

Financial support for this project was generously provided by the University of Toronto Doctoral Fellowship program, the Lorna Marshall Award in Cultural Anthropology, the Social Sciences and Humanities Research Council of Canada (SSHRC), and the Wenner-Gren Foundation for Anthropological Research. Portions of this book appear as revised versions of earlier manuscripts I published in *American Ethnologist; Medical Anthropology; Culture, Health, and Sexuality;* and a book chapter I published under the editorship of Douglas Feldman. I am thankful for the permission to reuse this work and for the feedback of its editors. Virginia Dominguez gave enormously helpful advice on publishing scholarly work that was instrumental to this book project.

Finally, I am deeply grateful for the emotional support of my family, especially my partner, Roger Grant; my mother, Celia; my sisters, Norah and Verne; and my brother, Charles. They have all loved and encouraged me throughout the process. I cannot imagine having completed this book without their unconditional support.

# Prologue:
# Approaching the Transnational

In JULY 2001 I walked into the feminist nongovernmental organization (NGO) known as Sister Namibia,[1] located just north of the central business district in Windhoek, capital of the Republic of Namibia, to access its gender resource library for medical anthropological research I was planning to undertake.[2] One of the young staff women, Anne, immediately asked, "Are you gay friendly?" to which I responded, "Well, I have a boyfriend in Canada." Anne, who was dressed in men's baggy pants and a long, loose T-shirt, with her hair styled in short dreadlocks, rushed excitedly to the back office and returned with a small, framed picture of her girlfriend. "She's my lover. . . . She's Damara like me," she said proudly. "I hear it is very gay friendly in Canada. Is it true that gay people there have their own town and even own their own businesses?" She went on to describe Toronto's gay village in some detail, bringing up a bookmarked web page of Church Street on the office computer. She seemed to know more about it than I did. Then she proceeded to teach me the proper pronunciation for the Damara word !gamas, which, she explained, referred to an animal (usually a goat) possessing both genitalia. I clumsily tried to articulate the click with my tongue when she said, "You hear some of the elders use this word [to refer to us] . . . but I know I am a lesbian!"

I continued to chat with Anne, explaining my interest in HIV prevention research. As a doctoral student at the time, my supervisor, Richard B. Lee, had invited me to assist with a research capacity–building project for the University of Namibia Faculty of Health Sciences, which involved methodological training on how to examine the social dimensions of the HIV epidemic. As I sat among students and faculty, not a single word about the same-sex transmission of HIV was uttered. This absence appeared striking to me at a time when the word "homosexuality" regularly seized front-page news headlines. Only a few weeks previously, the republic's president, Sam Nujoma, had publicly condemned the presence of gays and lesbians in Namibia—yet again.

After my explanation, Anne insisted on taking me to the main office and drop-in center of the LGBT (lesbian, gay, bisexual, transgender) rights NGO known as the Rainbow Project (TRP), assuring me that talking to members would be good for my research. "There are many gay men in the rainbow community that have died of AIDS," she told me. Restaurants, shopping centers, luxury hotels, gambling halls, bars, and a few discos surrounded TRP's center, which was located in the commercial district of Windhoek and within walking distance of the parliamentary grounds, government ministries, NGO offices, the police station, and other public institutions. After a warm introductory conversation, TRP's director, Ian Swartz, informed me that twenty of their members had tested HIV positive over the past year, and many others in this closely knit community worried that they too had contracted HIV. Then he showed me several pictures of young black men who had recently died from AIDS and said, "There is hardly any AIDS research on homosexuality in Namibia, or anywhere else in Africa for that matter!"[3] His face fell, and he grew silent. Regaining his composure, he continued: "Why not come to our meeting tonight? You must talk to our members about your research."

Later that evening the TRP director introduced me to a group of more than thirty "Rainbow Youth," as he called them, most of whom lived in the impoverished township of Katutura. Some of the young males were busily examining German pamphlets about safer sex, a gift from an older foreign supporter who recently had returned from a holiday in Frankfurt. The boys giggled at the sexually suggestive pictures of naked men. However, when the group began to talk about HIV and the rainbow community, a doleful tone filled the air. They began telling stories of family denial, rejection, and shame.

The atmosphere shifted again when the group turned its focus toward event planning—an upcoming poetry-reading night to be held at an upscale local bar that many of the more affluent Namibians and expatriates frequented. "I'm going to meet my future Dutch husband there and walk down the aisle in Amsterdam," said the shy seventeen-year-old Tuli, with dreamy eyes and a wide smile. Then, in a slightly more serious tone, Hanna, a young woman in the group who introduced herself as an LGBT-rights activist, asked me, "Robert, do you know any Canadian women who would like a Namibian lesbian like me?"

After the meeting I received three rather intense love letters and several offers for email pen pals from the young feminine males. I discovered over time that these same youths lavished similar attention upon most visiting gay foreigners. At the height of the ruling government's hate speeches, TRP became a focal point of international attention. The organization was deluged with letters and emails of support from across the globe. British, Dutch, German, and various African news media descended upon Namibia to cover the response to the hate speeches. Foreign journalists produced documentaries to spotlight local men and women's struggles with homophobia. And as TRP's visibility increased through numerous press releases and publicly staged political protests, gay and lesbian foreigners visiting and working in Namibia became closely affiliated with the organization. TRP offered plenty of opportunities and special events for local and foreign women and men to socialize. "We perform sort of a dating service here," the receptionist once told me with a grin. Much to my surprise, my initial fieldwork became entangled in this transnational economy of desires, as what happened during my very first preliminary interview illustrates.

One early Thursday afternoon, on a downtown sidewalk, I stood awaiting the arrival of Tuhaleni, a young member of TRP. He had contacted me because of his interest in the study, or so I thought. He kept sending text messages to my cell phone delaying the meeting time until it finally grew dark. When I returned his call, he suggested we meet up at TRP's office, where they were having a movie night, a screening of the Western queer cult classic *Bent*. I agreed.

I arrived to find Tuhaleni clad in a skintight black catsuit and large, chunky high-heeled boots. Slicked-back hair, bracelets, and makeup completed his ensemble. Fits of laughter came from the men and women attending the showing. My soon-to-be key informant, Hanna, took me aside and said, "*That one* is telling everyone that you are going on a date with him this evening." Feeling somewhat uneasy with this perception, the young man and I headed from TRP's center toward a nearby restaurant of his choice called Drös, where the more "high-end gays," as he called them, hung out. Sporting his catsuit, Tuhaleni certainly created a spectacle as we walked together down Independence Avenue. People's eyes widened as they passed us by on the street. Several derogatory comments were made, and some people looked at me, shaking their heads and turning up their faces in disapproval. But Tuhaleni seemed to relish all the attention. As we sat at the restaurant, he talked about all the places where he had performed drag, in Swakopmund, Johannesburg, Durban, and Cape Town, before crowds of admiring foreigners. His detailed stories continued relentlessly, to the point of excess, until they eclipsed any chance I would have to discuss my research project. Tuhaleni seemed far less interested in discussing HIV risk with me than finding out how he could migrate to Canada or the United States. The next day Hanna told me that Tuhaleni was known for making up stories and that now he was telling everyone that he and I were dating.

Hanna helped male research participants to realize that my interest in them was in examining their sexual risk practices, not the type of sexual interest shown by other foreigners. She became particularly interested in my research project because, as she explained, "I have lost many of my close gay friends to this disease." Eventually the confusion subsided. After a few months, as I came to know the Rainbow Youth well, I was invited into their homes to meet their families and friends. Toward the end of 2002, my fieldwork drifted from TRP and the Windhoek industrial area city core to the township of Katutura. There I came to share in the everyday lives of gays and lesbians in the *lokasies* (locations) of Goreangab, Damara, Nama, Herero, Hakahana, and Wanaheda. Although Katutura is considered part of Windhoek, it is located outside walking distance from the city's core, a result of the segregational urban planning practices of the early twentieth century.[4] For five Namibian dollars (approximately ninety cents

US), however, I moved about with participants between Windhoek and Katutura, taking the often dilapidated taxis, which several Afrikaners insisted were "the transportation system for blacks."

One of the reasons that these white Namibians claimed not to take these taxis was safety. Like many local people taking these taxis, I had the misfortune of being mugged on occasion while traveling alone. Some of the lesbians I worked with were quite vigilant about my safety as a foreigner traveling about Katutura, even at times when I was unconcerned with or unaware of potential threats. One event stands out in my memory. After sharing a taxi together, the driver dropped off Hanna at her home lokasie. Suddenly she began criticizing his choice of "*Vambos* [Oshivambo ethnic] music," and in a belligerent tone she continued to antagonize the driver, saying, "I know where your sister lives. I'm going to eat your sister. Yes, I will eat your sister!"

"Fucking *moffie* [queer]," the driver said after Hanna left the car. I was in complete shock: Why had she tried to goad him into a fight like this? The next day when I met up with Hanna, I asked her what had happened. She explained that she had sensed that the driver was very likely planning to mug me after he dropped her off, and she wanted to remind him that she knew where his family lived and where to find him if anything happened to me. I was most grateful.

Physical and other overt displays of violence frequently occurred in Katutura. Many of the Rainbow Youth carried knives and other weapons to protect themselves. Masculine-acting females proudly showed me scars from the small stab wounds they had received during fights with other males and females, usually at *shebeens* (small, informal, and sometimes unlicensed drinking establishments) during the consumption of much Tafel and Castle lager. Stabbing usually took place around the shoulder area, not always with the intent to kill, but to punish, inflict pain, and express anger. American rap cultural references supplied the glamour in the retelling of their impressive, violent encounters, in which people were sometimes identified as "gangsters" and "players." Hip-hop fashion at the time—wearing baggy pants and long, loose shirts, and filling teeth with silver and gold stars—helped to project their character in Katutura, a place that many affectionately referred to as "my ghetto."

However, although Katutura was certainly ghettoized from Windhoek's city core in terms of its location and infrastructure, it was not uniformly impoverished. Since Namibia's independence in 1990, Katutura has grown increasingly economically stratified (Pendleton 1993). For example, in Goreangab there are abundant and rapidly expanding squatter settlements comprised of small shacks clustered together made of burlap, cardboard, and corrugated steel sheets and tied together with wiring. Many of the shacks I saw had no flooring, running water, or electricity. In some places more than one hundred households shared a single water faucet, which, like electricity, was under private regulation. By contrast, in Damara one finds older concrete-block houses with well-worn lino-leum floors, as well as some indoor plumbing, electricity, and basic appliances. In Wanaheda, a newer subdivision of Katutura, residences are somewhat larger and more securely structured, and ceramic tiles, flush toilets, running water, and electricity can be found inside. However, these houses by no means compare to the opulence of the compounded mansions in the affluent suburb of the capital city known as Klein Windhoek.

During apartheid Katutura residents were legally prohibited from owning property. Although these restrictions have since been lifted and the municipal-ity has sold off many of its houses to private investors (Pendleton 1993, 113–114), most participants' families continued to rent houses from the municipality. The transition toward private real estate in Katutura was accompanied by a consider-able increase in rental and utility costs. To afford these high monthly fees, most families I knew rented out rooms and shared accommodations in their homes. When I first met Hanna in 2001, she was living in her aunt's relatively small house with her three children and several other relatives; one room was rented out to a cocaine dealer and another to a commercial sex worker and her newborn. Similar crowding was found in the homes of many of my other research participants.

Between 2002 and 2005 I stayed in Katutura at people's homes; went to social gatherings at shebeens, local discos, and funerals; and attended sexuality work-shops, parties, press releases, and political forums organized by TRP in the com-mercial district of Windhoek.[5] Lesbians from Katutura were particularly helpful in many aspects of my research. Over time they shared their personal struggles with trying to avoid becoming HIV infected from men. Initially I expected that it would be difficult for me, as a male, to speak with lesbian and transgender females about sexual health matters concerning their bodies—surely they would feel uncomfortable. However, when they learned I had a male partner, they be-came quite candid with me about their sexual relationships with women. Only after many months did they discuss their sexual relationships with men and their involvement in transactional sex. These practices seemed to hold considerable shame for the masculine females I came to know, as though it questioned their "authenticity" as lesbians. Even more hidden was the fact that many young lesbi-ans were mothers to one or more children. I came to learn this only after several months of conducting my research in the township of Katutura.

Lesbians took considerable initiative in educating me about gay and lesbian life in Namibia. They helped to organize interviews, set up focus groups, and introduced me to the Rainbow Youth who accessed TRP, as well as numerous others who refused to associate with the organization, claiming the organization was "too white." They offered advice about how to phrase questions so that peo-ple would be interested in responding. They aided with translations, explained cultural practices, gave language lessons, and helped me to interpret findings throughout my fieldwork. I am much indebted to them for their contributions. In short, the progress of my research relied greatly on the dedication of these females (see fig. 1 and fig. 2).

Between 2004 and 2008 my fieldwork branched out from Windhoek to the transport hub in the south known as Keetmanshoop; to the working-class coastal town of Walvis Bay in the west; and to the northern towns of Oshakati and Ongwadeva, overlapping with routes where TRP expanded its LGBT rights training work.[6] At that point I began to focus my research on how youths remade themselves in light of the universalistic rights discourses being promoted in TRP's self-discovery workshops. During TRP's political forums, local press engagements, and formal interviewing, the Rainbow Youth usually referred to their sexual desires using the words "lesbian" and "gay." Frequently these terms also referred to gender nonconformity, with the idea that lesbians "normally" act in a masculine way and gays tend to be effeminate. In turn, youths recognized that such gender performances would attract their object of desire—that is, lesbians acting in a masculine way would attract feminine women, and gays behaving effeminately would attract masculine men. Thus, gender and sexual desire were inextricably intertwined in their perceptions and practices.[7]

The local term "moffie," which referred to gender nonconformity, tended to be uttered more during informal social gatherings. According to Ken Cage (2003, 4), the word originated from the slang word "morphy" used by sailors to refer to the transvestite prostitutes working in Cape Town harbor.[8] The term primarily refers to feminine males within the rainbow community; however, it also refers, more broadly, to both males and females who are nonconforming in terms of gender and desire. Although usually pejorative when spoken by outsiders, the Rainbow Youth have reclaimed this word to signify community solidarity and affection. During my fieldwork in Namibia, youths sometimes labeled gender nonconformity with the words "butch" and "drag queen," terms they adopted from the more internationally well-traveled TRP staff and workshop facilitators. They also became familiar with these words through exposure to movies, pamphlets, and especially gay and lesbian magazines that TRP's resource center supplied.

TRP provided training that attempted to carefully distinguish between lesbian, gay, bisexual, and transgender identities, yet few Rainbow Youth openly proclaimed transgender and bisexual identities. Although the term "lesbian men" was featured in the title of an important book for scholars and activists in the region—*Tommy Boys, Lesbian Men, and Ancestral Wives* (Morgan and Wieringa 2005)—most youths rarely claimed this identity during my conversations and interviews with them. Two transgender females who did identify as "lesbian men" did so during political forums to express their solidarity with transnational rights networks such as the Coalition of African Lesbians, which linked organizations serving the interests of lesbians in Sierra Leone, Ghana, Nigeria, Liberia, Rwanda, Kenya, Uganda, Tanzania, Zambia, Zimbabwe, Botswana, South Africa, Mozambique, and Namibia.[9] Only two females and three males I spoke with, who were members of TRP, identified as bisexual, although certainly bisexual behavior was not limited to these individuals.[10] Generally the term "bisexual" was employed interchangeably with the word "straight," "real man," or "real lady" to refer to local people who sometimes engaged in same-sex sexual behavior but who neither (directly) associated with TRP's human rights projects nor practiced gender nonconformity. In addition to expatriates, these non-TRP members were often the desired and actual sexual partners of the Rainbow Youth.

Community elders tended to use the words *eshenge, !gamab* (masculine), and *!gamas* (feminine) as the traditional terms for gays and lesbians. The Damara words "!gamab" (masculine suffix) and "!gamas" (feminine suffix) joined together notions of gender, sexual desire, and anatomical difference.[11] Although most community elders I spoke with defined these terms as referring to anatomical ambiguity—a goat or cow that possessed both male and female genitalia—many of the Damara- and Nama-speaking Rainbow Youth remembered other children calling them these words primarily to belittle their gender nonconformity. The word "eshenge" derives from *eshenganga*, which, according to Finnish anthropologist Maija Hiltunen (1993), is the name for "homosexual diviners" among the Ondonga tribes around the Namibia-Angola border in the north. In *Good Magic in Ovambo*, Hiltunen describes an eshenganga as a young man who is "shy and feminine . . . with his sexual desires directed toward men and boys" (1993, 55). During my fieldwork in Oshakati and Ongwadeva, the idea circulated widely among Oshivambo-speaking people that eshenges had both male and female genitals. However, in the Oshivambo section of the *Namibian* newspaper, the word "eshenge" merely stood in as the translated word for "homosexual" or "gay."

Although I attempted to interact with participants from all ethnic communities, most of the Rainbow Youth identified with the Damara ethnic group, reflecting the disproportionate number of Damara youths who were members of TRP. This overrepresentation is linked to perceptions of gender nonconformity in Damara communities. In my experience among Damara youths and their families, I commonly encountered relative openness around expressions of gender nonconformity. The tensions that did erupt often related more directly to the ruling government's delivery of antihomosexual rhetoric and to the nationalistic anxieties that were subsequently unleashed. In contrast, Rainbow Youth who identified as Ovambo encountered intense discrimination in their communities owing to a "deeply entrenched . . . patriarchal culture" (Isaacks and Morgan 2005, 79). Public displays of gender nonconformity were much less common in this group.

Members and staff of TRP explained to me that tensions often ran high between young black members and the older "colored" (light-skinned) staff, who were commonly referred to as "white." None of the staff lived in Katutura and instead lived in more affluent parts of the city. Unlike the majority of the Rainbow

Youth, all of the staff had received a university education. Adding to this social distance, the director and head office administrator for TRP were South African nationals. TRP's management committee was comprised mainly of older and more affluent white and colored representatives. The tensions that existed across this divide, although marked by ethnic and color difference, were constituted in class-related terms. Because I was often identified as a colored (being Caribbean Canadian), I was concerned that this would impede the development of rapport with the youths. My attendance at funerals unintentionally distinguished me from other "coloreds" and helped me to build relationships with the Rainbow Youth. On one occasion a young woman told me, "You are the first 'white' person I know to come to a funeral here in Katutura."

There were also intentional ways I sought to build rapport with participants. During my attendance at many of the early membership meetings, I noticed that when refreshments were served, the masculine-acting females would rush to eat the *broetchens* (bread rolls) and cheese, but the young feminine males would not. I didn't bother to take food, because I assumed they needed to eat more than I did. When I eventually asked Hanna why the males never ate when refreshments were served, she laughed out loud and said, "They want you to think that they have class, because you are a foreigner." I wondered how I would unsettle this division. At the next lunch I attended, I was the first to move to the table and firmly grabbed a half broetchen in each hand. After a momentary silent pause and a few bursts of laughter, the men rushed to the tray and, along with the women, finished off the sandwiches.

Being in my twenties at the time I began my research also may have allowed me to gain rapport with the Rainbow Youth, as we were relatively close in age. It should be noted, however, that I use the terms "youth" and "young people" throughout this book not to invoke some kind of essentialist notion of age. I specifically use the term "youth" to suggest a significant axis that continually shapes similar experiences for participants: generation. Most participants were in their late teens to mid-twenties when I first met them. They did not have the direct experience of participating in the twenty-three years of armed struggle that gave Namibia its independence in 1990 and had little recollection of the events of the liberation movement (although, certainly, postcolonial liberation narratives imbued local political rhetoric since independence). Many of them had recently finished some degree of schooling and upon entering the workforce were confronted with slim opportunities for employment. Thus, this generation experienced the ambivalence of growing up in a country that is free from the oppressive laws and policing of colonialism while, at the same time, they were encountering the oppression of poverty, poor access to higher education, and limited prospects for employment. The structures that now exclude the majority of black people from sharing the country's wealthy economy operate through the less visible route of neoliberal government practices that favor the interests of foreign investors and postcolonial elites while draining public assets and social welfare resources.

From independence until 2007 the Namibian government had never accepted any loans from the World Bank and the International Monetary Fund (IMF), unlike other sub-Saharan African countries. However, after independence the government did receive technical assistance from both of these multilateral institutions to further develop the nation's economy. Under their advisory influence, Namibia eventually joined the larger neoliberal fold in Africa and moved increasingly toward economic liberalization and a reengineering of the state that favored more democratic and decentralized participation (Hilgers 2012, 83–84; Jauch 2002). Furthermore, conditions attached to official development assistance (ODA) from mostly Western nations similarly shaped Namibia's political landscape by promoting democratization, entrepreneurship, good governance, and local accountability.[12]

In 2003 TRP's programs came to align with this emerging neoliberal order in Namibia. After an external evaluation and policy reforms imposed by its principal funder, Hivos (Humanist Institute for Cooperation), in the Netherlands, TRP shifted from being a volunteer membership-based organization to a trust organization that claimed to be more professional in its approach to advocating for the rights of LGBT Namibians. In an interview with the press, the NGO's director portrayed this shift as enabling TRP to become more "strategic and proactive in working towards its vision of a society in which the human rights of all people are protected, affirmed and promoted, and the state fulfills its obligations to all citizens" (TRP 2003). Much to the dismay of the Rainbow Youth, the NGO soon halted the soup kitchen it was running as well as the delivery of other poverty and social welfare–related services. Regular membership meetings were disbanded, and temporary housing programs for the Rainbow Youth who had been thrown out of their homes were terminated. Instead, TRP programs began to concentrate more on good governance, organizational capacity building, legal advocacy, partnership building with NGO allies, and "mainstreaming" programs that promoted gay-straight alliances called "straight talk with straight friends." Programs also emphasized sexual and gender identity training, Christian spiritual counseling, and the geographic expansion of programs that sought to foster greater self-awareness and individual responsibility. Although this latter set of programs hindered possibilities for raising class awareness, they did intensify personal identity politics. In the coming years I watched as the budding hopefulness of the Rainbow Youth became replaced with intense frustration and disillusionment. By 2007, toward the end of my fieldwork, members began to openly express their deep dissatisfaction with TRP's leadership role. Amid these mounting tensions, I begin the story.

# NAMIBIA'S RAINBOW PROJECT

# Introduction

In AUGUST 2007 Hanna welcomed me into her home—a gift from her new European mother-in-law.[1] After we exchanged greetings, she took out her wedding photo album and began flipping through the pages with me. She halted when she came to one of the wedding photos in which she and her partner stood dressed in matching white "German frocks," as she referred to them in a displeased tone. She then said, "That was one of the saddest days of my life! None of my friends were there. They couldn't afford to go all the way to South Africa. I was feeling so, so sad that day." Our conversation was interrupted when Rubina, one of Hanna's masculine friends, called out, "*Satsa* [Hey, there, man]," as she entered through the open gate. The three of us decided to take a walk around Damara Lokasie, in the Namibian township of Katutura, to visit with friends.

We first stopped by to see Shane, who had recently been released from prison for having stabbed a man who didn't pay her for sex. Although it was the middle of the afternoon, Shane was just waking up after having had "a rough night of drinking and chasing women," she explained with a yawn. When we asked how she was doing, Shane said, "You know, the Rainbow Project [TRP, the national sexual minority rights NGO] really must do something—there are just no opportunities for us. We can either work cleaning houses and washing clothes or be security guards. Both of these jobs don't pay enough. Robert, you must find me a nice girlfriend in Canada that I can marry!" Shane was adamant in her request. Not knowing how to respond, I looked toward Hanna and noticed that Rubina had now vanished. Hanna explained that Rubina probably took off because she was very upset these days; her family had lost their small cinder block home and had to move out to the squatter settlements. "It's happening to many people in our location now," Hanna said.

Next we went to the home of Hillman, who was sitting quietly on her bed, with her young, withdrawn-looking girlfriend crouched with a baby in her arms in the corner of the small steel-sheet shack. The once very vital Hillman, who had always been admired by her fellow lesbians for her physical strength and numerous girlfriends, now looked frail and sick, having wasted down to well below 100 pounds. She managed a smile and said, "There's no freaking [flirting] with the ladies for me these days. I've got TB." Hanna interjected, "You know, it's [TB] worse now than it ever was during apartheid with all this overcrowding." Hillman then confided in Hanna and me that she also worried that she had contracted HIV, "but I am too afraid to go for the test."

The somber tone of the day continued when we met Damien, a well-known local drag performer. Like Hanna, Rubina, Shane, and Hillman, Damien regularly attended TRP's empowerment workshops, meetings, and special events when I first met him in 2001. In his late teens at that time, Damien performed in various local drag competitions, held aspirations of becoming a model and a fashion designer, and hoped to marry a wealthy, gay foreigner. When he greeted me, I noticed much sadness in his eyes. "Tomorrow I'm going to Sossusvlei [Desert]. I need to think about my life." He then added in a serious tone, "TRP really must do something, because the hopes and dreams of our [LGBT] community are going down the drain."

The growing disenfranchisement among the Rainbow Youth culminated in February 2008 during a meeting they organized with staff to air their complaints. Held at the Rössing Foundation Centre in Windhoek, the meeting drew a full house of youths. Most of them came from the outlying townships of Katutura and Khomasdal.[2] I was invited to observe and record the session as someone who was considered to be sympathetic to their struggles for social justice, having worked with their community for several years as a medical anthropologist (see fig. 3).

Amid the swiftly rising mid-morning heat, the buzz of the crowd gained momentum. The director finally called the meeting to order and began outlining the purpose of the gathering. After the group negotiated the ground rules, the participants introduced themselves in rather polite and reserved tones. When it came to Tuli, however, all tensions broke loose as he sharply exclaimed,

> I feel that TRP's objectives, TRP's main aim right now, and apparently for the past eleven years, has been for law reform and political-related legal matters—they try to fight for the rights of the LGBTI community. Have a look around here, people! Most of us do not need our rights to be fought for. Right now we need to be socially and economically emancipated!

Later during the meeting Tuli continued his line of criticism:

> We don't need legal reform, rights to adoptions, those kinds of things. Most of us have children we are responsible for. Our people are dying of AIDS, lesbians are getting raped, and most of us are unemployed. We need jobs and more opportunities. This is what TRP should be fighting for! Why can't we have more capacity-building workshops so that we can attend international workshops like you [the staff] do? Why can't I go to Washington, D.C., for conferences? We are the ones all along who've been fighting on the ground for LGBT rights.

Many of the others nodded, including Hanna, who exclaimed, "Yes. He is right!"

For as long as I have known the normally shy and soft-spoken Tuli, he has quietly devoted himself to attending the meetings, empowerment workshops, public forums, and social events organized by TRP. I often found him thumbing through the sexually provocative images of the Western gay and lesbian magazines and pamphlets on safer sex at TRP's resource center, where he consumed a steady diet of gay and lesbian erotica, pulp fiction, and books on how to come out to your parents and how to reconcile being gay and Christian. Tuli also devoured the reports on the Namibian constitution, the state of democracy in southern Africa, and other literature composed by Human Rights Watch, ILGA (International Lesbian and Gay Association), and Amnesty International. His searing criticism that day appeared as a long overdue response to all he had digested over the years.

TRP's director, a well-educated and self-identified colored born in South Africa, firmly and sedately dismissed Tuli's comments, asserting that the mandate of the organization was neither to deal with poverty nor find employment for TRP members; unemployment was a problem facing the wider Namibian society, "not just LGBT people."[3]

After the meeting I spoke with the director and his staff. It was clear that the staff felt some ambivalence about the director's statement, expressing considerable sympathy about the financial struggles of the Rainbow Youth. To reiterate the organization's position, though, the director reminded them of "what happened in Zimbabwe" some years ago and why organizers there had to shut down the shelter for homeless LGBT youths: some of the homeless youths who came to live there, he explained, were "*not* LGBT."

\* \* \*

What are the consequences when international interventions like the Rainbow Project try to save and protect LGBT people from discrimination with programs that treat their sexualities in isolation from the local conditions in which they are embedded? This book tells the story of what happened over time when a group of young men and women living in an impoverished Namibian township became drawn into the transnational project of LGBT rights mobilization. During my years of research among the Rainbow Youth, it became evident that TRP had a number of unintended consequences, many of which ran counter to the affirmative goals of local and international policy makers and organizers. Certainly, youths gained many immediate benefits from the intervention and the benevolent actions of the organizers. However, I argue that the way TRP's intervention deployed the neoliberal rationalities of individual autonomy and personal responsibility, as guided by Western directives regarding funding policy, has actually obscured opportunities for political mobilization that hold implications well beyond the rights of Namibians engaged in same-sex sexual behavior. Furthermore, TRP's programs not only inhibited important political possibilities but sometimes also reinforced social inequalities.

The story begins amid the storm of antihomosexual government rhetoric that swept across southern Africa in the mid-1990s. In the "safe spaces" created by TRP organizers, young men and women sought refuge. There, with the aid of sex-positive programs, the Rainbow Youth cultivated what I call *practices of freedom*—individual and collective projects that aspire toward the broad kind of emancipation that Tuli articulates above. These practices of freedom eventually appeared as open displays of gender nonconformity, assertions of lesbian and gay identities in their homes and communities, and participation in public protests and discussion forums through the delivery of "coming out" testimonials. As youths pursued their liberation projects, everyday forms of oppression—high HIV prevalence, sexual violence, gender discrimination, racism and tribalism, and intense poverty—subverted their practices of freedom at almost every turn. TRP's education and training programs, although closely tied to rights discourses assembled in Europe and the United States, initially enabled the Rainbow Youth to recognize the many local obstacles that lay on the road to freedom, and this only strengthened their resolve and defiance. But over the years, passions and enthusiasms turned to deep frustration and intense disappointment.

This cautionary tale shows how a form of violence may inadvertently operate in international interventions that seek to rescue and "free" the sexualities of poor people in postcolonial contexts like Namibia. This form of violence takes place along the avenues of people's desires and self-perceptions, because it acts on their very sense of political agency. While I am appreciative of the various strategic plays of visibility and invisibility staged by LGBT organizations in the region, so richly described by Ashley Currier (2012), in this ethnographic narrative I focus on the underside of social movements, bringing into view the perspectives of the Rainbow Youth and the forms of struggle, eroticism, irony, and intense longing that came to characterize their political engagements. Chronicling the various conflicts that emerged in their practices of freedom, I highlight the new challenges and forms of inequality created by TRP in its unwitting collusion with wider neoliberal power arrangements taking hold in southern Africa at the time of my fieldwork. Before I proceed, however, some brief words on the politicization of African sexuality in the region are necessary to understand the premise from which interventions like the Rainbow Project were designed and implemented.

When Zimbabwean president Robert Mugabe denounced the human rights of gays and lesbians at the opening of the Zimbabwean International Book Fair in 1995, he set off a barrage of antihomosexual government rhetoric across southern Africa (Dunton and Palmberg 1996), and dynamic public debates and social movements ensued. Southern African political leaders asserted that homosexuality, as a European cultural practice, had been "imported" to Africa and should be regarded as a neocolonial practice that threatened the destruction of African culture and society. In Namibia ruling party officials from the South West African People's Organization (SWAPO) fired various rounds of antihomosexual rhetoric, locally known as "the hate speeches," and even attempted (unsuccessfully) to draft antihomosexual legislation.[4] The response to these events drew a frenzy of outcry from local and global human rights organizations and national political lobbying networks, even those stretching back to the antiapartheid era. The subsequent public debate surrounding the authenticity of African homosexuality in Namibia culminated in 2001, when the SWAPO president called for the arrest, imprisonment, and even *deportation* of gays and lesbians in Namibia, reinforcing the idea that homosexuality was somehow imported from the West (and therefore needed to be returned to its supposed countries of origin). SWAPO's vilification of homosexuality continued until the end of Namibian president Sam Nujoma's reign in 2004, after which time it subsided.

Over the years this government rhetoric ignited an impressive array of scholarly rebuttal, most notably Murray and Roscoe (1998), Epprecht (2004) and Morgan and Wieringa (2005)—works that challenge the assertion that homosexuality is inauthentic to African culture and society.[5] Historian Marc Epprecht, for instance, suggests that the very notion of same-sex sexual behavior as being un-African likely has its origins in the West. Epprecht traces this idea to the writings and sexual cartography of the late-nineteenth-century explorer Sir Richard Burton, who, "on [the] eve of British imperialism expansion on the continent, located black Africa together with northern Europe in the non-Sotadic zone" (2004, 7), a geographic region where Burton imagined homosexuality to be nonindigenous. Scholars have also traced current repressive attitudes about homosexuality among southern African politicians to the legacy of colonial-era sodomy regulations (Phillips 1997).

In Namibia local journalists, human rights NGO directors, and lawyers I came to know commonly attributed the outbursts of Nujoma and his ministers to a blind adherence to "cultural traditions" (or sometimes the president's supposedly weakening mental state). This logic was reinforced in the global news media covering the hate speeches, which branded African homophobia as tied to cultural beliefs (Awondo et al. 2012). Generating the imaginary of Namibian primitivity and savagery, foreign journalists selected the most wildly sensationalistic examples of irrationality to characterize this homophobia. This is apparent in a 2004 piece in the *Chicago Tribune* by Laurie Goering: "Some Namibian gays find themselves subject to brutal 'cures.' Families arrange to have lesbian daughters raped to show them the 'right' way to behave. Gay men are held down by police and earrings are ripped from their ears. A leading government official has written a treatise describing how homosexuals can be 'cured' by sawing off the top of the skull and washing the brain with a chemical solution." In an article titled "Namibia Chips Away at African Taboos on Homosexuality," Emily Wax (2005) of the *Washington Post* published a local man's account of a brutal sexual assault committed by a teacher when he was a student. In the account, Wax writes, "Un-African. Un-Christian. Anti-family. Witchcraft. In many African countries, being gay is considered all of those things. It is also illegal in most of them, so taboo that a conviction for homosexual acts may bring more jail time than rape or murder." In these caricatures the language of homophobia and cultural taboo articulate together in their portrayal of Africans' irrational fears with respect to the subject of homosexuality. Furthermore, this portrayal of irrationality joins the larger chorus on African sexuality that echoes across the landscape of sexual health projects. In Namibia, as in many other parts of southern Africa, mantras call for greater sexual openness and awareness within African communities in the fight against the HIV epidemic. For example, at the height of SWAPO's anti-homosexual and xenophobic condemnation, French researcher and Namibian AIDS NGO director Philippe Talavera called for a sexual revolution in Namibia, declaring, "There is . . . an urgent need to break taboos" (2002, 342–343). By insisting that cultural taboos prohibit open public discussion of sexuality and pose the real problem for HIV prevention, Talavera constructs the object of sexual health intervention for the readers: "traditional beliefs." In his book *Challenging the Namibian Perception of Sexuality*, widely cited by local sexual health researchers and policy makers, Talavera explicitly adheres to a Freudian analysis in describing in intimate detail the traditional sexual beliefs and behaviors of Ovahimba and Ovaherero people living in northern Namibia. Although he acknowledges how Christianity historically altered sexual mores in the region, Talavera tends to describe traditional gender and sexual practices as though they were timeless cultural artifacts that stubbornly survive the influences of modernity.[6]

> It seems obvious that the sexuality of the Ovahimba and Ovaherero is shaped right from his/her early childhood. . . . From birth to age 4, the child lives in close contact with its mother and the other women in the homestead; hence it is a polygamous environment. Furthermore, the child appears to play a role in sexual relations between adults, at times passively (sleeping next to the couple having sex), at times actively (used as a tool by the mother to avoid sexual intercourse with her husband). . . .
>
> The first large-scale change [in "culturo-sexual structures"] was observed between the 1980s and early 1990s. This change opened doors towards the modern world and its promises. . . . However, such change has been incomplete because, for example, *gender relations have not evolved in rural areas . . . new economic influences and cultural elements have not replaced customary ones: they co-exist but at variance with each other.* The conflicting modern and traditional systems have offered a perfect ecological niche for HIV to spread. . . . In order to stop the spread of HIV, there is a need for a second large-

scale change. This change should break taboos and discuss sexuality openly as it is in fact practised in the Ovahimba and Ovaherero communities, and not in terms of the ... puritanical, monogamous, Christian model. (Talavera 2002, v; emphasis added)

Such so-called traditional or customary practices are, of course, likely more dynamic and ever changing than Talavera's depiction suggests and may be more recently invented than imagined (Ranger and Hobsbawm 1983). Although mindful of the ethnocentricity that underlies Western-framed educational discourses on sexual health in Namibia, the way Talavera questions ideas of culture and personhood with respect to these communities inadvertently depicts their "not yet shaped" erotic subjectivities as being circumscribed by an all subsuming ethnic identity.

Certainly the Ovahimba and Ovaherero communities have institutions (such as marriage), laws (traditional trials) and customs; and *they certainly contain the individual within its norms. Perhaps the individual self is also incorporated into these societies.* However, the two societies have often been qualified as acephalous by modern anthropologists. Under such conditions, what is the importance of ego? How can the self express itself, sexually and otherwise? Is there in fact a self? ... [7]

Because the notion of sexuality had *not yet been shaped in the Ovaherero and Ovahimba culture,* because it was limited neither to the individual nor to society ... no word even existed to describe such a notion. (Talavera 2002, 15–16; emphasis added)

Working among various sexual health NGO networks in Namibia over the years, I became familiar with how sexual health workers commonly viewed African traditional beliefs and traditional sexual practices as central obstacles to educational initiatives. One respected German sexual health worker who came to live in a predominantly Oshivambo-speaking community once told me in an exasperated tone, "I am so frustrated with their [Namibians'] ignorance ... and they take Christianity so literally here. ... Why can't they see that it's their traditional beliefs and their inability to talk about sex openly that keeps the [HIV] epidemic going here?" For this trained psychotherapist, naïve and blind adherence to Christian ideologies and traditional beliefs exemplify "*their* ignorance" and impede the educational progress of public health. Like homophobia, the problem centers on "lack of knowledge and awareness" and "resistance to reason" in sexual matters. Therefore, the reiterations of homophobia by human rights activists and journalists and the pervasive assertions of sexual health workers regarding traditional beliefs—as circumscribed by ethnicity—are in many ways strains of the same view that regard African people as being somehow backward in their (sexual) self-awareness.

The pervasive problem of homophobia outside the West has supplied international human rights organizations such as the International Lesbian and Gay Association (ILGA), the International Gay and Lesbian Human Rights Commission (IGLHRC), Amnesty International, and Human Rights Watch with a global measuring stick for ranking and classifying nations on a scale of rationality. At the time I began my fieldwork in 2001, Namibia was certainly graded very close to the bottom. Accordingly, TRP, like other LGBT rights interventions throughout Africa, invested considerable energy in raising the self-awareness of the Rainbow Youth under the assumption that an increased knowledge of "the self" would help liberate them and inevitably lead to improvements in their health and well-being. This work took the form of workshops on sexual and gender identity, self-esteem, body image, and safer sex, with the expressed aim of fostering subjects who are sexually liberated, self-possessed, and able to demand social justice for themselves and their community. Scholars who appeal to theories of "governmentality" inspired by the French thinker Michel Foucault rightly suspect such valorizations of the "self-actualized subject" as shifting the terrain of responsibility for social problems related to poverty away from social welfare institutions and toward the individual (Cruikshank 1999, Dean 1999, Rose 1999, Gordon 1991, Goldstein 2001). This line of thinking exposes self-empowerment projects directed at the poor as imposing their own unequal power relations, because "the subject must first be shaped, guided, and molded into one capable of responsibly exercising that freedom through systems of domination" (Dean 1999, 165).

The appropriateness of Foucault's theories in Africa has been questioned by scholars like Megan Vaughan (1991, 11), who asserts that unlike the European democratic societies that Foucault described, in colonial times "Africans were conceptualized, first and foremost, as members of groups (usually but not always defined in ethnic terms) and it was these groups, rather than individuals, who were said to possess distinctive psychologies and bodies."[8] In a postcolonial era, TRP's interventions certainly cultivate subjectivities through individualizing projects that foster self-awareness, but they do so through discourses that are also heavily mediated by notions of tradition, culture, and ethnicity. While publicly (and ironically) asserting Western gender and sexual identity terminologies to oppose government claims that homosexuality is "un-African" (Currier 2012), TRP's educational programs targeting the Rainbow Youth were, instead, most attentive to "indigenous" sexual identities, often drawing upon ethno-sexological texts from the late 1800s and early 1900s to invent traditional homosexual identities. Through its deployment of sometimes timeless ideas of ethnic traditions, these programs enacted a complex form of postcolonial governmentality, a mode of power that individualizes at the same time as it *de-temporalizes* African subjectivities. In many ways TRP's intervention approach repeats SWAPO's political logic that casts legitimate Namibian citizens as only those who adhere to traditional cultural practices.

Over the course of my fieldwork, I came to learn how TRP's intervention strategies created internal conflicts for the Rainbow Youth who struggled to find a place of belonging within the global LGBT community at the same time as they continually found themselves mired in primordial notions of traditional culture. These conflicts, as they manifest themselves in the daily lives of the Rainbow Youth, speak to contemporary debates on globalization and sexuality that move our thinking beyond simplistic perspectives that either celebrate emerging "queer" communities outside the West as benefiting from globalization or suspect their appearance as signs of cultural imperialism, a form of globalization that masks local "authentic" sexualities (Boellstorff 2005, 27–30, Manalansan 2003, 5–6, Wekker 2006, 223–224). Within the context of TRP, questions around "global-Western versus local-traditional" have emerged as an important social and political field in which the Rainbow Youth reflect upon and sometimes wrestle with LGBT empowerment discourses as they cultivate their everyday practices of freedom.

With respect to the Rainbow Project of Namibia, I have come to regard the concept of sexuality as a *technology of citizenship* that links the multitude of conflicts encountered by the Rainbow Youth to broader notions of freedom, liberal democracy, and national identity. Departing from notions of citizenship as a legal status bestowed upon the rights-bearing individual, this perspective instead shows how an emergent field of identity politics channels the Rainbow Youth's political desires into the project of remaking the boundaries of belonging in postcolonial Namibia.[9] Even though TRP's interventions operate to oppose the ruling government, the manner in which TRP's mobilizations cultivate "the self" as a political territory unwittingly abets the dispersion of state power by reconfirming "sexuality" as a key defining term of Namibian citizenship.

At a moment when Namibia's neoliberal economic restructuring and repositioning within global market systems drain social welfare resources (Jauch 2007), concatenations of sexuality and universalistic ideas of freedom inhibit wider forms of solidarity around the forms of oppression that Tuli mentioned earlier.[10] Many of the Rainbow Youth diligently followed the road to a healthier sexual life by getting to know and articulate their sexual identity, by celebrating open expressions of sexual desire, by reinterpreting "sexuality" through local cultural histories, and by participating in public protests that were being played out on a transnational stage. Yet they experienced profound ambivalence when their newly found sexual freedom collided against and collapsed before the stark material realities of extremely high HIV prevalence, sexual violence, gender inequality, tribalism, and underemployment. It is precisely at those moments when universalistic ideas of rights become well-worn and begin to tear that we see most vividly their socially and politically violent effects.

\* \* \*

In my attempt to gain a fuller understanding of the unintended consequences of the Rainbow Project in Namibia, I have felt compelled to develop a theoretical understanding of the social construction of desire, because, as a discipline, anthropology is certainly lacking in its theorizing around the subject (Moore 2007, 44). The work of Deborah Cameron and Don Kulick (2003, 108–114) is a notable exception here, drawing selectively on theories of desire from Lacan, Foucault, Butler, and Deleuze and Guattari to formulate a methodology for mapping and analyzing desire "conveyed through language." Although I too take cues from these critical discussions of psychoanalytic theory, I am less concerned in this book with theorizing "What is desire?" and more preoccupied with the question of "How is desire generated, understood, and utilized by social actors?" How do the Rainbow Youth come to see larger, global LGBT narratives of self-discovery and liberation as pertaining to themselves as if these identities were given by nature? What do narrative practices pertaining to desire, such as public coming out testimonials, actually accomplish for the Rainbow Youth? How does sharing intimate political space with TRP organizers, foreigners, and more affluent LGBT people compel and shape their expressions of desire?

During TRP's initial public protests, the Rainbow Youth became caught up in all the excitement. Their exuberance was understandable, for suddenly these young people, who came from impoverished locations, found themselves sitting among a host of international activists, Members of Parliament (MPs), government ministers, human rights lawyers, foreign embassy and NGO directors, and nationally renowned entertainers. They received entrée into social and political spaces that previously appeared far beyond their reach. In interviews, participants described the early days as brimming with hopefulness, believing they would soon see their community liberated. Indeed the immense international attention paid to their experiences of discrimination made liberation from oppression feel imminent to participants. Offering up their testimonials of discrimination and coming out in public seemed like worthy sacrifices for a social movement that was expected to radically transform and improve their lives. In the earlier days of my fieldwork, the Rainbow Youth I spoke with believed that the public exercise of coming out about one's sexuality in the form of testimonials (also see Boellstorff 2009) would enable them to achieve greater social and economic freedoms.[11] This bears some similarity to anthropologist Vinh-Kim Nguyen's (2010) account of "therapeutic citizenship" in Côte d'Ivoire in which the bartering of personal confessions of being HIV positive linked people to actual lifesaving medicines. However, in the case of the Rainbow Youth, offering up their public testimonials connected only a slim number to lifesaving resources (such as finding a wealthy partner who could pay for their education and help support their families). For most of these youths, these public testimonials never translated into the long-term material transformations they desired and imagined. Coming out narratives and the dynamic transnational spaces they inhabited with more affluent LGBT supporters, however, did serve to multiply the desires of the Rainbow Youth (Lorway 2008a; 2008b).

A key feature of TRP's intervention was the incorporation of sex-positive ideologies that embraced open sexual expression. Among many of the Rainbow Youth I came to know, I was struck by how their engagement with these ideologies came to display a devotion to the very production of desire itself. Reemploying the self-discovery techniques they had learned during TRP's sexual-identity training workshop, they sought ways to amplify their expressions of gender and sexual dissidence, thus ascribing a prime ethical and political value to desire. Their desires were made visible through provocative displays of gender and sexual defiance: in gestures, comportment, clothing, erotic behavior, and discursive practices and through reassertions of lesbian and gay (and, to a much lesser extent, transgender and bisexual) identifications in everyday life. These aesthetics of resistance, which came to characterize youths' practices of freedom, allowed them to forcefully enter into the transnational arenas where Namibia's democratic character was being contested and redefined. For example, at public forums held each year during Namibia's annual Human Rights Awareness Week in Windhoek, Tuli, Hanna, and their friends were quite visible in their attendance (in high numbers), in their appearance (by wearing drag), and in their vocal public commentary (by interrogating panelists and rising to give personal testimonials), even to the degree of annoying some of the expert panelists who reminded the audience that there are other human rights issues, besides those of sexual minorities, that need attention. The open display of their desires in this fashion played a pivotal role in their practices of freedom, as though making gender and sexual selfhood take on fuller expression would inevitably bring about a certain personal and collective emancipation. Thus, through their participation in the Rainbow Project, defiant desire came to be regarded as a vital resource for legitimation and political action, making the self a significant site of liberatory potential.[12]

The manner in which discourses on LGBT rights engaged and shaped the political desires of the Rainbow Youth appeared in everyday bodily politics. Youths commonly employed the Western terminology of "top" and "bottom" (to refer to insertive and receptive sexual practices, respectively) as a metonym for masculinity and femininity. More generally these terms were utilized to articulate various intersecting power struggles related to ideas of race, nationhood, gender, class, and age—conflicts they frequently confronted in their everyday practices of freedom. For example, a young man, Travis, who once gave his coming out testimonial before international journalists, later spoke candidly at a workshop about his relationship with a much older and wealthier British man. He complained, "Why must he always expect *me* to be the bottom? After all, *we* Africans, as men, you know, we are usually bigger than the Europeans. Just because he has more money! Why can't we just go fifty-fifty?"

The term "fifty-fifty" here refers to the practice of taking turns in playing active (insertive) and passive (receptive) sexual roles. Travis borrowed the term from a popular song playing in the region at the time, performed by DeMandoza and Mdu: "All the women, independent, let's go fifty-fifty."[13] Responding to the American R & B hit "Independent Women," performed by Destiny's Child, the refrain insists that men and women should meet each other halfway financially. In this way Travis employed the phrase to invoke the power inequalities he wanted to overcome in his relationship with the foreigner.

The term "fifty-fifty" also can be associated with the nationwide feminist campaign for "equality between the sexes" in political decision making—the 50/50 Campaign—which the feminist NGO Sister Namibia launched in October 2001. Sponsored by the Global Fund for Women, the initiative aimed to promote women's participation in all levels of government and drew together women's networks from more than twenty-one villages and towns in Namibia. Interestingly, some youths believed that European and North American gay and lesbian people were more likely to practice fifty-fifty sexual practices. When I asked why, I was often told "because they come from more democratic countries." The Rainbow Youth often made these kinds of connections between erotic bodily practices, transnational power relationships, and their political desires.

Through its interface with transnational LGBT networks, the Rainbow Project provided a steady stream of global images, discourses, values, practices, and people that represented forms of freedom that lay beyond the reach of the organization's mostly unemployed and working-class participants. Tied to the social production of desire in this community, then, are the following questions: In relation to more affluent local and foreign LGBT people, how does a lack of economic resources become reflected in ways of identifying and valuing the self? And where do the transnational trajectories of freedom projected by more privileged, cosmopolitan LGBT movement organizers ultimately leave impoverished young people like Hanna, Tuli, and their friends?

Over the course of seven years (2001–2008), I was able to witness the more long-term, unintended side effects of LGBT rights interventions, which were legible in participants' idioms of desire. In many instances their desires led them along a path toward their own self-exploitation. Here I am referring to the following ironic life trajectories of the Rainbow Youth: the pursuit of females to become "like men" in order to escape sexual violence that leads to the intensification of their oppression at the hands of men; the longings for "real men" by young feminine males who yearn for love, intimacy, and social acceptance that ends in their severe physical and sexual abuse; and the fetishization of foreign and local gay elites by impoverished young males in search of greater social mobility and erotic freedom that results in the loss of their bargaining power during negotiations about safer sex. I consider these unexpected and unintended consequences as arising from what I call "post-structural violence," which acts in ironic ways on peoples' desires and their perceptions of their own political agency. In the narratives of desire that fill the pages of this book, it becomes clear that TRP's interventions initially heighten political awareness and increase the tangibility and sense of imminence of liberation from multiple forms of oppression. Yet over time the very possibility of emancipation increasingly slips further outside the grasp of the Rainbow Youth. The marks left by post-structural violence became visible in participants' profound frustrations and nihilistic sentiments. These negative effects bring into view the deeply cutting ambivalence wrought by an assemblage of liberal democratic, humanitarian, and universalistic rights discourses, raising a number of critical political concerns: Does the diverse and contradictory field of sexual politics in which many Namibians find themselves today—ranging from black lesbian feminist to Christian fundamentalist—signal the arrival of what Ernesto Laclau (1996) calls "the beginning of freedom" and "the end of radical emancipation"? Are these the kind of extensive political solidarities that once led to the overthrow of the colonial regime? As intervention discourses gather momentum in freeing Africans from sexual oppression, do they do so at the cost of diminishing radically transformative political possibilities? The story of the Rainbow Project in postcolonial Namibia is important, then, for understanding the location of sexuality in emerging forms of political domination and resistance in Africa. What arises in my retelling is the view that sexuality is much more than a strategy utilized by ruling governments to deflect the attention of citizens away from "real" political matters, as some scholars have insisted. Rather, the potency with which sexuality is able to mobilize multiple political positions suggests its vital place at the very heart of contemporary political governance in the makings of traditional authority, postcolonialism, and liberal democracy. To borrow the words of Deborah Posel, "Sexuality is perhaps the most revealing marker of the complexities and vulnerabilities of the drive to produce a newly democratic, unified nation" (2005, 127).

# 1  The Instrumentality of Sex

Tradition, understood as a set of political principles and strategies forged
through struggle, can and should be mobilized in the debate about African gay
and lesbian identities. But tradition, homosexual or heterosexual, imagined as
the repository of an authentic racial or national essence, despite its considerable
affective power, should be viewed with a little more circumspection.

—Neville Hoad, *African Intimacies*

SEVENTY-YEAR-OLD WAYNE WITNESSED significant social transformations
in Katutura with the birth of Namibia's independence in 1990. When Hanna and
I visited his home in late 2002, Wayne spoke about how "gay life" had changed
since the end of colonial apartheid. He reminisced about the many secret affairs
he had had in the late 1960s with men from the mining companies' bachelor compounds.[1] In particular, he enjoyed having sex with the migrating Oshivambo laborers living behind the walled compound located near the entrance to Katutura.
"There were only a few 'women' like me then . . . so I had a very active sex life,"
Wayne said as a gentle smile folded back the deep expression lines along his face.
"Now there are *so* many moffies." Wayne's silver-haired friend who lived with
him added in a quiet tone, "Yes, there are so many moffies in Katutura now. You
see them with their short, tight shirts walking around in Katutura—they are very
open these days. There are even the ones you see as young as ten years old now."

What was striking for both of these elders was the growing visibility of
young, feminine-acting men in Katutura. This stood in contrast to "couples like
us," Wayne explained, who lived together in Damara Lokasie for many years
without arousing commentary in the community. Although Wayne and his
friend were well known for their work—cooking for weddings and funerals—no
one ever bothered them about their living situation. Wayne said, "People knew
about us, definitely, but we were left alone. We weren't exactly coming out like
the young people these days." When I asked Wayne why he thought there were,
as he put it, "so many moffies now," his eyes gleamed as he exclaimed, "It's *!Noras

[freedom] . . . it's liberation; there's freedom to be with anyone you want to be with and to have sex with whoever you want—at least until Nujoma started with his hate speeches!"[2]

Characterizing sexual life before SWAPO's onslaught of antihomosexual rhetoric, several local gay and lesbian activists living in Windhoek repeated what Wayne had told me: national liberation gave one the "freedom to be with whoever you want to be with." This kind of statement associates the colonial apartheid era with sexual oppression, which is not surprising when one considers the preoccupation of the former colonial regime with regulating sexuality for citizenship purposes. The criminalization of interracial sexual relationships sought to prohibit mixed-race children from claiming European citizenship, as well as the confinement of various ethnic groups to "traditional homelands" (*bantustans*) aimed at preventing racial mixing. Even Katutura was divided into five ethnic group sections. The relinquishment of these prohibitions with the end of apartheid for many Namibians opened up new possibilities for intimacy across the historically constructed boundaries of tribe, race, and nationhood.

LGBT activists living in the Windhoek urban area who were old enough to remember the early 1990s recalled the scene of "beautiful colored drag queens" from the township of Khomasdal parading down the sidewalks of Windhoek's newly renamed Independence Avenue, walking with pride and poise. In 1990 the once popular Club Thriller in Katutura even advertised a three-night drag contest known as "Miss Mavies Beauty Competition." To further invoke an atmosphere of sexual freedom, interview participants referred to the prevalence of interracial same-sex couples openly holding hands in public spaces. Seasoned activists reminded me that the ruling party did in fact legally recognize sexual freedom by writing "protection on the basis of sexual orientation" into the Labour Act of 1992 (Section 107, Subsection 1b). It seemed that Namibia would parallel neighboring South Africa, where the efforts of famous black gay activist Simon Nikoli, imprisoned like Nelson Mandela, gave way to the world's first constitution that explicitly granted citizenship rights according to sexual orientation. But as Wayne explains, this atmosphere of freedom came to an abrupt end when SWAPO officials began launching the hate speeches in 1995.

This chapter provides a brief overview of the controversy surrounding the hate speeches. These debates occupied immense public space for almost a decade, between 1995 and 2004, filling the pages of local newspapers with articles, editorials, opinion pieces, and front-page headlines on the subject of homosexuality.[3] I demonstrate how SWAPO deployed sexuality as part of a larger strategy to reaffirm its political power. This political economic context played a crucial role in the story of what happened to the Rainbow Youth as it set the parameters of acceptable citizenship in relation to traditional culture and forms of legitimacy that shaped their practices of freedom.

The public debate between SWAPO politicians and the defenders of LGBT rights played out against a broader backdrop in which the democratic character of Namibia was already being brought into question. In the first decade following independence, Namibia had begun to exhibit characteristics of a nation "under increasingly autocratic rule" (Melber 2003, 18). Henning Melber's (13–21) examination of Namibia's liberation notes how SWAPO denigrated democratic principles on a number of counts. First, the constitution was changed in 1998 to allow Nujoma to stand for a third term. Although the change took place through a legitimate political process, it still signaled to the international community that Namibia might be heading in the direction of a single-party state. Second, in the run-up to the elections in 1999, SWAPO discredited the newly formed opposition party, the Congress of Democrats (CoD), by aligning its political agenda with the foreign interests that putatively sought to "civilize natives" (18). Third, SWAPO failed to reconcile its history of human rights violations, in the form of torture and forced exile, committed within its own ranks (see Nathanael 2002). Fourth, postcolonial land distribution policies were exploited to benefit high-ranking state officials, including those serving public office. Furthermore, the privatization of national wealth mostly served the interests of an emerging class of postcolonial elites. Finally, SWAPO's nation-building efforts sidelined minorities, unleashed xenophobia, and silenced dissenting voices (Melber 2003).

In defense of its political performance, SWAPO attempted to revitalize its masculinist role as the liberator and protector of Namibia (Currier 2010). Sexuality proved instrumental to this aim. The instrumentality of sex is evident in the following newspaper headline from the *Namibian,* in which President Sam Nujoma officially addressed regional governors, councilors, and traditional leaders at Okahao in the Omusati region:[4]

> Nujoma called upon Regional Governors, Councilors and traditional leaders in the North to single out gays and lesbians and common criminals in their areas. He said they should be condemned by the whole nation and arrested. "Traditional leaders, Governors see to it that there are no criminals, gays and lesbians in your villages and regions," he said. "We in SWAPO have not fought for an independent Namibia that gives rights to botsotsos (criminals), gays and lesbians to do their bad things here."
> . . . He also hit out at Namibian women who fall in love with foreigners. He urged Namibian parents to tell their children not to sleep with foreigners. "I have children and if it happened that my child comes to me and tells me that she or he is going to marry a foreigner, I will advise her or him not to do so." Nujoma reiterated his call for Namibians to return to the institution of traditional marriage as a means of combating HIV-AIDS. His calls have caused consternation among some church leaders in the North who do not recognize the practice.
> Yesterday Nujoma said traditional marriages had been discouraged by missionaries and should be revived so that Namibian communities return to

their traditional values and norms. "If we do not go back to our traditional marriage culture and practices, this killing disease of HIV/AIDS will continue to kill our people." Nujoma argued that traditional marriages would prevent sex before marriage and lead to monogamy—thus reducing the spread of HIV-AIDS. (Shivute 2001)

Similar government pronouncements, rife with sexual content, abounded during the earlier part of my fieldwork between 2001 and 2004.[5] For example, ruling government officials of SWAPO asserted that Americans had created HIV and tested it on homosexuals, who were "responsible for spreading the epidemic" in Africa. Numerous parliamentary debates concerning sex with foreigners, prostitution, and homosexuality placed sex under suspicion as a significant point of entry for lurking neocolonial forces that threatened the integrity of the nation and postponed a truly emancipated Namibia. Such xenophobic state rhetoric called upon Namibians, as "responsible citizens," to exercise libidinal restraint in defense of a society under foreign threat. Because Namibia's HIV seroprevalence has hovered around 20 percent of the adult population (ages 15–49) since 1996 (MoHSS 2009), the deployment of "sexuality" to invoke the vulnerability of national security was particularly effective for policing the perimeters of citizenship and the boundaries of being.[6] SWAPO refounded its role in safeguarding territory, nation rebuilding, and decolonization by exploiting the grand narrative of a nation at risk of losing control to external forces (if citizens did not carefully control their internal sexual desires). Under Nujoma's rule, SWAPO politicians located political remedies for Namibia's social and economic problems in the return to a "traditional sexual life"—the nostalgic evocation of a primordial time when sexual practices could be imagined as tied to a "natural" moral order of reproduction. The instrumentality of sex in the deployment of this precolonial utopian vision, then, lies in its ability to articulate a political ethic of collective recuperation from colonialism. Therefore, through this articulation, SWAPO forged what would be considered as admissible and acceptable forms of political existence in the postcolonial era. Through ensuing debates, sexuality in Namibia effectively (and affectively) linked the sexual conduct of citizens with notions of the future economic prosperity or peril of the nation.

Ironically, SWAPO laid claim to the moral superiority and the vulnerability of traditional sexuality by calling upon Christian ideologies—a colonial religion. Deputy of Lands, Resettlement, and Rehabilitation Minister Hadino Hishongwa and Finance Minister Helmut Angula, for instance, made an attack by employing an Adam and Eve–like narrative, along with notions of "nature" and "traditional culture," to portray Namibia's innocence and vulnerability to foreign corruption.

In an emphatic tone, Hishongwa said he did not take up arms to fight for an immoral society, neither does he want his children to live in such a corrupt state. "It is against God and our traditional values. God created man and woman. There was no middle creation. Where do homosexuals and lesbians come from, if we all come from God?" he said. "They are abnormal and should be operated to remove unnatural hormones in them."

Finance Minister Helmut Angula shares Hishongwa's opposition to homosexuals and lesbians. Angula warns that though alien, homosexuality has infiltrated Namibian society, and if not fought will "lead to social disorder. In my tradition this is never heard of. We must watch out so that we are not corrupted by this Western influence." (Mwilima 1995, 2)

This invocation of religious ideologies accomplished two rhetorical tasks: (1) it cast Namibian sexuality as morally superior to Western sexuality, and (2) it shored up support from its political base, a base that church leaders historically shepherded in political matters. Indeed, many prominent antiapartheid leaders in Namibia were also prominent church leaders. Moreover, local and international Anglican, Catholic, Methodist, Episcopalian, and Lutheran pastors and priests—as members and important allies of SWAPO—brought thousands of Namibians into SWAPO's fold during the antiapartheid movement (Vigne 1987). In today's postcolonial era, Christian ideologies continue to hold considerable sway over SWAPO constituents.

Although the LGBT organizers I interacted with were acutely aware of the contradiction of using a colonial religion to define "traditional Namibia culture," they claimed it would not be politically strategic to target this subject. As one Sister Namibia representative explained, "If we attack SWAPO's use of Christianity, we risk further aliening the Namibians whose minds we actually want to change." To retaliate against SWAPO's remarks, the feminist NGO instead released a press statement in the most widely read local newspaper, the *Namibian,* drawing an analogy between the government's discriminatory rhetoric and former German Nazi propaganda:

> Hishongwa and Helmut Angula claimed in the article that homosexuality was a western phenomenon as alien to Namibian culture. In response Sister Namibia quoted Kurt Falk [a German ethno-sexologist] who lived in Namibia for 10 years early in this century [early 1900s]. He found homosexuality in all cultural groups and lesbianism in most and provided a list of terms used in Oshiwambo, Otjiherero and Nama/Damara for the homosexual acts and relationships and described relevant customs and practices.
>
> This research was done at a time when western countries were still criminalizing homosexuality and trying to "cure" gays and lesbians with electro shocks and brain operations, Sister said. "Thousands of homosexuals were killed together with Jews, gypsies[,] trade unionists[,] communists and social democrats in German concentration camps during the reign of Nazism. This puts the remarks made by Minister Hishongwa in a frightening perspective." (Anonymous 1995)

By questioning SWAPO's historiography here, Sister Namibia exposes the ruling party's political ambitions as repeating the logic of previous colonial regimes. On the other hand, by employing Western interpretations of African sexual culture, lifted from the pages of early twentieth-century German ethno-sexology, Sister Namibia also repeats SWAPO's political logic of what constitutes authentic citizenship, drawing attention to the presence of ethnic-specific words in order to authenticate the existence of Namibian homosexuality.

The ensuing eruption of public debate concerning sexuality, human rights, and authenticity continued to grow in 1995. The reactivity around "homosexuality"—particularly lesbian sexuality—was fueled by two highly politicized and contentious events. First, the famous black South African lesbian activist Bev Palesa Ditsie made a historic address at the United Nations Conference on Women held in Beijing in 1995. She was the first person to address gay and lesbian rights before a U.N. assembly. This was met with a great deal of controversy throughout international women's networks to which Namibian women's groups held active ties (Iipinge and LeBeau 2005). Second, in October 1995 German national and former antiapartheid activist Liz Frank applied for permanent residence in Namibia on the basis of her committed same-sex relationship with Elizabeth Khaxas, a renowned local black social activist (and the director of Sister Namibia). In 1997 the Namibian Supreme Court rejected Liz Frank's application for permanent residence in Namibia on the grounds of her lesbian relationship with Khaxas (Hancox 2000). The government's refusal to recognize the relationship of two prominent former antiapartheid activists fueled civil protests against SWAPO. Politically savvy local activists and academics such as Ian Swartz, André du Pisani, Elizabeth Khaxas, Liz Frank, Henning Melber, and Wolfram Hartmann commanded several public forums in Windhoek that directly challenged—and at times ridiculed—the remarks made by the SWAPO government. TRP's director, Ian Swartz, even participated in a nationally televised debate with the minister of home affairs that at times took on a humorous tone, draining "officialdom of meaning" (Mbembe 2001, 129) on the issue of homosexuality. Many of the activists, though, also remembered the fear that the hate speeches created. As one of the founders of TRP told me, "Suddenly you didn't see gay and lesbian couples holding hands in public, especially the mixed couples. The beautiful colored drag queens walking down the streets were no longer to be seen." Famous Namibian drag queen "La Rochelle" explained, "Many of the coloreds like me left for South Africa—at least those who could afford it."

Between 1995 and 1997 a number of international LGBT rights networks rose to support Namibia's sexual minorities. Indeed, these heated disputes over homosexuality in Namibia exposed the multiple and powerful lobbying ties that LGBT groups had established with the foreign ministries of various governments. The Swedish Federation of Gay and Lesbian Rights, for instance, announced in a press release that it had requested the Swedish Ministry of Foreign Affairs to launch a formal investigation into the hate speeches. The details of this press release, carried by the *Namibian*, raised the issue of withdrawing Swedish aid calculated at the annual amount of 122,5 million Swedish kronor. In early 1997 the European Union expressed similar concerns over the hate speeches and the possible withdrawal of development funds. Dutch and British embassies in Namibia followed suit. Amid growing international disapproval and publicized threats of economic sanctions, Namibia's economic dependence on Western development aid became clearly revealed. In response to this public exposure of economic vulnerability, SWAPO released a press statement in 1997, which read in part:

> It should be noted that most of the ardent supporters of these perverts [homosexuals] are Europeans who imagine themselves to be the bulwarks of civilization and enlightenment. They are not only appropriating foreign ideas in our society but also destroying the local culture by hiding behind the facade of the very democracy and human rights we have created. . . . We are convinced that homosexuality is not a natural and objective form of moral history but a hideous deviation of decrepit and inhuman social behaviour. In reality lessons learned from the morals of our Namibian culture demonstrate that our morals are far more superior [to Europeans] and acceptable to the vast majority of our people who are adhering to Christianity. (SWAPO 1997)

The iteration of these discourses significantly reified overlapping binary oppositions such as modern/traditional, European/African, white/black, wealthy/poor, innocent/corrupt at the same time as it established sexuality as a moral and political territory under its rule. Furthermore, the concatenation of sexuality with notions of national identity, human rights, democracy, and neocolonialism pushed "sex" into conversations about the emergent problems of the postcolonial era such as the encroachment of globalizing forces. Take, for example, Nujoma's official address before SWAPO supporters outside the Okuyangava Women's Center:

> The enemy is still trying to come back with sinister manoeuvres called lesbians and homosexuality and globalization. . . . They colonized us and now they claim human rights, when we condemn and reject them. . . . Those who want to do that [practice homosexuality] must pack up and go back to Europe. (Maletsky 2001)

Homosexuality, as a colonial residue, became instrumental to the government's normative prescription for economic recovery from colonial apartheid. This can be noted in Nujoma's address to Prime Minister Theo-Ben Gurirab and Foreign Affairs Minister Hidipo Hamutenya upon returning from the World Summit on Sustainable Development in Johannesburg, South Africa:

> We are tired of insults (from) these people. I told them they can keep their money. I told them that these political good governance, human rights, lesbians . . . that they want to impose on our culture . . . they must keep those things in Europe.
> Even in Namibia we have enough wealth. We have already enough meat, we are exporting meat. We have enough fish, we are exporting fish to other

countries. Now, why should we cry to these imperialists? I told them today that we don't need your money. We can develop ourselves. (Amupadhi 2002a)[7]

By casting types of sexual subjects (homosexuals) as suspected foreign objects that threatened the nation's economy, antihomosexual rhetoric both internalized and externalized immediate local struggles surrounding economic hardship. For Namibians who engaged in same-sex practices, this xenophobic rhetoric constituted internal conflicts as it questioned their status as citizens.

Thus, the very damning and damaging remarks made by SWAPO were undergirded not by a thoughtless, culturally circumscribed irrationality—what LGBT and other human rights activists commonly refer to as "homophobia." Instead, SWAPO's instrumentalization of sexuality advanced a political rationality that was highly effective in the way it masked the organization's role in widening disparities of wealth accumulation by (re)connecting contemporary social suffering to the colonial past.

Amid the blaze of government hate speeches moving across southern Africa, impressive scholarly interventions were forged, culminating in the publication of a rich anthology devoted to the study of non-normative African genders and sexualities titled *Boy-Wives and Female Husbands* (Murray and Roscoe 1998). In general this scholarship sought to challenge the idea that homosexuality was an imported European cultural practice, and for this reason it soon became a key resource for TRP organizers in their training and educational work among the Rainbow Youth.

One important scholarly intervention examined the colonial prosecution of sodomy that was alleged to have occurred in labor compounds and prisons (Epprecht 1998; 2003, 53–55, 97–98). Marc Epprecht (1998) and Oliver Phillips (1997) unsettled the racialized image of homosexuality as a "white man's disease" in Zimbabwe by referring to the changing social contexts in which sodomy was enforced. In the first thirty years of colonial rule, sodomy cases involved mostly black men, but more recent years (1966–1994) saw the trials of white men as the primary offenders. Following on this work, I began to examine sodomy court cases in 2001, hoping to catch a glimpse of how the regulation of same-sex sexual behavior in Namibia might have looked during the colonial era. Interestingly, the cases I was able to retrieve show intriguing continuities with SWAPO's postcolonial deployment of sexuality. Specifically, the morality dramas that played out in sodomy trials during the transition from German to South African government in the early twentieth century reveal an important formative period for contemporary inventions of traditional sexuality. Moreover, these court cases suggest how sexuality served as a linchpin in the arrangements of opposing national, racial, and tribal political positions in former South West Africa (Namibia).

In 1915 German troops were defeated by South African military forces, ending thirty years of German colonial rule in South West Africa (SWA) (Emmett

1999, 65). At this time SWA was relegated as a province of South Africa and valued for its rich mineral deposits of copper, gold, uranium, and diamonds. Over the next five years SWA remained under South African military martial law, awaiting the final imperial settlements of World War I. South African rule was considerably more difficult to execute than the rule of the previous colonial regime, because in addition to regulating a large "native" migrant labor force (primarily from "Ovamboland" in northern Namibia), administrators had to contend with a white (German) settler population. Though sixty-four hundred Germans were repatriated (mainly military police and former administrative officials), six thousand German settlers were permitted to stay and keep their land under the Treaty of Khorab (Wallace 2002, 72).

Against this context a number of sodomy trials appear as a cluster in the South West African colonial archival record between 1919 and 1930. Virtually no cases of sodomy appear before or after this period (until the Immorality Act was instituted in 1957). (These absences may partially stem from the incompleteness of the Namibian archival record.) The legal framing of these sodomy cases reveals an underlying logic in that the moral boundaries and obligations of citizenship are differentially marked according to race in the building of the South African empire. Moreover, these cases occurred as an atmosphere of resentment toward South African rule was building within the German settlement community and within the black migrant labor force. While the former German colonial administration had previously regulated Ovamboland by indirect rule, South African administrators increasingly sought to exercise more direct control over the flow of black migrant laborers (Emmett 1999, 81).

When South West Africa was placed under the South African protectorate in 1915, it was considered more efficient to maintain earlier elements of the German criminal code. However, South African administrators added Act 31 (1917), regarding sodomy, to the code as one of a number of serious *criminal acts*, which included the offenses of robbery, murder, and rape (IGLHRC 2003, 256–266). Legal discourses acknowledged *only* the existence of same-sex sexual behavior between men, altogether excluding women and heterosexual couples from legal definitions of sodomy. Moreover, cases of sodomy tried in court were primarily confined to two contexts: between black male laborers and between German settlers and their black employees.[8] Both were considered serious criminal offenses, with the convicted "native" receiving between six and eighteen months of imprisonment with hard labor and, in some instances, physical lashes; whites received even stiffer penalties, of up to three years, as they were usually tried for multiple offenses. To some extent this parallels Epprecht's (1998, 217) analysis of sodomy trials that took place in Southern Rhodesia (now Zimbabwe) between 1892 and 1923. However, Epprecht's findings differ somewhat, as only whites who committed sodomy generally received harsh penalties, of usually more than a year, whereas the courts treated sodomy among Africans as "a fairly common misdemeanor" and imposed minimal fines.[9]

Acts of sodomy between African laborers in SWA were alleged to have taken place in bachelor residences, such as those found at railway, fishing, and mining compounds, where black migrant laborers slept. Sodomy was constructed as punishable *only* where it could be proven that anal sex had taken place. In other words, the threat of "unnatural carnal knowledge," realized through penetrative sex, had to be traceable to physical evidence such as the "emitting of sperm" and "damage to the anus." Such evidence would have to be provided by medical officers in order for the crime to be successfully prosecuted. Sexual practices between black men such as oral sex, thigh (intercrural) sex, and mutual masturbation, which were detailed throughout the sodomy trials, were not prosecuted as criminal acts.[10] In this way the narrow definition of sodomy under the SWA colonial regime was not exercised simply to eradicate same-sex sexual practices between laborers but operated more to establish the *acceptable limits of physical intimacy between men,* as men were still expected to return to their homesteads and reproduce in order to replenish the required young and plentiful workforce. Therefore, the precise enforcement of sodomy regulations worked in tandem with efforts to tighten regulations involving the migratory labor system.

Although the law wrote sodomy as an act committed against the *will* of others, many of the court transcripts suggest that regular sexual intimacies between men on the compounds were consensual rather than purely coercive, even though many of the arguments in the cases involved nonpayment for sex.[11] The case involving thirty-year-old Dwasbasam (accused No. 1) and twenty-year-old Standato (accused No. 2), both identified as "Xhosa laborers" at a mining compound in Lüderitz, exemplifies this point.

The sodomy hearing opens with the testimony of the "native" Albert Mgele—the key witness to the alleged act. He provides his account of the clandestine rendezvous he witnessed between the two accused men, which occurred just outside the labor compound at 10:00 PM. After following the men, he watched them from behind the packing cases.

> The accused No. 2 was on his stomach on the ground and No. 1 was on the top of him. They were naked and were lying on the blankets. Accused No. 1 was moving up and down as if having connection. I watched for five minutes and then spoke to them. . . . No. 1 stood up and took his blanket. I saw his penis in erection. It was moonlight and I could see plainly. Then No. 2 took up his blanket and ran away with no. 1.

This testimony is followed up with an account from a police officer, Constable Ferdinand Samuel Conway, who pursued the charge of sodomy reported by Mgele the morning after the incident. Fulfilling the mining authorities' request to have the laborers medically examined, the constable led an investigation that by the late afternoon tracked them down in the neighboring town of Elizabeth Bay. The medical officer who worked for the mining company in Lüderitz that employed the two men examined Standato and Dwasbasam and concluded that sodomy had occurred:

> No. 2 accused, I examined microscopically and took slides. On the slides was spermatozoa. In the anus I inserted my finger and pulled out mucus which I drew across the slide. This showed the spermatozoa. There were no abrasions.

Standato, who had already pleaded guilty along with Dwasbasam, essentially confirmed the prosecution's allegations, but in his own defense stated that it was only his first time performing the act. Curiously, he also commented on his lack of payment for the act.

> Accused [No. 1] got on top of me and put his penis in my anus. He first put his penis between my legs and after a time he told me to stretch my legs and then he put his penis in my anus and it hurt me. I was wet in my anus when I got up. I got no money for it.

When it was Dwasbasam's turn to testify in his own defense, he also mentioned payment in exchange for sex; however, he denied the charge of having anally penetrated the young man.

> Accused No. 2 came to my hut at the compound and said we should meet privately as he had heard I was fond of having connection with small boys. I then asked him that both of us should go and sleep together and we did so. Then Albert Mgele came and caught us together. I had connection with accused No. 2. *I promised to pay accused No. 2* for letting me do this to him. . . . I admit to emitting semen between accused No. 2's legs but I did not penetrate his anus [emphasis added].[12]

The candid nature of Dwasbasam's testimony suggests that sexual intimacies between men—as long as they do not involve anal penetration and money is not exchanged—are not particularly remarkable to the court; in fact, Dwasbasam's persistent desire for "young boys," which he openly professes, is never interrogated during the entire trial. The prosecution of this "venereal affair" was not necessarily considered a grave crime in court because a victim was harmed or because it contravened "the order of nature" and violated codes of greater social responsibility, as it was worded in the legal act. Instead, the narrow and precise definition of sodomy, as anal penetration, was enforced by mining and police authorities more to maintain order and control over the black labor force so as to secure economic productivity for the South African state.

Managing an all-male labor force was certainly more cost-effective than accommodating entire families of women and children, who were considered unable to contribute to the mines' productivity given the physical requirements of labor. For this reason, few mining hostels included marriage or family accommodations, forcing most men to be separated from kinship networks for many months at a time.[13] According to Kurt Falk (1998, 188), young "kitchen boys" often accompanied the miners on the railway cars to Lüderitz, serving as "passive pederasts on the journey and during the term of service at the mine field. . . . These boys are given to the young men usually by their wives or betrothed" to ensure their fidelity.

While this may suggest that male-male sexual practices were relied upon by black communities for the protection of "traditional" social institutions from colonial influence, the intent here is not to reduce these sexual intimacies to a functionalist view, as "a mechanical or necessary substitute for heterosexual life" (McLean and Ngcobo 1995, 166; also see Spurlin 2001, 190–191). The possibility certainly exists that these new spaces of possibility for male-male erotic expression were *not* tied solely to social and economic relations in rural areas, a possibility provocatively argued by Zackie Achmat (1993) in relation to colonial South Africa. Furthermore, one should not assume that these male-male sexual relationships, in terms of pleasure, were preferred over male-female ones (McLean and Ngcobo 1995, 166). Rather, the point being made here is that *the policing* of "immoral practices"—the disciplining of libidos in the governing of the migrant labor system—proved instrumental in the instantiation of South African colonial power during the transition period. The precise enforcement of sodomy laws not only contributed to South African empire building, but it also inadvertently created the conditions in which Ovambo defendants could forge the anticolonial political discourse of "traditional (Ovambo) sexuality" as being heterosexual.

The transition between German and South African colonial rule was certainly not straightforward. Instead, "South Africa's status as an occupying power was both temporary and ambiguous" (Emmett 1999, 65–70). To establish their claim to this territory, South African administrators set out to prove to Britain that German colonial rule was costly, inefficient, and unjust. In 1918 South African administrators collected evidence on the "injustices and atrocities" committed under German rule and published it as an official report in London (70).[14] Sodomy also served as evidence of such gross misconduct. Prominent German members of society were tried for sodomy and given severe penalties by the South African state. For example, the sentencing of a German businessman who was given three years imprisonment read:

> Wilhelm Liechert, it is pathetic to see a man like you in the dock found guilty of such serious offenses as you have been found guilty of. These offences are amongst the most serious offences which are known to the law. . . . The Court has taken into consideration that on each occasion you were under the influence of liquor. The Court has also remembered that you are a man of standing

... but as against that a man in your position should have known better. But the court has also not lost sight of the fact that the [black] complainants were of a very low moral character and intelligence.[15]

Wilhelm was found guilty on four counts of criminal acts. Yet, unlike cases involving black laborers, the court criminalized Wilhelm's non-penetrative sexual acts such as oral or manual sex as forms of assault. This differential prosecution hinged on a particular racialized legal assumption pertaining to the relations of consent between men: sexual behavior between black men might be consensual, but sex between white and black men could never be considered consensual, with white men found guilty of the supposed assault.

The lengthy trial of German expatriate and physician Hermann Schneidenberger, one of only nineteen medical practitioners licensed to practice in South West Africa, further illustrates the social and legal construction of consent between black and white men. Doctor Schneidenberger was eventually sentenced to three years in prison after having had "connections" with several black men in his employ at the state hospital.

The mine hospital in Tsumeb in 1920 provided the setting for Schneidenberger's alleged acts, in the district of Grootfontein. Five "native" witnesses attested to the indecent assaults committed by the doctor. Although intended as accusatory, their testimonies often read as though each of the witnesses had been involved in ongoing consensual sexual relationships with the doctor, even though they were mediated by material transactions. Note the testimony of the first witness for the prosecution, Huske Kumbuku:

One night during the month of December, the accused came to me where I was on night duty at the hospital. It was early in the evening but it was before midnight. . . . The accused said to me I must accompany him to his house. I rose and accompanied him. Arriving at accused's private dwelling, we entered by the front door and then proceeded to the bedroom of the accused. Accused then gave me some work to do. I had to serve beer to a few gentlemen visitors. I did not count the guests but I know there were several including Messr. Bentheim and Sachs. I served them with beer and finish[ed] my duties at about 11 PM. When I finished, the guest left; the accused alone remained. I did not return to the hospital but remained in the house with the Doctor (accused). All the guest[s] having left, he ordered me to go into his bedroom. I did as he told me. . . . Accused told me to strip and I stripped. Accused did likewise. We were both nude. Having stripped[,] the accused switched off the electric light and the room was in darkness. Accused then went and lay on the bed and I came and sat next to him. Accused spoke to me and caught my penis in his hand and showed me how to play with his penis. Accused took my penis and played with it until I emitted semen. I dressed again and returned to the hospital. He gave me a three penny piece. Arriving at the hospital I went to sleep.

A month later the accused and I did the same to one another again. This was on a day on which accused gave a dinner to which he invited friends. The native who helped me to wait at the table was Micus. After the guest left, the accused told me to sleep with him and that if I did not sleep with him, native Micus should. I refused to sleep with him and that night he did not play with me nor I with him. When the accused told me to play with him again it was on a day sometime later at noon . . . in his office. This was after I had cleaned his motor car. He fetched me to his house; accused then played with my penis and told me to play with his. I did as he told me. I did not get paid on the second occasion, because I refused, but on the third time he again paid me three pence. . . . Nobody instructed me to report the accused. I went and reported to Mr. Pfafferot because I had heard that the accused had done the same things to other natives.[16]

While such accounts are suggestive of mutual sexual gratification, possible jealousy, and mutual consent (or at least that the sexual practices were part of mutually agreed upon transactions), under the racist logic of colonial legal discourse, sex between white and black men could never be regarded as consensual. To define such acts as consensual (or to even accuse black men of sexual initiation) was not possible by legal definition, because black men were disqualified as equals according to their "low moral character and intelligence." Throughout the trial, verification of German indecency, coercion, and corruption was supported through the iterations of black male witnesses: "I did as he told me"; "He is a white man, I must listen"; and "He showed me how to do it."[17]

Black men, however, were not simply complicit within the colonial moral arenas of sodomy trials; they certainly were also in a position to blackmail white men.[18] It is possible, too, that Schneidenberger, who had pled "not guilty," had given an "examination of all hospital natives for venereal diseases" as he claimed—a practice not uncommon with the enforcement of the new Public Health Act of 1919.

But what is important to understand here is how the legal regulation of intimacy between black and white men through sodomy trials made the courtroom into a site where the colonial logic of racial and moral supremacy could be turned on its head by Africans. Instead of affirming the depraved moral nature of "the native," black witnesses often revealed the immoral nature of colonial power relations. Black men who were tried for sodomy exposed colonial immoralities through the employment of what I refer to as "narratives of proximity," which described the appalling living conditions that black men experienced in migrant labor camps. Similarly, African witnesses to the act of sodomy articulated the inhuman conditions in which black bodies were housed, within cramped quarters and an insufficient numbers of beds—if there were beds at all (see figure 4).

In the sodomy case against thirty-two-year-old Petrus, an "Ovambo [Oshivambo] laborer" working in the mines of Lüderitz, the alleged victim, Jeremia, is the first to testify for the Crown. Much of his testimony paints a picture of the close proximity shared between the laborers.

Accused and I sleep on one bed under same blanket. We came down from Ovamboland together. We came from the same place. We have always slept together [at the compound]. We had no clothes on in bed. Ovambos generally take off clothes when going to bed and just keep one rag over their private parts. It is the first time the accused has done this [anal penetration] to me. The *Ovambos think it is a bad thing to do. They don't do it in Ovamboland* . . .

[The sleeping quarters] is on one raised platform all along the compound that we sleep on. We don't have mattresses. We all get two blankets, but I have sent one of mine to Ovamboland. . . . I did not sleep alone . . . but with the accused [emphasis added].

And the supporting witness stated:

We all three sleep in the same compound at [Lüderitz]. . . . There are a great number of Ovambos sleeping there. We sleep on a long platform all along the side of the compound. It is usual for 2 or 3 to sleep together. I sleep with 2 others under the same blanket. We each get two blankets. But we put some [of the blankets] on the boards, as we have no mattresses. The accused looks after Jeremia's. I have never seen them quarrel. . . . The other Ovambos woke up when Jeremia [the victim] shouted. They laughed because they were surprised to hear that a big man had had connections with a boy. *Ovambos do not have connections like that in Ovamboland. . . . If accused did such a thing in Ovamboland he [the accused] would be killed.* We can't do anything here, so we just laughed [emphasis added].[19]

One could infer that the assertion "in Ovamboland he would be killed" suggests there was some cultural recognition, although negative, of such acts. More important to note, however, is how the colonial legal regulation of sexuality, which portrayed black men as "powerless," "vulnerable," and "complicit," had a *generative effect* by unwittingly producing the formal space that black men could seize to construct the supposed truth of Ovambo cultural morality as *superior* to colonial moral systems—and free from "unnatural" offenses.

Sporadic migrant labor protests began in the "chaotic conditions" of SWA's transition to South African rule (Emmett 1999, 260). As exemplified in the sodomy trials during this period, a politics of "traditional sexuality" began to form among Ovambo laborers, buttressed by colonial programs to Christianize and manage indigenous institutions in the north from a distance. Sodomy between male migrant workers became emblematic of colonial exploitation and corruption, of separation from kinship relations, and of the erosion of indigenous economic and social life. The reiteration of authentic Ovambo sexual practices as heterosexual during sodomy trials must be viewed, then, as part of a larger political narrative unifying migrant laborers at that time, one that later establishes them as a significant contingent in SWAPO's nationalist movement for liberation (260–261). Disavowing same-sex relationships during the transition period thus appears less a testament to Africans' blind adherence to cultural taboos than an effective political tactic that cleaves the boundaries of tribal identity from the colonial state as an act of anticolonial resistance.

Returning to the contemporary period, the employment of "traditional sexuality" in the art of government has enabled SWAPO to reiterate its role in safeguarding the nation-state and to stir great support from its political base. During a SWAPO rally before the national labor union in 2003, former president Nujoma successfully whipped the crowd into uproarious applause when he denounced the rights of gays and lesbians. In the postcolonial era SWAPO has consistently fired rounds of antihomosexual rhetoric during highly publicized economic crises.[20] In September 2005, as allegations of corruption in the management of public funds and assets were linked back to SWAPO party officials, "homosexuality" proved effective once again for managing low public approval ratings when Deputy Minister of Home Affairs and Immigration Theopolina Mushelenga publicly claimed that "gays and lesbians created the AIDS epidemic in Namibia" (IGL-HRC 2005). "Traditional sexuality" as a tool of statecraft, however, is more than just a deceptive political maneuver, even though it has been made to serve such ends. The broader implication is how its contemporary redeployments operate to diffuse and intensify the project of governing the Namibian body politic.

# 2   Subjectivity as a Political Territory

Democratic politics is not out there in the public sphere or in
a realm, but in here, at the very soul of subjectivity.
— Barbara Cruikshank

IN THE WINDHOEK urban area, abundant transnationally orchestrated NGOs display striking diversity and dissonance in their approaches to sexual health and have staged numerous contests related to Namibian sexuality in the arenas of AIDS prevention, reproductive health, the decriminalization of prostitution, gender rights and inheritance, and homosexuality and authenticity. This chapter examines the last of these by taking a critical look at how TRP's intervention techniques unwittingly play into the dispersion and intensification of postcolonial state power. By emphasizing self-knowledge and self-possession in their intervention, democratic politics are projected into the personal and away from an awareness of how wider neoliberal practices enacted by the state shape the material ground of their social suffering.

Following SWAPO's press release in 1997 that condemned homosexuality as an imported European cultural practice, a gay and lesbian rights movement mobilized. The initial collective of approximately fifty individuals calling itself the Rainbow Project drew its membership from pre-existing gay and lesbian social groups in Windhoek. According to a journalist I spoke with working for the Afrikaans newspaper known as *Die Republikein,* the Social Committee of Gays and Lesbians (SCOG), which had existed before the government hate speeches, primarily organized local parties and other social events. However, after Mugabe's hate speeches in 1995, SCOG gave rise to Gays and Lesbians of Namibia (GLON), a group that began to focus on constitutional and legal matters as homosexuality became a larger political concern in southern Africa. Former organizers explained that GLON quickly dissolved "because of a lack of unified vision." Some members wanted to participate in formal legal action; others wanted to focus their activities on establishing LGBT social spaces. There were also unresolved racial and class tensions.

With the establishment of the Rainbow Project, most of the decision makers continued to be whites or colored. Many were well traveled in Europe and North America, highly credentialed, and employed in middle- to upper-income jobs as teachers, NGO directors, lawyers, and local embassy representatives (Palmberg 1998). A number of the core organizers were non-Namibian. In 1998 TRP received operational funding from SIDA (Swedish International Development Agency); the Heinrich Böll Foundation, based in Germany; and both Mama Cash and Hivos of the Netherlands. During the barrage of hate speeches, leading officials from Amnesty International, lesbian and gay associations based in Europe and North America, and local and transnational NGO networks released a flurry of press statements later carried by the nationally distributed newspaper the *Namibian*. Under the watchful eye of international human rights societies, this emergent social movement developed through an organized effort "to globalize from below" (Appadurai 2001, 17).

Between November 21 and December 2, 2000, TRP held its first LGBT Human Rights Awareness Week in Windhoek, which was comprised of a series of public panel discussions. For example, Norman Tjombe of the Legal Assistance Center (LAC), sponsored by the Ford Foundation, carefully reemphasized Namibia's obligations to international human rights agreements. The major themes raised during this week of events also included perspectives on homosexuality in relation to Christianity. The week commenced with a church service led by Nokuthula Dhladla, a black and openly lesbian pastor from the Hope and Unity Metropolitan Community Church in Johannesburg (Sister Namibia 2000–2001). The following day, a panel debated the question "Can one be gay and a Christian?"[1] Panelists included Pastor Dhladla; Douglas Torr, an openly gay Anglican priest and theologian from South Africa; local Methodist minister Lynita Conradie from Windhoek; and a theology professor from the University of Namibia, Jannie Hunter. In general they offered alternative interpretations to passages of the Bible often cited to condemn homosexuality (Sister Namibia 2000–2001). This display of support by church leaders and scholars carried great strategic importance, because the prominent political role of Christian churches during the antiapartheid era continued to hold great influence in postcolonial Namibia. (As mentioned in chapter 1, SWAPO also relied upon Christian ideologies to fortify their image as the nation's protector.)

These public panel discussions, Hanna told me, drew a great deal of interest and attendance among black people from Katutura, particularly those pertaining to Christianity. During "LGBT Week," TRP also held an open house, attracting 150 young black men and women mostly from Katutura Township (Sister Namibia 2000–2001). When President Sam Nujoma called for the arrest, imprisonment, and deportation of all gays and lesbians in Namibia in 2001, these vibrant youths flooded the national Human Rights March held on April 28 of that year.

During my earliest interviews, most of the Rainbow Youth had some awareness of non-normative sexualities and genders in their communities before the hate speeches: most claimed to have heard of local terms for gender and sexual nonconformity, like "!gamas" and "eshenge"; some had already begun to practice gender nonconformity; a few had previously known of a shebeen where moffies would gather in Katutura (Club Thriller); and others remembered hearing about or seeing drag queen competitions in Katutura and the neighboring colored township of Khomasdal in the early 1990s. But most of the youths insisted that the strongest realization they had had of their own sense of difference occurred amid the discrimination they encountered at the hands of relatives, religious and community leaders, and paramilitary police officers in Katutura.

> The announcement [calling for the deportation of gays and lesbians by Nujoma] was in the night, and the next morning I went to the shop in Katutura for a smoke, and people were looking at me and saying, "That moffie is going to be deported, exported!" They were pointing at me because they are very Christian. And I thought . . . they could even kill me! I was very scared. I took my bags and got out of there and went home and I just sat there. The people that I was staying with did not notice that I was gay. They said, "What is wrong?" and I said, "The president's speeches!" and they said, "Oh, are you [gay]"? And I told them I was. Then there was this space between us, and I felt [pauses], I felt like I was thrown away. I wanted to cry. I wanted to take the president and kill him. It took a lot of courage to convince [my relatives] that no matter what the president says or does, I cannot change. (twenty-year-old Namibian woman from Damara location, Katutura)

Despite the level of vitriol that the government unleashed upon Namibian gays and lesbians, no arrests, imprisonment, or deportations actually occurred. The more affluent white and colored gay and lesbian organizers generally did not experience overt violence from the hate speeches, because the international human rights community carefully guarded them. However, this was not the case for black Namibians living in the impoverished township of Katutura. Many young men and women received immediate negative repercussions within their community. Jason, a twenty-year-old male, explained how antihomosexual rhetoric ignited tensions within his family:

> When the president made that speech, my mother said, "He's doing the right thing. When they start to arrest or deport people, I will personally bring you to the police or to whoever will do the job!" I was hurt. I was scared, so I moved to my grandmother's place from my mother's. My grandmother sent me to the shops, and the people were saying, "Sam [Nujoma] is saying you must go out of our country, you must be deported." I felt like . . . I wish we [he and his two best friends] could just go somewhere. I felt like we had nowhere to go.

As contestations concerning homosexuality worked their way through township cultural life, tensions took shape within local fields of ethnic-identity politics. The president's condemnations of homosexuality were accompanied by a call for a return to traditional ways of life (Menges 2001). Yet many viewed the mention of "traditional" by the president as indexing Ovambo and Herero cultural practices. Thus, the LGBT social movement also provided a platform from which members of other ethnic groups (particularly Damara and Nama) could protest the tribalism associated with SWAPO's homophobic rhetoric. One TRP member in his early twenties who identified as Nama/Damara said:

> From the [heterosexual] Damaras you won't really get discrimination or sharp words; you will just get, "Hey, ladies, where are you going?" or "Can I fuck you tonight?" or "Did you hear what the president said?" But the Ovambos, they go deep into your skin and they work their way out with words.
>
> The Ovambo and Herero people, [some of them] are also moffies like us, but they are just hiding it . . . they are very scared. Our friends who are Ovambo and Herero guys, if they get drunk, they will get like this, "Girlfriend" [said with camp]. But if he is sober, he is very masculine.

Participants who identified as Ovambo or Herero and engaged in same-sex sexual practices, however, experienced extreme isolation and stigmatization within their communities.[2] One twenty-six-year-old who identified as being both Damara and Ovambo described how his social support circles began to dwindle after a series of announcements made by the president:

> I have been very close to Ovambo guys. So they knew I was gay. But after the hate speeches I could see that they were starting to withdraw from me, moving away slowly but surely. Many are cousins to me, but they don't want to be seen with me and go out with me clubbing like they use to.

For eighteen-year-old Winston, whose Oshivambo-speaking family held strong political ties to the SWAPO party, the hate speeches incited acts of violence: his father and brother beat him and his uncle's friend raped him. In 2002 he described his tumultuous journey of fleeing his village in the north to take up residence in the township of Katutura:

> My father was hating me, sometimes beating me. He is not supporting me anymore. My mother understands [my sexuality], but she cannot do anything, because they [his father and brothers] are men. My family, when they found out about me [being sexually attracted to other men], they thought I had a mental illness. My father put me in the mental hospital for two months. I remember the psychologist was giving me a pill and injections every day. . . . I do not know what was in it. My parents signed the forms to put me in there. But there was nothing wrong with me except that I was gay. I was locked in a room with only a toilet. I escaped from there and came to TRP. That is where I learned that I was a gay.

My uncle's friend, he [pauses] . . . he was the one who raped me. He is not a gay; he is married [and a prominent SWAPO politician]. He used a gun and I was stabbed twice. My father wanted to solve the problem in the family, but [the rapist] had pointed the gun at my head and he stabbed me here twice [shows his long scars on his head and shoulder]. Sometimes I want to go to Ovamboland to visit my mother, but I cannot, because of my father.

As black youths began to participate in the LGBT rights movement, they increasingly asserted gay and lesbian identifications and practiced gender non-conformity to confront hegemonic interpretations of their bodies. However, such strategies often broke down in local arenas where gender discrimination refracted through ethnic identity politics. Kelly, who regularly dressed in men's clothes and who proudly identified as Nama/Damara, relayed her experience of discrimination in her neighborhood grocery store:

I have the most difficult time with Ovambo people. The president is Ovambo, and he said that there were no Ovambo gays or lesbians. The other day I was walking just after the president's last speech at the labor union [August 2002]. I went to shop. I was in the front of the line and the teller wouldn't wait on me; she served the other lady. And these Ovambo guys were just looking at me, and I said, "Yes, I am proud to be a gay." The lady wouldn't serve me, and I said, "What the fuck is the problem?" I went over to the other Damara lady and said, "What is going on with the staff? She doesn't want to help me. I am standing in the queue, [and] she's serving the other person. It is because I am gay." She said, "Oh! Oh! Just take your stuff and leave." On my way home these same guys, the Ovambos, came toward me to touch my breast, and I said, "*Eina!*"[Afrikaans word signifying pain], pushed away his hand, and he said, "Oh, moffie," and the other one said, "You deserve to be fucked to become straight." This one Ovambo guy in Katutura promises me that one day he is going to rape me to make me straight.

Participants described their encounters with antihomosexual discrimination as occurring within institutional, community, and familial settings. Spaces that they once considered private became public and politicized when police and church representatives intruded upon their daily lives. As the regulatory power of institutions denied gays and lesbians the rights of privacy accorded to heterosexuals (McElhinny 2002, 118), sexual desire became the site of personal and national conflict, stirring political consciousness. For example, twenty-two-year-old Francis described his experiences of harassment by the paramilitary police, known as the Special Field Forces, at the height of the homophobic government rhetoric:

We were at a shebeen in Katutura, me and my friends . . . even the one who is a drag queen. After a while we decided to go to my aunt's place because she was selling some beer, and on our way to the house while we entered we just saw a car coming with the lights off, and they [the Special Field Forces] stopped and said that all of us would have to come out from the yard. Then my aunt said, "No, they are staying here"! And then one said, "Yah, it's eshenges. Eshenges are not allowed in Namibia!" Then they began to speak in [Oshivambo] and my friend, who was also Ovambo, said, "I am Ovambo eshenge," and they started to beat him, and my aunt said she was going to call the LAC [Legal Assistance Center], so they drove off. We filed a report after that, but nothing happened.[3]

Christian associations, which wield great symbolic capital in Namibian society, also took cues from government hate speeches. At the time the speeches began, many church leaders took up the issue of the "evils of homosexuality" in public sermons addressed to local congregations. Twenty-year-old John discussed his feelings of devastation when he faced discrimination in his church:

I grew up as a Pentecostal churchgoer. At the moment the hate speeches started in church, pastors, the deacons, the elders started preaching that homosexuality was a sin. And every Sunday when I go to church, there was a thing about homosexuality as a sin. It was after the human rights weekend. It was a pressure for me; I couldn't stand it. Usually I would be singing in the choir. I moved away from the church because my mum was an elder in the church and people were saying, "Oh, that elder's son is a gay person." The choir would have worshiping practice and they would move from house to house but would not tell me, and they said, "No, you are a gay, you are not supposed to sing in the worship." It made me sick for a while; you are so depressed, it is as if God is chasing you away. The way the pastors preach, the way the elders would speak, I would feel that God doesn't want me and I am excluded from the human race.

Gay and lesbian youths described how they were chased out of their churches for not conforming to gender-based conventions in their attire. Daphne, who was in her late teens when I first met her, recounted her negative experiences with church officials in Katutura:

Some church leaders were telling us that we could not wear pants. Sometimes when you walk into the church, there are people sitting at the door and they will chase you out. I have noticed this with my [lesbian] friends. . . . I have also experienced this myself. You are not supposed to come to church in pants if you are a woman.

With respect to health care, participants generally perceived the state-funded system as ignoring the needs of gay and lesbian people. As one young man explained: "If you go to the health officer and tell them about your sexuality, they will say that 'Oh, you sleep with a man. That is not allowed.' I once had a health officer tell me when I wanted some condoms, 'Oh, you are a gay man? *You* also use condoms?'" Lesbian youths expressed similar apprehensions. Hanna, for example, recounted experiencing great embarrassment when the attending nurse requested that her "boyfriend" come to the public clinic to be tested. When she explained that she had a girlfriend, the nurse became exasperated: "She looked at me as if there was something not right with me, and she said, 'Are you telling me that you got this from a woman?'"

The myriad denials of rights neither stifled nor immobilized these youths, but fueled their political desires to participate in the LGBT rights movement. When I returned to Namibia in July 2002, TRP's membership had grown to 190 and consisted mostly of people who were poor, unemployed, young, and black. A regular soup kitchen was then running twice weekly. The staff and management committee of TRP, however, continued to be primarily composed of people who were over thirty, white or colored, and lived in more affluent areas of Windhoek. As the membership base came to be dominated by young black people, many of the older founding members began to withdraw their involvement from the organization.[4]

Channeling the enthusiasm of these youths, TRP organizers began to deliver various self-awareness training workshops before a most eager group of participants, thus giving coherence to their emerging practices of freedom. In addition to work on improving self-esteem and body image, TRP's self-awareness programs focused on the following activities: teaching how to distinguish between lesbian, gay, bisexual, and transgender identities; exploring ideas of traditional homosexuality in ethnic identity terms; reconciling being lesbian or gay and a Christian; and encouraging open discussion about sexual desires in order to combat vulnerability to HIV infection. Although TRP's awareness-raising techniques aimed to protect and empower the Rainbow Youth, they also enacted a complex mode of power, operating at the level of subjectivity. By compelling these youths to regard selfhood as a vital resource for political action, TRP's interventions cultivated subjectivity as a political territory. What follows is a description of one of the many sexuality and gender identity training workshops I attended.

\* \* \*

About thirty of us took our seats around a half circle that opened toward the front of the conference room, where a confident eighteen-year-old named Travis stood and welcomed us in English, Afrikaans, and Damara. Despite his young age, Travis had already demonstrated his political commitment when he gave his coming out story to the national newspaper, the *Namibian,* and later recited it during a public poetry-reading night organized by TRP, Sister Namibia, and the National Human Rights Society of Namibia (NHRS).

This was a special meeting, for it was the first time that family members of lesbian, gay, bisexual, and transgender youths had been invited to attend a TRP workshop. Lionel, the facilitator, who during an earlier interview identified himself as a "colored" born into a wealthy South African family, rose to assure everyone in Afrikaans, "It's *not* a workshop, it's a talk shop. We talk openly about the issues here."

Then a respected elder, the grandmother of a well-known local drag queen, stood and spoke in Damara:

> I was supposed to go to a funeral, but because of this workshop I came here instead. I came here because of questions and answers—it is difficult for me. In 1940 I was born in the old location [of Katutura Township]. These days I see things—girls who look like boys, boys who look like girls, and now they are calling them homosexuals. In the old days it might have been true that homosexuality existed there, but we didn't see it. And when I see it here now in my surroundings, I am asking myself why. It's so hard to accept that women like to be men and men like to be women when in the beginning it was Eve and Adam. How do they become like what they are?

The director then said in Afrikaans, "To look at that question, we must explain gender and sexual identity."

The grandmother again interrupted the facilitator: "What we have done wrong is to begin without a prayer." She then led our group in a prayer, saying in Damara: "Holy Father, I thank you. We don't know about [homosexuality], so God, I am involving you in this: You created Adam and Eve, but there is a different lust among us, God. Let us understand this, God. I am asking this in Jesus Christ, the Saviour's name, who has no beginning and no end. I thank you for being part of this. Amen."

The facilitator thanked the grandmother with a mildly uncomfortable smile and then opened the floor for questions.

The first question came from a twenty-three-year-old male participant, who directed his query to the grandmother: "I want to know if homosexuality started now or is it an age-old thing?"

The grandmother responded by saying: "I didn't know things like this. Me personally, I don't like it. It was me taking care of my grandson when he was a child. I saw him. He is a man, not a woman, and only now do I see these things. . . . He's dressing up like a lady."

Daphne, a seventeen-year-old who describes herself as a "butch lesbian," pressed the question further in English, then switched to Afrikaans when she realized the elder was not following: "But what about the traditional words '!gamas' in Damara and the Ovambo word 'eshenge'? Doesn't that prove that homosexuality exists in Namibia?"

The grandmother conceded and said she remembered hearing the word "!gamas" used when she was a child. She said it referred to a goat that had both male and female organs.

Another elder made a correction: "No. It's a sheep."

Then another parent argued that "!gamas" referred to any animal that has both genitalia, while one of the youths insisted that it is the traditional name for a homosexual.

An intense debate broke out over the correct meaning of the word "!gamas," and it continued until the facilitator tried to settle the argument by referring to the research of Kurt Falk, an anthropologist who conducted studies in ethno-sexology throughout southern Africa during the late nineteenth and early twentieth centuries. The facilitator explained that Falk had recorded traditional names for homosexuality in all of Namibia's ethnic groups.

Daphne then said, in a stern tone, that parents know when their child is homosexual, because one girl may be good with cooking and cleaning in the home and another will be good outside, doing yard work and fixing cars (both considered to be men's work). The parents and relatives silently nodded and seemed convinced by her explanation.

Next the South African facilitator began the education portion of the "talk shop." First he distinguished between animals that are sexual and those that are asexual by explaining how fish, unlike humans, do not have sexual intercourse during their reproductive cycle. Then, referring to humans, he drew a horizontal line across the flip chart with three points, one at each end and one in the center. He referred to it as the "spectrum of sexual identity," labeling each point with sexual-identity categories: heterosexuality on the left, bisexuality in the middle, and homosexuality on the right. He explained the differences in sexual identities by referring to the corresponding object of desire. "Heterosexuals are attracted to the opposite gender. A homosexual is someone who is attracted to the same gender," he said, and so on.[5] After asking the participants to think about where they felt they fit within the spectrum, the facilitator told them that homosexual prevalence is "10 percent of all people"—a number once advanced by U.S. sexologist Alfred Kinsey in the 1940s and 1950s (see Kinsey et al. 1948). Amid a few giggles, the youths asked numerous questions, such as how to distinguish between a person who is transgender and one who is a butch lesbian. Then the facilitator continued his delineations by defining different forms of transgenderism: transsexuality, cross-dressing, transvestitism, and "gender bending." The talk shop continued for more than two hours and ended with a round of applause for the facilitator and the translators. The elders seemed grateful, politely thanking TRP for imparting this information to them, and then closed with another prayer.

\* \* \*

This vignette illustrates the kind of politics that sprang to life around TRP's training programs. The grandmother in the account refers to "Adam and Eve" to question the authenticity of Namibian gender and sexual nonconformity. This biblical narrative invokes the notion of a "universal humanity," one that is in keeping with the version of universal humanity proclaimed by SWAPO political leaders, as we saw in the last chapter. When the grandmother reminds everyone to start with a prayer, she is not simply declaring how religiously devout she is; rather, she is setting out the ethical parameters of a proper political discussion, for beginning with a prayer is a standard practice during local political meetings in the township of Katutura.

TRP's talk shops engage the subjectivities of their participants within a number of interlocking temporal and geographic conceptual registers. The first register is the present and the local. By reaffirming the existence of homosexuality in Namibian society with the use of contemporary local words such as "!gamas" and "eshenge," TRP's talk shops locate homosexuality within the boundaries of ethnicity. The second register is the archaic and the national. Citing the ethnological work of Kurt Falk allows TRP facilitators to invent traditional Namibian homosexualities as enduring and timeless. The third register is futuristic and global. In accordance with Dutch, German, and U.S. development policies, TRP's sexuality training programs draw explicitly upon the authoritative claims of sexology to teach participants how to distinguish between gay, lesbian, bisexual, and transgender identities. Referencing the sexual sciences, LGBT identities can be understood as a naturally occurring part of universal humanity, thus challenging the Christian version of universality put forth by the community elders.[6]

The idea of universal LGBT identities traverses the boundaries of nationhood to assert the legitimacy of Namibian gender and sexual nonconformity. Although local words and ideas filled TRP's many talk shop discussions, there is, nonetheless, a tacit (and therefore insidious) form of subjugation exercised here. When facilitators employ authoritative sexological discourses to rescue uncertainties regarding the "correct meaning" of "traditional" names for gender and sexual nonconformity, local gender and sexual knowledge becomes repositioned as being *undifferentiated*—that is, not fully recognized and in need of elevation to the more secure status of LGBT identities. In effect, this employment of universalistic logic recasts the local knowledge of the talk shop participants as being somehow backward.

When Sister Namibia activists first appealed to the work of the German ethno-sexologist Kurt Falk in the *Namibian*—privileging, ironically, racist literature to challenge SWAPO's claims—they set in motion a transhistorical knowledge-production process that warrants critical examination. Using ethnocentric ethnographic data to invent "traditional homosexuality," of course, serves as a form of "strategic essentialism" (Spivak 1990): by calling attention to the existence of "traditional homosexualities," lesbian and gay Namibians could fit within SWAPO's definition of what constitutes a legitimate citizen. Here TRP facilitators strategically comply with SWAPO's authority by reinforcing the importance of traditional sexuality in an effort to create a space of belonging. Yet, despite the immediate strategic end it appears to serve in countering state discourses, the resurrection of Falk's scientific authority combines with TRP's rights discourses in ways that create new inequalities for the Rainbow Youth at the level of self-conceptualization. To demonstrate what I mean here, it is necessary to provide a short synopsis of Falk's work based upon the translated texts that appear in Stephen O. Murray and Will Roscoe's (1998) anthology of "African homosexualities," *Boy-Wives and Female Husbands,* which was published to oppose the vilifying antihomosexual rhetoric that occurred in southern Africa in the mid to late 1990s.

Falk's research sought to contribute to the destigmatization of European homosexuals by drawing upon Magnus Hirschfield's typology of homosexuality (Bleys 1995).[7] In former South West Africa (now Namibia), Falk recorded traditional names that not only described homosexual acts but also homosexual roles and relationships. For example, Falk described one man "who was active as a wizard and medicine man" and whose "love of men" was known by his Ovahimba tribe (Falk 1998, 190). Falk also discussed homoerotic relationships among young Herero boys. These *oupanga,* as they were called at the time of Falk's research, continued until marriage. At such time, Falk maintained, "[they] naturally turn to heterosexual intercourse" (191). However, he goes on to say that when adult Herero men left on long journeys, they were often accompanied by their former *epanga* (singular form of oupanga), with whom they engaged in sexual intercourse (mainly mutual masturbation). Although Falk's documentation of *tribadie* (same-sex practices between women) was less extensive, he did refer to "newly married" black women living in northern and southern regions of SWA who "practiced intercourse with each other almost insatiably" (193).[8]

Situated within larger European sexological debates, Falk's research spoke to tensions related to the proximity of settlers and Africans. At that time German sexologists who regarded South West Africans as the unspoiled and pristine "other" expressed concern over the possible negative effects on natives who came into contact with European (particularly German) homosexuals (Falk 1998, 195). Falk's ethnographic work attempted to settle this debate by demonstrating that "homoerotic" behavior was not only present but was also "so widely practiced among the natives" that it could even pose a potential threat to colonial residents.

> Thus, the fear that "the morality of the native is done harm" [by contact with white homosexuals (translator's insert)] is baseless. *It would be correct to say that the harm is to the whites by their proximity to the natives.* But then sexual intercourse between whites and coloreds is completely prohibited and untolerated, indeed, it is penalized. To the natives having sex is as normal as eating and drinking, and by all means tobacco smoking. They understand it as something wholly natural that whites also require and seek. And so they see nothing special in same-sex intercourse, provided only it is kept secret. As

long as this happens, all is in order. Because they view homosexual intercourse with unbiased eyes and find nothing monstrous there, they have known and practiced it the same way in the time immemorial [emphasis added].

Falk's work conceived of African homosexualities within an imperialistic framework that portrayed African sexuality as archaic (not to mention hypersexual). While he delineated same-sex sexual practices along ethnic lines, his overarching analysis spoke of a more singular, essentialized "native" sexuality. For Falk, "native sexuality" was devoid of subjectivity—a timeless, precolonial artifact that remained tied to nature and instinct and contained within ethnic groups. Positioned within sexological discourse as an original form of human sexuality, "native homosexuality" allowed Falk to raise protest against paragraph 175, a provision in the German criminal code prohibiting sex between males, which was later enlarged under Nazi German rule: "Everyone who has worked as a sexologist among natives must instinctively shake his head when certain representatives and supporters of the ominous Paragraph 175 want to deny the inborn nature of the homoerotic. . . . Anyone denying inborn homosexuality should without prejudice make inquiries hereabout with the natives and he will soon have another opinion" (Falk 1998, 195–196).

Falk's work was not the only colonial source to which Sister Namibia activists subscribed. In 2001 they published a three-page article on African homosexuality as a "litmus [test] for human rights" in their bimonthly magazine, also named *Sister Namibia*.[9] The author, freelance journalist Erika von Wietersheim, cites South African activist and scholar Linda Ngcobo to argue for the existence of "traditional" African homosexuality (Sister Namibia 2001, April-May). In the foreground of this article is a photo that depicts an *ekola* player wearing traditional Kwanyama garb.[10] According to the work of ethnomusicologist Percival Kirby in the early 1940s, von Wietersheim notes, the ekola was played by "sodomites." Legal scholar Dianne Hubbard of the Legal Assistance Center also took up this historiography during a discussion of sodomy laws titled "Why the Law on Sodomy Should Be Repealed" for TRP's LGBT Rights Awareness Week held in 2000. At the end of Hubbard's speech, she references the Kwanyama ekola player to evidence the existence of homosexuality in northern Namibia. She also adds the fact that seventeenth-century Italian missionary Giovanni Cavazzi had published a drawing of the same instrument in 1694 (citing Kirby 1942), thus pointing to the supposed enduring tradition of homosexuality among Ovambo communities in this region. This postcolonial invention of traditional homosexuality tends to mute the overt colonial overtones that are evident in the original sources. In the original text, Kirby mentions that Cavazzi "emphasized the 'indecent' nature of many native dances and rites which he saw" (1942, 350). A closer examination of Kirby's text reveals a series of colonial-style interrogations with local people in an attempt to elicit the "true" meanings surrounding the playing of the instrument.

> Mr. A. C. Logie, of Windhoek . . . discovered after prolonged cross-question-ing, that the natives' reference to "half man, half woman" did not mean "her-maphrodite," as we had supposed, but "sodomite." His final description of the instrument is as follows: "Although not itself a particularly attractive instru-ment, the *ekola* plays a most interesting part in the life of the Ovakuanyama. It is essentially connected with sodomy, and is played in the first instance by the medicine man, who encourages this practice. To him it is a source of revenue, as he obtains a 'fee' from every man he has enticed to be a partaker. . . . When an Ukuanyama man falls a prey to this practice he discards his weapons, his bow, his arrow and his assegai (the distinguishing marks of manhood) and plays the *ekola*. He is no longer regarded as a man . . . but who is after all only 'half man, half woman.'" (349)

Trimming off the colonial context from these ethnocentric sexological texts, writers and activists affiliated with *Sister Namibia* magazine strategically inter-vened in the idea of homosexuality as being un-African. However, the contempo-rary re-presentation of sexual archetypes, frozen in the photo of "the Kwanyama Sodomite" (see figure 5) and in Falk's sexual cartography, also positions ordinary Namibians within this epistemological terrain as being unaware of their own sexual history, thus displacing local sexual knowledge.

Interestingly, the Rainbow Youth I spoke with had never heard of many of the words that Falk had documented, or else they considered the words to be unrelated to gender nonconformity or same-sex sexual behavior. For instance, Herero-speaking participants recognized "oupanga" as a name for friendship but maintained that it held no erotic denotation or connotation. As well, Falk never recorded "!gamas" or "!gamab" as traditional words among Damara speakers nor other, similar words with which elders living in Katutura were familiar. This is not to say that local people or Falk misnamed Namibian homosexualities or failed to recount an accurate version of Namibia's history of gender and sexual noncon-formity. Instead, local uncertainties over "the correct names and meanings" for homosexuality point more to a noncontinuous and perhaps even ephemeral his-tory of naming same-sex erotic practices in Namibia due to its changing moral-political significance within colonial and indigenous institutions since the turn of the twentieth century.[11]

The idea that Damara ethnic communities were less discriminatory toward homosexuality compared to Oshivambo communities was a widely held assertion among TRP organizers and the Rainbow Youth alike, and it certainly matched my observations in Katutura. But the idea of sexuality as tied to ethnic cultural origins was reified in the book *Tommy Boys, Lesbian Men, and Ancestral Wives* (Morgan and Wieringa 2005). In the chapter composed by the self-identified Damara feminist writer Elizabeth Khaxas and her co-author, Saskia Wieringa, they attempt to explain "the fact that many women in same-sex relationships among the Damara live their lives more openly than women of other communities in Namibia" (123). The authors trace contemporary gender relationships and familial arrangements among Damara people to precolonial Damara culture—that is, an "egalitarian" sexual division of labor; a "matrilocal system in which the children reside with the women"; and "bilinear inheritance" patterns that provides "a very democratic space for all its people" (124). Although giving a nod to the influence of Christianity, colonialism, and apartheid, the authors insist that the less discriminatory ways of Damara people continue to exist as part of the "remnants of these values [that] have remained in the collective consciousness of the Damara people" (125).

I witnessed Khaxas deliver this form of culturalist narrative during various public forums attended by the Rainbow Youth. I have also heard TRP and Sister Namibia organizers and workshop facilitators repeat different versions of these ethnic-origin narratives pertaining to sexuality and gender in Namibia. The significance here is how the mostly Damara-speaking Rainbow Youth receive these essentialist narratives and how these discourses compel them to see their difference through the primordial lens of what Khaxas and Wieringa refer to as "the old kinship system" (2005, 125).

Articulating with Sister Namibia's historiographies of traditional sexuality and gender, Namibia's most widely read newspaper, the *Namibian*, provided a regular space for organizers from TRP, Sister Namibia, and other allies to express opposing views to SWAPO's antihomosexual rhetoric. Known for taking a critical stance on SWAPO's political practices in editorial opinion pieces, the *Namibian* regularly headlined queer news items from Europe and other economically advantaged countries. Such headlines during the period of my fieldwork, for instance, have read "Germany Opens Door for Gay Marriages," "Blair Backs Gay Minister," and "Gay Politicians Told to Come Out" (like the openly gay mayor of Berlin). These examples of European "progressivity" are held out for Namibians to highlight the need for "liberation" in the area of gay rights; notably, these articles spoke considerably less about the intense racism and xenophobia that was occurring in Germany at this time.

The deployment of "sexuality" by Sister Namibia, TRP, and the *Namibian* together imagine a cultural evolutionary trajectory for Namibians engaged in same-sex sexual practices. Sister Namibia reveals how to be the legitimate, authentic Namibian—by first rooting oneself in archaic terms. TRP's sexuality lessons teach about the nature of one's being, which in the case of queer youths is not yet fully realized. And the *Namibian* directs and inspires LGBT youths toward a path that is more "progressive," more "modern," and more "enlightened." This posits the recognition of (Western) sexual identities as a modern and progressive cultural achievement. Subjectivities emerge along this temporal trajectory of enlightenment as participants "discover" themselves within LGBT identities. Take Francis's explanation to me during an interview in 2001:

> *Now I know I am a gay,* but I think I started to realize I was different from other boys when I was about in grade seven. Because I can remember . . . I came back from school on a specific date, then I talked with my parents and I said, "Even though I stay with girls, I didn't have this strange [sexual] feeling, but when I saw this certain guy today, I was feeling like this" [gestures to indicate being sexually excited]. I told them that. That was where it started.
>
> My dad was a little bit angry. I shouldn't say a little bit; he was very furious. But luckily I grew up with my grandmum, and she had already observed all these things even while I was still a child. My grandmum said that "in our language there is a word that they used to say for it," but even at that stage I was too young to make it out—!gamas. It is like you were meant for something but you don't go for that—you are the other part. Luckily she was there when I told my parents.

After describing the torrent of discrimination he survived, Winston, who grew up in a small village in northern Namibia, remembers his earlier experiences of gender nonconformity:

> *Before I came out and realized I was a gay,* there was this guy at my place. Normally the people, they say that I look like a girl in my face. One time we were looking after the cattle (this is what the men must do). [The other villagers] used to say that when I come to the house I must bring him some *ongome*— you make it in a pot with *Mahangu* [a root crop] and put sugar and salt; it is what a woman brings to the man. One day he comes home and he was saying, "This one is my girlfriend." They were saying that I must bring the ongome to the man like a woman. When people used to want to beat me, he would say, "No, he's my girlfriend," because I looked like a girl.

Travis, who was nineteen years old, said that growing up he did not have many troubles because of his "difference." However, he did remember at times being called names like "!gamab" by other children. He said that before his coming out, which happened after he joined TRP at the age of sixteen, "*I didn't even know what my sexuality was.* I always knew I was attracted to boys, but I was thinking I must be the woman. I don't identify as a woman anymore. I identify as a gay man now—a man who loves other men."[12]

In such coming out narratives, local words and practices that refer to gender and sexual nonconformity re-signify in memory to represent a period when selfhood is undifferentiated. Realization of a gay or lesbian identity as a discrete property of the self, then, brings certain local anxieties about gender and sexual nonconformity into relief as it ties together local knowledges, memories, pleasures, and experiences of discrimination to the global project of LGBT rights.

Francis, Winston, and Travis, like many others I spoke with, found the process of self-realization, fostered during TRP sexuality training workshops, extremely liberating and felt compelled to come out publicly by actively delivering their testimonials of discrimination during Human Rights Awareness Week, meetings with the press, and poetry readings between 2001 and 2003. Indeed, the cultivation of subjectivity during TRP training workshops sparked new ways of understanding and valuing the self for the Rainbow Youth, redefining how they related to the nation-state and the global human rights community. These workshops were instrumental in making selfhood into a vital territory for LGBT political mobilization.

In particular, TRP organizers utilized two key interrelated technologies to channel the desires of youths in the service of LGBT rights mobilizations—"sexual identity categories" and "the coming-out narrative." They can be regarded as "technologies of the self" in the sense that they "permit individuals to effect by their own means, or with the help of others, a certain number of operations on their own bodies and souls, thoughts, conduct, and way of being, so as to transform themselves in order to attain a certain sense of [liberation]" (Foucault 1997, 225). LGBT identifications were not passively accepted by these youths, but emerged through careful, critical rumination. And it was not uncommon during talk shops for participants to debate, sometimes almost endlessly, the various possible meanings of and boundaries between sexual- and gender-identity categories. These flourishing identity politics form the ground from which the Rainbow Youth cultivated their practices of freedom. They also display the effects of neoliberal logics that give primacy to the resources of self-determination over the everyday materialities that constitute their oppression (Comaroff and Comaroff 2001, 11, 15).

\* \* \*

One day Jennifer came into the office with long, braided hair extensions. She announced to all of us that she was feeling like a "lady." There were a few giggles from some of the other youths, because only yesterday she had styled her hair in a short, masculine-looking Afro and generally carried her body in a masculine manner. One of the onlookers, Kelly, turned to me with a grin and muttered under her breath, "How can she be a lady when she's the captain of our football [soccer] team?"

I had the chance to interview Jennifer later that day and asked her what she thought about TRP's training workshops. She responded:

> For me I really can't say I define myself as something. Today you identify yourself as—what? And then tomorrow you don't feel the same. . . . I don't agree with the categories sometimes, sometimes you have to call yourself something so that people won't be confused. But I wouldn't mind if people think I am confused, because I know who I am [*laughs*].

TRP sponsored Jennifer and several other young women to go to South Africa for additional training in sexuality. She expressed her ambivalence about the categories used by facilitators by saying:

> I was against something there; it was a debate. There were people who identified as "lesbian men" and "transgenders." Me, I am just a woman who likes other women; if that makes me a lesbian—that's fine. But it doesn't make me a man. Now, because I have my hair long (I have extensions now), people think I am going back to men.

By the afternoon, the braids started to come undone, and Jennifer began removing them in a piecemeal fashion until it was time for her to head out with her lesbian teammates for football practice. The next day she returned to the office with a shaved head. But this was certainly not the last time Jennifer made declarations regarding her gender ambiguity.

When I interviewed other lesbian participants about what they thought about the sexual-identity categories taught to them, most expressed similar reservations about the typological scheme drawn by TRP. Another member of the football team, Daphne, said:

> Me, I knew I was a tomboy. But when I hear the different terms—lesbian, bisexual, transgender—you think, I have a little bit of this, a bit of that. But at the end you have to make up your mind. Some people don't want to identify; they don't want any identity. Sometimes I feel I don't want any identity but just want to be part [of society]. So I identify as "bisexual" and sometimes a "butch lesbian." I feel I am 70 percent lesbian and 30 percent heterosexual. Over time it has changed. First I identified as a "butch"—as a man. Now I see myself as a woman that loves other women.

Although most female participants contested these categories, they still continued to engage enthusiastically in debates on sexual and gender identity during training workshops, thereby repeatedly placing attention on the self. However, participants displayed far less uncertainty about lesbian and gay identities during more political forums and rallies such as annual human rights awareness weeks or public storytelling events held outside of Namibia. Youths indeed recognized the strategic benefit of unambiguously asserting lesbian and gay identifications to form the kinds of transnational political solidarities that might help to bring greater focus to the oppression of queer Namibians. In this respect Jennifer and Daphne greatly excelled in narrating the struggles of being a lesbian in Namibia in 2002 before an international audience at the Gay Games in Australia. Jennifer gushed about her experiences upon returning from the Gay Games while sitting in the van that drove her from the airport to her home in Herero Lokasie. Along the way, she said to a group of us, "You wouldn't believe it. After I told my story all these white lesbians were coming up to me and congratulating me. They really understood me. And I got a lot of emails [addresses]. God, this one lesbian—ah, I fell in love with her."

However, once we arrived in front of her home in Katutura, I watched Jennifer's excitement vanish when she left the van and saw her mother, who was waiting inside the front door with a stern look on her face. Her mother looked at the van with great disapproval. Soon after, Jennifer stopped going to TRP meetings, workshops, and political forums. When I bumped into her one day on Independence Avenue, Jennifer explained that her family had forbidden her from going to TRP's workshops, because they had noticed, as she put it, "too much of a change in me," and they had pressured her into dating men who were friends of the family. When the subject of Jennifer's withdrawal from TRP came up at the office, Hanna insisted that Jennifer was "going with these men [for paid sex], so she can support her family. They are Herero, you know, and so they pressure you like this." Then, pausing to reflect, she continued: "Anyway, Jennifer is too confused about herself. She doesn't really know who she is! That is why she is going with those men." Daphne and a few others nodded silently. In this way an identity politics that privileges notions of autonomy and self-determination elides the exigencies of poverty.

In addition to sexual-identity training, TRP's workshops provide a "safe space" where people could tell and retell their coming out stories. For most of lesbian participants, coming out stories followed a similar structure, from a state of naïveté and uncertainty to a state of self-awareness and self-transformation.

> When I was young, I was rough—kind of what you call a tomboy. And then I went to high school; I became feminine, a woman. I was also interested in boys. I was in boarding school when I realized I was attracted to women *but didn't know that it* [being a lesbian] *was possible*. I mean, people are saying you are influenced by others, but I don't feel I was influenced by others, because when I first felt for a woman *I didn't know what it was, and I didn't know that it happens somewhere else.* And for me it was very abnormal and wrong. I felt I mustn't do this. I felt I should take men, because this is how it should be and everyone is doing it.
>
> I was playing soccer and a friend saw me playing on the street and said, "Oh. You are a nice soccer player!" She brought me to the Rainbow Warriors [women's soccer team]. She was not gay, but most of the players were gay, and that is where I learned about what a lesbian was. I got to know those people when I went on tour and a woman made a move on me, and from there I knew I liked women. When I first went to a lesbian workshop put on by TRP and Sister Namibia, the workshops broadened out my mind. Now I can look at things from many sides. . . . I had too many questions. I get a lot from reading [TRP's] magazines, books, videos and even blue movies [*laughs*]. (Jennifer, 2002)

> I remember playing mummy and daddy games when I was five or six. I remember clearly that I made love to a girl . . . we were kissing. My mum knew I

was a big tomboy. She bought me shorts and T-shirts. Just when I got to high school I was supposed to be like a girl. I grew up only with girls, so there were pressures to be like a girl. I grew up in a very Christian house. At church and school I had to wear a dress. In high school I got involved with this girl for four years. *I didn't know it was a lesbian relationship until I came here to TRP.* . . . Last year when I came to TRP I learned what a lesbian was. But I didn't really come out because of my family name and ethnic group [Ovambo]. After being involved [with TRP], I wrote a letter for their newsletter. They asked if I would be brave enough to give my coming out story publicly. So I did and it has changed how I felt about myself. I feel I know myself now. (Daphne, 2002)

Kelly's rather triumphant narrative, below, demonstrates how TRP's workshops facilitate the process of "uncovering" self-knowledge, a process that propelled Kelly's entry into political activism.

I was very "womanly"—long hair, very beautiful girl. But after I came to grade eight, I met one girl in school who cut her hair like a man and was talking "like that" [*lowers her voice to imitate a man*]. And I thought, okay, I feel like that also. . . . I cut my hair and changed my clothes, and then I felt much more comfortable. . . .

This one schoolteacher, who called me into the staff room, told me, "[Kelly], wear a skirt." And the next day I still wore trousers and she called me in again. I told her, "I feel I must do this because I am a boy." I got sent home for two weeks' suspension. So I did eventually wear the skirt, and the students, they were laughing. . . . They were loving it when I was wearing a skirt, because I was walking more like a man. I looked like I was in the circus.

The first time I heard the word "lesbian" was 1998, when I was hearing about TRP in the news [during the hate speeches]. And I was wondering: What is a lesbian? How does she look? Is she a man? [TRP] said, "No. She likes dressing in men's clothes. She is 'like a man' and she only dates women." And I thought, okay, I am a lesbian because I only dress like a man and I like women. But I was afraid . . . because I thought if I am a lesbian, I won't go to heaven; I will go straight direct to hell.

There was a workshop at TRP in 1998. There was the thing of labeling, and I said, "Don't label me, because I don't want to be labeled." I met this friend of mine at a lesbian workshop [organized by Sister Namibia] where there was only women. I went along with her, and at this workshop we talked about this labeling, identity stuff. Actually, it was there that I thought I will join TRP and learn more about myself, and to know how to defend myself and how to deal with people who are being homophobic.

The pamphlets that [TRP] had helped me with my self-esteem—very much. Even when I was feeling confused about myself, I would sit down and take this pamphlet; it would give me this strong courage to be myself. When I came to TRP I was meeting new people. They were telling their story, how they experienced it. Some were worse than mine, and I would think if these people could go through this struggle, why can't I? TRP is a place where you can know yourself and identify yourself; they won't sit there and tell you, "No, you are like this." But when they are doing workshops . . . they show you the [spectrum of sexualities] and you know that you are there or there [*gestures*].

Every day I am getting stronger. I was even involved in the march. Pictures were taken. I was in the front holding the sign. I was screaming "I am gay"—this is who I am. Because first I was ashamed of myself, I could not accept who I was. I went home after the march, [and] I thought, *This is the way forward, and this is the next step.* (Kelly, 2002)

Like Kelly, most participants claimed to feel transformed in how they understood and valued themselves after participating in TRP workshops, even while they held sexual- and gender-identity categories to be problematic. As a technology of the self, the coming out narrative had dramatic psychological effects on the Rainbow Youth as a range of ambivalent personal historical events were brought into a coherent narrative structure. By invoking the coming out narrative, previously undifferentiated experiences became consolidated, knowable, and, therefore, available for self-valuation and legitimation.

During this earlier period of fieldwork, I witnessed numerous versions of the coming out narrative offered as testimonials during TRP workshops, press conferences, and interviews with media and foreign researchers. They were also employed to settle disputes with peers, relatives, and elders in Katutura. But these narrative practices must be distinguished from the recitation of bounded texts or fixed scripts because, over time, they unfold, alter, and enlarge as social actors become caught up in the spiraling of interpretations (Antze and Lambek 1996, xix). In its connection to bodily desires, which can be ambiguous to decipher, the coming out narrative allows for a sense of continual self-discovery; for this reason, participants often expressed their surprise in learning something new about their self in each retelling of their story.

In cultivating a sense of self-recognition, the coming out narrative structure generates desire as it bridges past struggles with gender and sexual nonconformity with the future possibility of freedom in Namibia. Articulating with TRP's inventions of "traditional homosexuality," as described earlier in the chapter, coming-out narratives detemporalize subjectivities, producing a sense of lack between where one is in the present and where one could (and should) be in terms of liberation in the future. Sharing these narratives with one another during workshops also intensifies participants' desires, such that what emerges from the relationship of individuals and groups with the self is a collective political project: the emancipation of LGBT Namibians. As demonstrated by Kelly, hearing the coming out stories of others and remembering her own gender and sexual troubles in a narrative of triumphant self-discovery compels her participation in political protests for the benefit of her community. Therefore, these "self-liberations" provide the ethical ground from which the Rainbow Youth conceive of and enact politics.

What is important to note here is how sexual desire is *positively valued* in TRP's interventions and is intensified through disciplined attention to the self. In SWAPO's rhetoric on homosexuality, sexual desire stands in opposition to morality: it must be repressed for the "greater good" of the nation (see Introduction). According to Namibia's ubiquitous AIDS campaigns, sexual desire must be self-regulated and controlled for the benefit of public health.[13] In the latter two instances, desire is constructed in somewhat Freudian, libidinal terms—it is what threatens the safety and stability of society. By contrast, within the context of the Rainbow Project of Namibia, *a form of ethics is constituted around sexual desire.* TRP organizers and staff members invest considerable effort in activities that aim to heighten consciousness about and encourage acceptance and expression of sexual desire. These practices are undergirded by a different moral logic: embracing one's inner sexual desires will lead to greater self-knowledge and self-possession, thereby enabling the individual to more effectively pursue social justice for herself and for her community.

The practice of reflecting on one's sexual desires helped to supply the Rainbow Youth with the internal resources for contending with state oppression. For example, twenty-year-old Roxy wrestled with her sense of sexual difference, keeping it a secret for many years. After taking part in several sexuality training workshops, she felt confident in defying President Nujoma's interdictions regarding homosexuality by coming out publicly at a human rights event. During an interview she explained how her inner desires legitimated her resistance to the president's antihomosexual rhetoric. "The president was saying that homosexuality is un-African. I would say it is untrue. I cannot sit here today and say I want to be gay tomorrow. It is not something you can learn from somebody. *It is something that comes from inside you.* No one is telling me that I should be gay or I should be heterosexual. I feel I am attracted to women, not to men. Why should I be attracted to men?"

Although this internal focus makes "the self" a critical site for liberation, the Western-informed intervention discourses, practices, and power relations that induce these *inward* practices of self-reflection and legitimation go unacknowledged, as though they are forgotten. As such, self-knowledge becomes experienced as if it is hidden in layers of consciousness. Because the sense of self gained through this type of self-reflection can be somewhat ephemeral, in order to more fully grasp that sense the Rainbow Youth displayed an almost ritualistic devotion to reconfirming their desires—through repeated acts of reflection and resistance, such as re-attending workshops, reading and rereading pamphlets and other literature, giving personal testimonials, debating questions of sexual identity with peers and staff, protesting for sexual minority rights, and dressing in drag.[14]

* * *

Early one morning in 2002, I arrived at the TRP's office and found several of the Rainbow Youth looking upset, with their heads hanging low. "What happened here?" I asked with concern. Travis immediately handed me a small booklet and told me to read it. The booklet condemned homosexuality. It asked questions like "What is a penis for?" and "What is a vagina for?" and supplied the definitive response—"procreation." A staff member of a Christian NGO whose office was adjacent to TRP had placed the booklet under TRP's office door. Travis and the small group took me to the front of the NGO and pointed out where the booklet had originated. Hanging outside the door was a rainbow sign to signify the mandate of the NGO: to address racial/ethnic diversity in Namibian churches. "That is not our rainbow!" Kelly exclaimed. Travis said, "I can't believe they are right next door to us and they would do this to us. It doesn't feel like it's a safe space here anymore." Witnessing the degree of outrage and upset that day rather than dismissal, I realized the extent to which the Rainbow Youth remained invested in Christian religious values.

Indeed, to fully understand the gravity of church condemnation of homosexuality, it is necessary to understand how Christian regulatory power has come to operate in contemporary Namibian society. During the apartheid era, the Church was one of the few spaces where racial segregation could be transcended. Antiapartheid political strategies drew on liberation theology to mobilize the universalizing discursive potential of Christian ideologies (Katjavivi et al. 1989). During the liberation struggle, therefore, Christian and antiapartheid ideologies became inexorably linked. In postcolonial Namibia, significant national and community solidarity continues to come through daily participation in church ritual and social activity. For this reason, TRP organizers, political allies, and academics worked hard with church leaders to negotiate a political platform that was less damning to the cause of LGBT rights. After a series of public forums in 2001, the Council of Churches in Namibia (CCN) did eventually support the protection of the constitutional rights of gays and lesbians (however, they have continued to maintain that homosexuality is a sin).

The importance of reconciling sexual identity with Christian doctrines was apparent during TRP workshops and special human rights events that deliberately included members of the clergy or theologians. One workshop in 2003, led by an openly gay Anglican South African priest, was especially lively. This was one of the best-attended workshops I had witnessed. After the priest asked each participant to introduce herself or himself, he discussed his struggle to be accepted as an openly gay priest in the Anglican Church in South Africa. Next he opened up the floor for the Rainbow Youth to relay their own experiences. Intense testimonials of discrimination were then fervently shared by a number of individuals, the audience listening with rapt attention to each person's experi-

ence. Dion recounted his painful experience after he moved in with his Oshivambo-speaking boyfriend in Wanaheda, Katutura:

> We visited [my partner's] church. His brother-in-law was also a member of
> the church, but he did not greet us. In the middle of the ceremony, my lover
> decided to move up to the front to confess [his homosexuality]. The pastor put
> his hand on his head and started praying for him. I was still sitting there and I
> saw his brother-in-law stand up and move towards me. He asked me to get out
> of the church. I asked "Why?" And he said, "Just get out of the church!" This is
> during the service! So I got up, I stood up—my lover is in the front confessing
> [his sin of homosexuality]—and on my way out [the brother-in-law] picked up
> a chair and hit me with the chair [breaking my collarbone]. I fell down and I
> got up again and ran out of the church.

This particular testimonial struck a chord with the young audience. The Anglican priest, responding to the rapidly rising energy in the room, asked the youths
to break into groups to identify their major concerns with respect to religion and
sexuality. Topping their lists was the concern "How can I be gay and a Christian?" This subject was discussed for more than an hour, circling around feelings
of shame and self-devaluation, which the participants struggled to overcome. Offering a critical interpretation of Sodom and Gomorrah and a few passages in
Leviticus, the priest helped the group to try to reconcile their sexual desires as
gays and lesbians with their desire to belong within "the Christian family," as he
called it.

In June 2003 TRP project manager Madeline Isaacs networked with members of the South African queer religious NGO called IAM (Inclusive and Affirming Ministries) at the "Sex and Secrecy" conference in Johannesburg, organized by the International Association for the Study of Sexuality, Culture, and
Society. Under the auspices of IAM, TRP soon initiated the Namibian Assistance
Project to help Namibian gays and lesbians to cope with religious persecution.
Although Christian religious training offered by TRP helped to ease the moral
uncertainties between sexual and Christian identities, this rescuing of "souls" in
some instances unintentionally contributed to feelings of insecurity among the
Rainbow Youth in relation to their place of belonging within the global gay and
lesbian community.

On July 14, 2007, a white, South African lesbian pastor from IAM held a
public talk at TRP's head office in Windhoek titled "My Child Is Gay—What
Now?" This well-attended presentation was offered to help parents cope with the
"loss" of discovering that their child is gay. "Such loss," the pastor emphasized,
"includes the loss of the dream of grandchildren."

This presentation followed a series of training workshops that taught spiritual (Christian-based) counseling techniques to young TRP members. Drawing
upon Craig O'Neill and Kathleen Ritter's (1992) eight stages of "spiritual awaken-

ing for lesbians and gay men," the lesbian pastor, with a rousing tone, insisted that parents and youths could "transform loss into a liberation. The journey doesn't have to end in victimization. There can be freedom at the end!"

What I found interesting was that unlike TRP's other workshops, which generally set forth delineations between lesbian, gay, bisexual, and transgender identities, the religious workshops, by contrast, *rarely* referenced bisexuality (and altogether ignored transgender identities). Knowing that many of the lesbian women sitting in the audience practiced bisexual behavior (and in fact had children), I posed the following question to the pastor during the discussion period: "How would O'Neill's stages work for parents who discover that their child is *bisexual?*" Some of the women nodded in agreement with my question; a few grinned at me slightly. The pastor paused, looked mildly perplexed, and began muttering for a few moments. Then, with a tone of conviction, she cited the term "pseudo-homosexuality," asserting that "some people are not true homosexuals. . . . For example, if a woman is sexually abused [by a man], she may think that she is a lesbian. But she is not a true lesbian and she must therefore seek counseling." A few of the women, especially Kelly, squirmed in their seats; others crinkled their faces. However, the usually vocal Rainbow Youth remained respectfully silent.

The issue of sexual abuse and lesbian authenticity resurfaced in 2008 during TRP's public forum held in conjunction with the Media Institute of Southern Africa as part of their new gay-straight alliance initiative called Straight Talk with Straight Friends. The forum began with a presentation by Daphne, now a prominent, young lesbian activist who defined a range of sexual identity terms: anatomical sex, gender, sexual identity, bisexuality, transgenderism, transvestitism, intersexuality, and so on. Then, during the question period, a male audience member asked, "Can a woman become a lesbian if she is raped by a man?" This question captured the audience's interest as a lively debate on the subject ensued. Attempting to settle the debate authoritatively, a European lesbian psychotherapist who worked at the violence and trauma counseling NGO known as PEACE (People's Education, Assistance, and Counseling for Empowerment) responded firmly, "Yes, it is possible for a woman who has become sexually abused by a man to *believe* that she is a lesbian."

The notion of pseudo-homosexuality asserted by the pastor and the psychotherapist offers a problematic interpretation for many local lesbians. The discourse of "pseudo-homosexuality" proffers a degenerative narrative whereby sexual abuse damages the integrity of heterosexuality—posited, tacitly, as an original and impressionable surface—corrupting its "natural" separation from homosexuality. This implies a psychopathological state in which the sexually abused individual falsely recognizes herself as a homosexual to escape anxieties surrounding the sexual abuse event(s). Employing this logic, the pastor and the psychotherapist not only position heterosexuality as the normal, pristine, healthy "default" sexuality, but they also frame African female bisexuality as a conflicted sexual subject position: where heterosexual remnants continually return to resist the foreclosure of a "false" lesbian identity enforced by traumatic memories. In other words, their deployment here calls into question the authenticity of the lesbian identifications taken up by many of the women in her audience, thus undermining their space of political belonging. Although these women hold a firm connection to global lesbian activism in their personal and collective pursuits of self-determination, many have shared (and continue to share) sexual intimacies with men, engage in transactional sex, and encounter various forms of sexual violence at the hands of men over their lifetime.[15] But what I find salient in the discourse of pseudo-homosexuality pertains not only to concerns over authenticity and belonging per se. Most troubling is how its redeployment seals over potentially wider political resonances between these women's struggles and other non-lesbian-identifying women, effectively erasing possibilities for wider political solidarity.

* * *

In a time of AIDS the Rainbow Project's HIV prevention workshops proceeded according to the logic that talking about sex more openly would empower the individual to overcome her vulnerability to HIV infection. This reasoning is, of course, consistent with TRP's investment in liberating the self-awareness of the Rainbow Youth to improve their well-being. In the ethnographic portrait of Louami that follows, I discuss how her subjectivity opened up to new ideas of freedom through her various engagements with LGBT mobilizations. Over time, however, the realities of HIV prevalence in her community and economic hardship eventually eroded her practices of freedom.

"I like my men like I like my bread—fresh and white!" said Louami as she helped kick off the two-day safer-sex education weekend called "Let's Talk about Sex, Baby." This sharing of local pickup lines to express sexual interest in others served as the warm-up exercise to begin the workshop series. Organized by TRP staff members in 2003, these workshops were held at the Harmony Center, a picturesque training venue on the outskirts of Windhoek.

In the evening, after the first session of workshops finished for the day, everyone made their way to the outdoor courtyard, where technicians were setting up a sound system for dancing. The young males first held an impromptu drag performance for the title of "Miss Africa." After grabbing the microphone, the emcee asked me to be one of the "international judges" for the competition, along with a couple of European expats. Contestants then began to creatively wrap and twist towels into different shapes for the costumes. At the pageant's conclusion, Louami asked me to dance along with her friends. She led me in the slower *kasamba* and was very forceful, although she seemed unaware of her considerable strength. "*Wie is de Vrou* [Who is the woman]?" I asked jokingly. She smiled widely. Six-foot-three Louami is indeed very strong despite her delicate and feminine physical presentation; the other members told me that she was transgender.

Later Louami confided in me, describing how she dressed up when she practiced sex work on the streets in the business district of Windhoek. She would wear her foundation makeup a few shades lighter than her natural facial complexion, with her hair piled up into a hive of dark waves to draw all eyes upon her. Her success as a sex worker, which she attributed to her beauty, once brought her as far as Germany, where she accompanied one of her "international clients" and received her first taste of "European gay life." As she told me, "It was so amazing, Robert, to see all those gay people in the same room!"

A couple of weeks after these workshops, Louami contacted me to do an interview at her home in Katutura. During our first conversation, I asked her about her life in Katutura, and she responded by talking about her gender and sexual identity: "At six years old I knew I was different than other boys. I was playing with the dolls and I was only playing the mother side in 'mummy and daddies' games, and small boys were touching my buttocks. My mum talked to me when I was young as if I was a girl. They were telling me at the [TRP] office that I am transgender, but I will never have the operation! I like how I look." Louami had attended many of TRP's workshops and explained during an interview that she had benefited from them, as it "really gave me the confidence to be myself and to love myself." Later that day, after the interview was completed, Louami insisted on showing me several photos that reminded her of meaningful life events. First she held out a photo of her local gay friends: three had died of AIDS, and the remaining two (whom I also knew), she told me, were quite sick with AIDS. Then she showed me a picture of herself in a drag performance, during which she had stripped down to a thong-like bikini bottom before a cheering audience in a local shebeen.[16] She picked out a recent newspaper photograph of her mother, who was actively involved in the antipoverty protest for people living in Katutura, many of whom were losing their homes because of their inability to pay steeply rising property taxes and utility fees.

Next Louami showed me a picture in which she was wearing a striking Herero women's gown and a distinctive head wrap. She had worn this dress in the human rights march in 2001 to protest the hate speeches of President Nujoma and other SWAPO party officials. Louami's mother had made the dress for her, staying up the entire night before the march to painstakingly sew together the fabrics whose colors signified SWAPO. But this "traditional drag" and the donning of blue, red, and green was not intended to mock or ridicule SWAPO as I first thought. Instead, Louami's dress allowed her to express her deep disappointment with the ruling government. As she told me, "My father died fighting for

SWAPO in the liberation army." She remembered how her father had very much accepted her as a girl at a young age.

Louami then showed me a small turtle shell with a piece of animal fur stuffed inside. She held it to my nose to smell the ladies' powder it contained. "My mother gave it to me. She told me that if I put it under my arms, then the men will chase after me [*laughs*]." In early 2003 Louami's mother died. And several months later Louami's closest friend, who worked on the streets with her, died of AIDS. These two events were to have a profound effect on Louami's practices of freedom.

Over the coming year Louami's celebrations of self-expression grew troubled and strained as she struggled with the effects of financial hardship, fear of HIV infection, and the death of her mother. When I visited her in June 2004, I found Louami without makeup and wearing men's clothing. She seemed so different that day. I looked over at her bed, which was in the center of her room, and saw that a Bible had been left open as though someone had been reading it. She explained to me that she had quit drinking and prostitution and was going to church regularly. I asked why she had changed the way she looked. It was then that she told me about how her friend had died from AIDS: "He would sometimes let German men take him without a condom, because they usually offered more money for it." Louami was terrified because she had also done this on occasion: "I am too, too afraid to get tested. If I find out I am positive, I will get sick faster." When I asked why she had stopped wearing women's clothing, she said, "I am thirty now, and my sister's children . . . I don't want them to grow up seeing me dressing like a woman. What will they think . . . if they see their uncle dressing like a woman?"

One Sunday in September 2004 as I approached Louami's home, I saw her leaving the church across the street from a funeral. She was dressed up in a suit with her hair cut short. She told me she had received much praise from her fellow parishioners. They still knew she had boyfriends, she said, but they were quite pleased with her new masculine look. "Inside I am a woman, still, but outside I am now like a man," she joked. Louami told me that TRP staff were giving her a tough time about her more masculine appearance, saying she had gone "back into the closet." Louami responded: "They don't understand. . . . I can't find work if I'm dressed like a woman, and with my mother gone, I am the oldest. I have responsibilities."

Although Louami had changed her appearance drastically and quit sex work, she continued to be unemployed. She was looking for work cleaning houses or ironing clothing. And finding work was an urgent matter for her, because the utilities on the house left to her by her mother were piling up. She showed me the letter from the municipality in which they threatened to take the house if she did not work out a payment plan of at least 700 Namibian dollars (approximately 64USD) a month. This was far out of reach for Louami. Previously she made

1000 Namibian dollars (approximately 91USD) in a typical week of sex work. Now, even if she did find work cleaning or ironing clothes, it would not be nearly enough to pay for the expenses on her house. I wondered how long it would be before she would have to return to sex work.

By early July 2005 Louami had indeed returned to sex work and was drinking alcohol to cope with her impending financial problems. It was now quite evident that her body had undergone considerable wasting, and rumors had spread that she was sick with AIDS. She had also just broken up with her boyfriend, Arnold, who lived down the road from her. Previously, Louami and I had regularly hung out together with Arnold at his family's home. Louami often brought him new clothes that she had purchased from unlicensed street vendors and gave him money to help support his family. Arnold was helpful in recruiting various other young bisexual men living in Damara Lokasie for educational sessions and focus groups led by TRP's HIV/AIDS awareness groups, which began to meet at Louami's place regularly. But Arnold was quite sick now, Louami told me, and in a worried tone added, "All the fingers of Katutura are pointing at me, because *I am the prostitute*. But he has slept with so many moffies, and I always wore a condom with him, even when he was not wanting me to."

One morning in late 2007, when I met Louami at her house to join her for church, she greeted me at the doorway as she made the last adjustment to her outfit. She was wearing pants, a shirt with a thin tie, and long, braided hair extensions held in place under a man's hat. She seemed to have struck a balance between a masculine and feminine style. Once we entered the Lutheran church, I walked toward the pews situated in the main sitting area for the congregation, as there was plenty of seating there. Louami quickly steered me toward the smaller and more crowded bench directly against the back wall, where older women unaccompanied by family members sat.

During the three-hour-long service the pastor made several announcements concerning would-be and recently married couples. Both the couples and their families were asked to stand to receive the congregation's applause and affirmation. Two of the newly married couples were invited to stand at the front altar of the church and encouraged to kiss, receiving another round of applause. Louami looked to me and quietly whispered, "Robert, could you imagine? If only gays and lesbians could be married in Namibia."

* * *

There are marked discrepancies between the sexual "openness" and autonomy promoted in TRP's HIV prevention workshops and the forms of "structural violence" (Farmer 1996; Schoepf 2001; Parker 2001) that limit Louami's ability to practice safer sex. Louami works through the lived contradictions in the territory of subjectivity, continually modulating her outward expressions of femininity and masculinity. Her changing gender expressions portray a complex interplay in subjectivity, moving between financial necessity; erotic pleasure; political protestation; and yearnings to belong within family, tribe, the nation-state, and the global LGBT community. Louami's portrait exemplifies the way the Rainbow Youth invest in projects of self-liberation introduced by TRP and the toll that social suffering takes on their practices of freedom over the years.

In her earlier days, sex work brought Louami into contact with international clients, furnishing her with the opportunity to travel to Germany, where the scene of "all those gay people in one room together" stirred her desires and stretched her sense of belonging and identity across national borders (Johnson 1998).[17] With the rise of the LGTB rights movement in Namibia, and after her regular attendance at TRP political events, it would appear that greater freedom, much like the kind Louami had tasted in Germany, would soon arrive in Namibia. Publicly proclaiming her gender difference during LGBT rights demonstrations, she aspires to emancipate herself and her community. Over the years, though, financial necessity has frustrated her practices of freedom and TRP's identity politics have become overbearing, eventually forcing her to withdraw from the organization and to turn to a local church to find self-affirmation. But even in the depths of her struggles with discrimination, the fear surrounding the HIV epidemic, and impending financial ruin, Louami continues to long for a freedom that has yet to arrive in Namibia—the freedom to marry someone of the same sex.

In this chapter we have seen how TRP's interventions cultivate subjectivity as a political territory and how the Rainbow Youth invest in LGBT rights perspectives through their repeated reflections and debates pertaining to the nature of selfhood. Furthermore, the mode of power exercised through TRP's interventions de-temporalizes the subjectivities of the Rainbow Youth, continually shifting their attention between archaic notions of "the traditional" and a sexual modernity that has yet to come. Thus there are complex temporalities at play in the subjectivities of the Rainbow Youth, complexities that call to mind the ideas of postcolonial theorist Achille Mbembe (2001, 11–18) on the close relationship between time and subjectivity: "such that one can envision subjectivity itself as temporality." According to Mbembe, "the time of African existence" cannot be thought of as simply linear. Rather, subjectivity is a complex combination of temporalities, "an interlocking of presents, pasts and futures" (17).

Wearing a traditional Herero woman's dress donned in the SWAPO party colors to protest the hate speeches, Louami simultaneously references various temporalities: the historical period in which SWAPO fought and won the liberation struggle; the "timelessness" of ethnic authenticity; the recent memories of her father and the support of her mother; and the future possibility of LGBT emancipation. Her show of "authenticity" vividly lays her claim to belonging in Namibian society as she attempts to rewrite SWAPO's heterosexist account of

Namibia's history of independence. As Louami reminds me, her father fought in the antiapartheid struggle for *her* freedom too. Nevertheless, this form of protest, inspired by TRP's inventions of "traditional homosexuality," also complies with the way SWAPO governs the Namibian citizenry. Because TRP's techniques elide the wider material grounds that constitute the everyday social suffering of youths, strategic essentialism inadvertently aligns with SWAPO's mode of post-colonial governmentality, which extols the virtues of primordial displays of authenticity while it simultaneously conceals the government's role in serving the interests of political elites at the cost of public infrastructure, social services, and equitable housing and labor conditions for working-class people (Klerck 2008).

At this point one might think of the subjectivities of the Rainbow Youth, as I have described them, as solely hemmed in by uncertainty, by an imagined pre-coloniality that can never be experienced and a future that is yet to arrive; however, scholars remind us that care must be taken not to depict postcolonial African subjectivities as a result of absence and lack (Mbembe 2001; Ferguson 2006, 10, 192). Certainly the attempt in this story is not to produce an understanding that reduces states of being to an economically deprived present and a material future to which youths can hardly gain access—an understanding of *what Africans are not* (Mbembe 2001, 9). For as the Rainbow Youth live out their desires in the concrete world, subjectivities gain a realness and vitality in confrontation with poverty, unemployment, AIDS, discrimination, sexual violence, and other forms of oppression. It is this emerging vitality that helps us to understand how the Rainbow Youth come to enlist their political energies and their practices of freedom in the service of remaking Namibian citizenship.

Figure 1. Dedicated research assistants and committed activists—"Silver," "Whoopi," and "Trouble," 2004.

Figure 2. "Cutie" and "Trouble" in an affectionate embrace, 2004.

Figure 3. HIV prevention working group, Katutura, 2004.

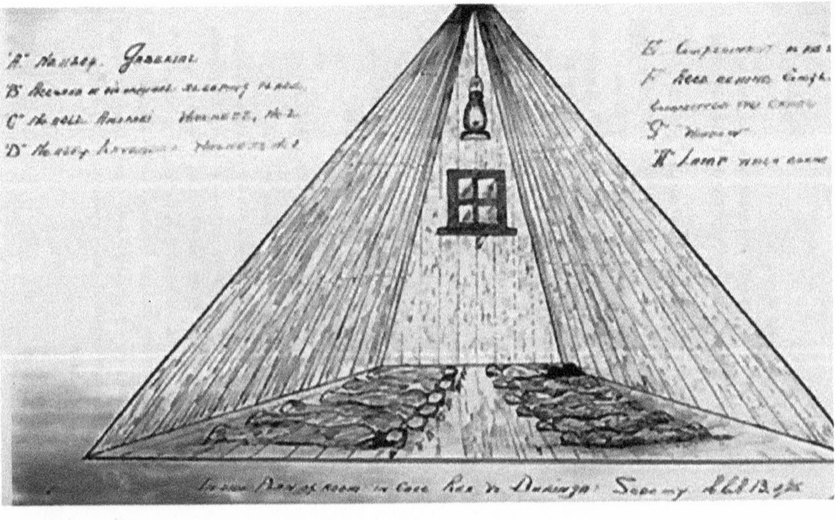

Figure 4. Housing conditions at a migrant labor camp in Lüderitz.

Figure 5. "The Kwanyama Sodomite" (holding an ekola) as traditional homosexual, in *Sister Namibia* magazine, April-May 2001. Courtesy of *South African Journal of Science* 38: 345–351.

# 3   Remaking Female Citizenship

> Life gains its vitality, its essential productivity, in
> the course of struggle and resistance.
>
> —Judith Butler, *Subjects of Desire*

COMMENTING ON THE oppression of gays and lesbians in the Bahamas, the postcolonial feminist M. Jacqui Alexander describes citizenship as "premised within heterosexuality and principally within heteromasculinity," posing a broader question of salience to this chapter: "In the absence of visible lesbian and gay movements, can feminist political struggles radically transform these historically repressive structures?" (Alexander 1994, 7). I consider this question alongside the modes of gender and sexual defiance enacted by lesbian youths, modes that continually collide against the oppressive structural forces that privilege heterosexual males. In Katutura Township I observed how groups of young females who took up lesbian identifications confronted daily oppressions with vivid displays of gender and sexual dissidence—dressing and carrying themselves like men and chasing after and professing their love for women. During interviews and informal conversations with these youths, they described how their practices of freedom fared outside the protected "safe spaces" of TRP's self-awareness workshops, where they faced myriad forms of oppression.

The subordination of Namibian women has been traced to precolonial times (Becker 2007); however, gendered economic inequality greatly intensified under German and South African colonial rule (Jauch et al. 2011). In particular, the imposed male migratory labor system fixed black women's lives in economic spheres where financial resources were limited to meager pay and informal economic exchanges. Where formal employment was available to black women, it was limited to domestic work and to menial employment in cleaning companies, where they faced long work hours, extremely low wages, and a complete lack of benefits or job security (Jauch et al. 2011). Although reforms have been made to the colonial labor system with establishment of the Labor Act of 1992, the act tended to benefit more the workers in industrial sectors of the mining and fishing industry and in public institutions (Jauch et al. 2009) than those who were unemployed or working as informal, casual, or domestic workers. Women comprised the majority of the latter class of workers. According to statistics from the Ministry of Labour, while mass unemployment was steadily increasing in Namibia between 1997 and 2008, from 34.5 percent to 51.2 percent, women's unemployment rate rose even higher than men's, from 40.4 percent to 58.4 percent, while youth unemployment rates rose from 58 percent to 75 percent (Jauch et al. 2011). Eventually Namibia came to show one of the highest levels of income disparity in the world.[1] Herbert Jauch and his colleagues (2011) tie this abysmal economic picture to the government's move toward the adoption of an economic strategy of becoming more competitive in global markets, an approach that utilized significant amounts of public assets to build infrastructure to attract foreign private enterprise. With poor returns in terms of job creation, low salaries, and unsafe working conditions, Namibia followed wider neoliberal economic trends in southern Africa (Lurie et al. 2004, 204–212); over time, these strategies of free enterprise further eroded local economic systems, leaving women even more financially subordinate. In postcolonial Namibia the work of many black women continues to be limited to low-paying jobs such as selling beer, food, crafts, and domestic service (Østreng 1997, 36), which pay far less than men's work, and many women's efforts to break free from economic oppression have been confined to forms of transactional sex (often to pay for educational advancement and to increase social mobility).

These striking forms of oppression continually thwart the projects of self-determination enacted by lesbian youths, as they do for many other working-class Namibian females. But lesbian youths' practices of freedom should not be regarded merely as failed attempts. Instead, what should be stressed is how the conflicts provoked by gender and sexual defiance in Katutura *render visible* the very workings of postcolonial female citizenship in local power relations, exposing the way it further secures men's dominant position in social and economic spheres at the cost of women's. The larger significance of these local modes of defiance tends to go unnoticed both in the national women's movement and the transnational rights discourses that inform interventions aimed at improving the lives of lesbians.

\* \* \*

When I met with twenty-eight-year-old Hanna for an interview at TRP's main office in July 2002, she was sporting a mock army vest over a baggy T-shirt, her hair in short twists to be grown into dreadlocks. That day I watched as she and her close friend Kelly furiously cut and buttered broetchens with a jagged knife, readying the soup kitchen for their fellow members. They too took advantage of the meal service once all the others were fed. Although Hanna lived in Damara Lokasie in Katutura, she regularly walked the long distance to TRP's office in Ausspannplatz, the commercial district of Windhoek. She was boastful of this ability, flexing her muscles to show me the excellent physical condition she had maintained.

When I first started to get to know Hanna in 2001, I would find her each day reading about and admiring the masculine lesbians featured in the international gay and lesbian magazines at TRP's resource center, which took the form of a large cabinet and a few bookshelves filled with queer magazines, educational manuals, queer pulp-fiction books, films, pamphlets, human rights reports, and materials on safer sex. One of Hanna's good friends from Walvis Bay, whose picture was taken by a German lesbian photographer in Namibia, appeared in a full-page spread in one of the issues of the South African lesbian magazine *DIVA*. Hanna handed me the magazine one day, saying, "I want to have my picture in there too—like that." She then showed me the pose she would make if her photo were included in an issue, folding her arms in a masculine way. What was particularly appealing to Hanna was how "strong and independent" these models looked to her. Remarking one day on a picture of a masculine-looking female model in the U.S.-based lesbian magazine *Curve,* she said, "*She* doesn't have to put up with the problems of men!" In this way Hanna often interpreted a lesbian identification not only as referring to sexual desires but also as a project of self-determination and resistance to male domination.

At human rights forums Hanna always rose to her feet in the audience to give her compelling story of coming out in Namibia, a story that always began with an account of living as one of the street children who slept in the concrete construction pipes. During our first interview, she proudly identified herself by saying, "I am a very, very sexy Nama lesbian. I don't know why that is. . . . The girls just find me very sexy [*laughs*]. I am a woman who likes to fuck other women. Most people think that I am transgender . . . because of my style, the clothes that I am wearing." Before her exposure to sexuality training delivered by TRP and Sister Namibia staff, Hanna said, "I never heard of this word, a lesbian," although, she continued, "I already began to dress like a man." Like many youths, Hanna frequently used the term "lesbian" interchangeably with notions of gender identity and sexual desire, as though there were a unity between them. However, she frequently made a clear distinction between "dressing like a man" and actually *being* a man.

From her childhood, Hanna did remember how her sexual desires and gender identity were different from those of other young girls:

> Mostly in my teenage life I did fight with my feelings. But I did not know people *like me* in the location where I lived. But I usually did fall in love with my female teachers at school. I was a child, I was eight years old when I knew I was different. I liked mostly to be with guys and to play soccer.

There was a while when I wanted to hang out with these gay guys. They were very strange, but I was very interested in talking to them. They talked a lot with their hands—very girlish, you know. These two guys were older; they were elders staying in my location.

No one said anything about them being gay or anything, but they had this girlish way about them, the way they walked, you know. People used to hire them to cook for these marriage and funeral things. They said they knew that I was a funny person like them [*laughs*].

When I asked how she felt about the hate speeches made by Nujoma, she said:

It hurts me a lot, very emotionally. But those [hate speeches] have made me very strong. At first I thought, "This is my country, it is our land, it is my land, and now he is saying that he is going to deport me." And the thing is, he can go ahead and deport me as long as it is somewhere I would like [*laughs*].

At her first "lesbian workshop," held at Sister Namibia, Hanna was truly amazed to see so many other females "like her."

So many lesbians! That was the first time I felt like I belonged, somewhere, you know. I felt we could really change our country [and] what the president was saying.

Hanna's association with the LGBT movement eventually gave her the confidence to openly celebrate her gender and sexual difference. Among her peers in Katutura, Hanna soon became well known as a fighter, and she proudly showed me the scars on her shoulder and neck she had received from angry men who stabbed her for flirting with their girlfriends. On more than one occasion, she retaliated with a fist or a knife.

I was in a shebeen in Katutura and I was freaking with this girl on the dance floor . . . and her boyfriend came and started beating on me. . . . So I pulled out my knife and stabbed him in the face and ran. When he later came to my place, he was looking for the "man" who had stabbed him. But I was wearing my T-shirt, so he didn't know that it was me. He couldn't find the "man" he was looking for anywhere [*laughs*].

Only her fluid dancing style rivaled her fighting ability. At the local clubs and shebeens she could be found dancing with numerous women. These feminine females, who Hanna referred to as "the ladies," also loved dancing with her. In particular, female sex workers at the clubs were drawn to Hanna because of her charisma and the humor with which she delivered her performances of masculinity. They would all have their chance to dance with her.

Hanna's love of women was quite evident and it did not matter if they identified as lesbians or did not. In fact most of the "the ladies" Hanna dated did not claim a lesbian identity. And after attending several TRP workshops Hanna felt confident in openly professing her desires to any woman she found attractive.

As we walked along the streets in her lokasie, we frequently stopped to visit the many young "straight women," she sometimes called them, with whom she was pursuing or having secret affairs. "[For] most of these girls, I am the one who must do everything [penetrate and go down on them], they are just one-night stands, but I would love to have a real relationship with a woman who will go fifty-fifty. You must bring me a woman from Canada," she said with a laugh.

During one of our many strolls through her lokasie in late 2002, Hanna led me to a small, single-room, steel-sheet shack, where she introduced me to three young, feminine Damara women who were sitting on a bed and carrying on a rather intense conversation about their sexual relationships with men. Hanna then went to find one of her lesbian friends, Shane, leaving me in the company of the women. I apologized for interrupting their conversation, to which they responded as they giggled, "It's okay; you're a moffie. You can hear." The women returned to their conversation about the difficulties they were having with men. One woman in particular was upset because her boyfriend would beat her when he was feeling jealous: "Even if he *thinks* I am looking at another man he hits me!" The other women nodded with agreement. When Hanna returned to the shack with Shane, the women halted their discussion of men and began to flirt with the two masculine females without any hesitation. When I later asked Hanna about the identities of these women, she said, "Those straight ladies are bisexuals." *A puzzling way of putting it,* I thought. Eventually I came to learn that this rather contradictory way of labeling these women suggested not only that they were feminine and shared sexual intimacies with women as well as men but also that they remained financially and emotionally dependent on men, as Hanna explained to me. Hanna's labeling, in other words, was as much about autonomy and power in relation to men as it was about gender identity and sexual desire.

In conversations with feminine women who were having secret affairs with masculine lesbians, most of whom identified as "straight," I was frequently told that they felt safer with masculine lesbians than with men. One woman told me that she greatly admired "the butches," because "they are able to stand up to men." She recounted how Hanna had once fought off her boyfriend for her when he attempted to rape her: "[Hanna] is like a man . . . but different, you know?" However, Hanna had not always been "like a man," her grandmother insisted one day, pointing to the framed collage of family pictures on the wall of her home: "Look at how beautiful a girl she was [*points to a picture of Hanna with longer hair and wearing a dress*]. There she is fourteen. Isn't she a beautiful girl?"

Shortly after the picture was taken, Hanna had left home to live on the street to escape the sexual abuse she had experienced from an older male family member since the age of seven. As she approached her late teens, she returned to live with her mum. She told her mother that she was opposed to having sex with men. As a consequence, her mother called numerous family meetings, bringing together several relatives to discuss the problem of her attire and unwillingness to be with men. Hanna's brother recounted how one family meeting culminated with Hanna shouting, "I want to be the man! Why can't I be the man?" Instead, they insisted that she must have children to be a "real African woman": "I got involved with men because of pressure! The pressure I got from my family, my mum, my brothers, my aunts—these people were driving me very crazy! I did it while I was drunk [*pauses*]. I didn't want to . . . but I was depressed. [Sex with the men] was very, very bad for me!" These sorts of events resulted in Hanna's giving birth to three children, whom she raised with the help of her mother. Although she never brought one of her female lovers home to meet her family, she spoke very openly to her children about her love of women: "Sometimes the kiddies asked questions . . . and I just tell them I like other women. Sometimes [my daughter] asks, 'Do you have a penis? 'Cause you wear men's clothes.' And I say, 'No! I am a woman; your mum just loves other women.'"

After a couple of months, Hanna invited me to meet her three children at her mother's place. We chatted about school classes with the young children, who were showing much affection toward their mother. But when Hanna's mother came home, everyone tensed up as she shot an angry glare at Hanna while going to the bedroom to start packing for an upcoming trip. Hanna's mom was taking the kids with her on a two-week visit to the farm down south and was annoyed that Hanna was not joining them. She said to me that Hanna was not properly assuming her duties as a mother: "All *this* one wants to do these days is go out dancing and do these gay and lesbian political things!" she said. After everyone had left, Hanna explained that her mothering of the three children was an ongoing source of tension with her mother. "I will always love my children, but, you know, this is not the life I chose for myself—having sex with men, getting pregnant, you know, it's not what I wanted."

Another bone of contention between them related to the children's contribution to household economic activities.[2] At the age of eleven Hanna's daughter had already begun to help her grandmother with generating household income, helping to wash the neighbor's clothing. Hanna was angered by this because she felt that her daughter should be spending the time on her studies "so she can have a better life than we have." Quarreling also broke out when Hanna's nine-year-old son began hanging out with the drug dealer who was renting a room at Hanna's mother's place. One evening I watched as Hanna reprimanded the man and threatened to beat him if she saw him around her son again. She then pulled her son aside to give him a stiff scolding. Despite these conflicts, what Hanna and her mother both shared, like many other people in Katutura I came to know, was the hope that their children would provide a better economic future for the family.

When I returned to Namibia in 2003, Hanna told me she was very concerned that she had contracted HIV through her experiences of unsafe sex with men.

She was also quite irritated with TRP because their HIV prevention work mainly focused on the males, and when the staff did consider women, they only spoke about dental dams and finger cots, which protect female-to-female sexual practices. Although Hanna realized that these resources could help prevent various sexually transmitted infections between women, she felt more concerned that most lesbian women in Katutura become vulnerable to HIV infection through unsafe sex with men. "You know lesbians are doing it too, like the other [heterosexual] women are, having sex for money with men, and they're not using condoms."

One day in late August 2003, Hanna seemed particularly agitated. She explained to me that she liked to dress like a man because it offered her a sense of safety: "If you are a woman in Katutura, you get raped, you get sexually assaulted, you get HIV/AIDS. . . . This way I don't have those kinds of problems." This idea recurred later that day when she and I bumped into a young sixteen-year-old friend called "Oabbie" (Damara Nama nickname for "boy"), who was wearing baggy pants, cornrows, and walking with a hip-hop gangster-style swagger. However, her baggy masculine clothing could not hide her delicately featured face and feminine physique. Unlike Hanna and many other masculine lesbians, Oabbie's performance of masculinity did not appear convincing. Like Hanna, Oabbie explained that she feared any kind of male sexual attention because of HIV. Yet her drag brought even more intense sexual attention from men. This became evident when men passing by aggressively called out with sexually suggestive remarks. A few months later Oabbie became pregnant because of "family pressure," Hanna explained, but when we later met with Oabbie, she still confidently asserted her claim to a lesbian identity. A month later I learned that Oabbie had tested positive for HIV.

Despite Hanna's convincing performances of masculinity, she too was not always able to escape unwanted male attention. She had been trained as a carpenter and bricklayer and had tried to work in this male-dominated industry but said the other men always wanted to touch her breasts to verify that she was "just a woman." Because of this problem she stopped working as a bricklayer. By the end of 2003 Hanna had joined the military and was in the middle of completing her training as a soldier. She was greatly enjoying the work although somewhat angered that she had to shave off her dreadlocks because they looked too jagged and masculine; braids would have been acceptable, she explained. When a senior military official had touched her buttocks and breasts on more than one occasion, Hanna finally retaliated by slapping him. She was dismissed from work by early 2004 when she later refused to apologize to him: "I couldn't be like many of the other women in the military who were having sex with their commanders and senior officers to get money." Again Hanna found herself unemployed. "I really loved that job so much; I was so good at gun handling. You should have seen me."

One afternoon in 2005, Hanna invited me to her new place, a small tin-sheet shack adjacent to a family home, which she called "my ghetto." It was up the road from her grandmother's home, where she had previously lived. I asked why she had moved out, and she told me the harrowing tale of when her grandmother had found her and Sylvia, her new girlfriend at the time, who was living at the house, naked and in bed together. The grandmother screamed at the top of her lungs until a crowd of neighbors gathered and the two women were forced out of the house in a half-dressed state. The grandmother, still screeching to the crowd exclaimed, "Have you ever seen this?—two girls together like this!" Meanwhile the crowd hurled insults at the two women as they were chased from the house, disgraced, partly naked, and crying.

Sylvia, who wore women's clothes and acted feminine, had come to stay with Hanna after she had come out to her boyfriend about her love of women. He beat her and tried to rape her: "It was Hanna who fought him off when he tried to break in here and rape me." Unfortunately, Hanna's relationship with Sylvia ended after being chased out of Hanna's grandmother's place, for Sylvia went back to live with her relatives. "Now she is back to going [*pauses and signs sadly*], sleeping with those German guys at Chez Ntemba [nightclub], you know." But soon after these series of events, another window to romance would open for Hanna.

Next door to Hanna's new place, a beautiful fifteen-year-old "straight" girl soon caught her eye. Each day when we returned to Hanna's place after conducting interviews and focus groups, she would go around the back and flirt intensely with the young, giddy teenager, pressing in against the tall makeshift wire fencing with her arms above her head in a masculine way.

Three weeks later, as I was speaking with an elder, I could hear Hanna softly exclaim, "Oh, sorry, sorry, sorry!" as a slight chill came over me. While I was talking with the grandmother, Hanna had gone around the back to flirt with the neighbor's daughter through the wire fence, as she usually did. This time, however, the young girl's mother appeared and told Hanna that her daughter had died. Suddenly the tones grew low between them. Hanna came around the front to meet up with me, and as we left, she said in a rather resigned manner, "AIDS is normal. You know that girl next door to my grandmother's place who's fifteen? She also died last week from AIDS."

Hanna's pitch began to rise as she instructed me to look down the dusty un-paved street at the houses that formed an irregular row and said, "Those crosses [small white flags with black crosses] . . . *that's* how many people have died here recently." The flags fixed to the corrugated steel-sheet roofs were indeed abundantly scattered. But these symbols of death, though plentiful, by now did not surprise me, for most Namibians I knew went to funerals almost every weekend. To avoid further dwelling on the subject, Hanna suggested we go visit Kelly, who was looking after her sister's baby. "That will lift our spirits," she assured me.

When we arrived at Kelly's home, we overheard her giggling as we peered in through the open door. Kelly, who was dressed in men's clothing and sporting a freshly shaved head, was gently bouncing an infant on her lap while making foolish faces. As we entered her house, Hanna remarked on the humorous scene of someone "so butch" playing so tenderly with a baby. We all broke up with laughter. Then Kelly gave the baby to Hanna and me to watch while she completed a number of household chores in the kitchen and backyard. The baby seemed so bright and alert, with his eyes darting around the room at the slightest movement or noise. I did notice, however, that the baby had a very mild croupy cough, which I attributed to the dust from the dry heat of that day. Two days later the baby died.

Hanna and I returned to Kelly's home shortly after the death announcement for the burial service. From the small, dilapidated taxi we watched as Kelly's family brought out the small casket from the house to take to the graveyard. Kelly participated as one of the pallbearers, helping to lift the casket into her uncle's truck. The casket was very small but extremely ornate and expensive-looking. Hanna told me that even though "we are poor in Katutura, but when it comes to funerals, everyone in the community gives something to the cost of the casket. It turns into a big competition."

We got out of the taxi and headed toward Kelly, who warmly greeted us through her tear-stained face. I asked her what had happened to the baby—it all seemed so sudden. She explained that it was "≠oab" that had brought about the sudden death. I didn't ask further what she meant, as she seemed quite upset. We all piled into the small open backs of the awaiting *bakkies* (pickup trucks) and slowly headed toward the graveyard. Sitting in the back together, I asked Hanna to explain further what "≠oab" meant. She described it as an "old Damara belief. If a wind blows from a certain direction, it can cause a sudden death to a healthy person." Hanna, however, did not believe this to be true and mumbled out of the side of her mouth: "That's the problem with us Damaras—we believe in too many things."

We eventually arrived at the funeral and moved to the "children's graveyard." The sheer number of small burial sites was astonishing: there were rows upon rows of freshly piled burial mounds. We made our way over to Kelly's nephew's burial site. Kelly was placed off to one side with the other children, even though she was older than one of her sisters who stood with the other adult relatives in the forefront of the ceremony. Explaining the positioning, Hanna whispered to me that Kelly was still regarded as a child—"not a real African woman, because she's not a mother and does not have a boyfriend." Several other lesbian youths, who arrived soon after us, made a point of moving into the children's side of the ceremony to stand in support of Kelly.

Finally the ceremony concluded with the burying of the coffin, accompanied by loud wailing from female relatives. As the crowd started to disperse, I overheard several discussions from people referring to how the baby had certainly died from ≠oab. Noticing my puzzlement, Hanna looked at me and said quietly but sternly, "Did you see the man standing by himself over there behind the others?" I said yes, and she continued, "He's the father. He is the one who gave the mother AIDS. Everyone knows that! That is why no one will talk with him. Look at how skinny and sick he is. Everyone knows that the baby died of AIDS! Don't you remember the cough the baby had? He died of pneumonia!" Feeling somewhat confused, I asked, "But why does everyone continue to refer to ≠oab if no one really believes it's true?" Hanna replied plainly, "It's [out of] respect for the mother's family."

A couple of days after the funeral, Hanna told me I needed to meet an HIV-positive friend of hers, Monica, telling me, "She's one of Kelly's old girlfriends." She said that Monica had heard about my research and asked to do an interview with me. In addition to rescuing women from sexual violence, Hanna's ongoing support of women living with HIV earned her great admiration from other women in her lokasie.

As Hanna and I approached Monica's small makeshift home, we could smell the aroma of freshly fried fish wafting out from the open front door. Monica, dressed in women's clothes, stood over a small cooking range tending to the food. Each day she baked fish and sold it to local men who dropped by her home around lunchtime.

Hanna began flirting, and Monica smiled shyly as she carefully rolled the pieces of fish in flour and then dropped them into a skillet, where they sizzled in the heated oil. Concerned that I would interrupt her business, I asked if she would prefer my conducting the interview at a time that was more convenient for her. However, she insisted that she would talk with me while she cooked. "I'm relaxed when I'm cooking," she said.

Monica told me that she really admired how Hanna and some of the other lesbian women walked around Katutura behaving like men.

> They are so brave. I have never been to TRP yet, but someday I want to go there to attend their sexuality workshops. But I am just not ready for that. I am too afraid of what people will think of me around here if they know I am a lesbian. Maybe people will stop coming to buy food from me if they find out.

Monica, who turned twenty-one years old that day, recounted her early experiences of sexual coercion:

> When I was eleven, if a man tried to touch me, I always had a fist for him. If a woman did, that was a different thing [*smiles*]. A friend of my family, he came and told me I must do it [have sex]. . . . I was fifteen. I didn't want to. He forced me, and that day I was pregnant. That was the only time I had ever had sex with a man. That day I also became HIV positive.

Over the course of a few months, as I came to know her better, Monica admitted that she occasionally had sex with some of her clients for money: "I just don't make enough selling fish, you know. I have to pay school fees for [my child] and my younger brother and sister. I am the eldest daughter." Eventually Monica attended a few of TRP's special events with Hanna and told me she had started to feel more confident about herself. However, she still continued to have sex with men in exchange for money not only to help support family members but also to afford the foods required to be taken with the antiretroviral drugs that had been prescribed for her when her CD4 cell count dropped significantly in 2005.

Later that year Hanna finally decided to get tested for HIV and wanted me to join her. As we arrived at the steps leading up to the New Start HIV Testing and Treatment Centre, Hanna's elder Wayne was just leaving with some nutritional supplements and a package of oatmeal that he needed to take with his HIV antiretroviral medications. Once inside the reception area, Hanna asked if I would remain in the waiting room until she received her diagnosis. When she came out of the office, she was overjoyed and began to cry with relief: "I can't believe it, I'm going to live!"

Toward the end of August 2005, Hanna met and fell in love with an older European lesbian woman, Georgina, whom she met at a social gathering organized by TRP. Georgina, who had just arrived in Namibia, was eager to begin her feminist development work, which was, she explained quite confidently to me, "to teach Namibians that they cannot be so violent!" I was somewhat surprised by Hanna's choice of new sexual partner, as Georgina presented herself in a masculine way in her attire and comportment—not the usual feminine object of Hanna's desires. Hanna explained to me, however, that she was excited to be in this relationship, because she was finally in a relationship that was fifty-fifty.

As her new relationship began to blossom, Hanna, on the strict advice of Georgina, stopped drinking alcohol and started to undergo regular counseling to deal with some of the sexual abuse she had encountered when she was younger. She began regularly attending the NGO known as PEACE, which was originally set up to treat posttraumatic stress among detainees returning to Namibia after the war of independence. A year later Hanna and Georgina got married in South Africa, following the legalization of same-sex marriage there in 2006.

When I returned to visit them at their new place in Katutura in 2007, after showing me her wedding photos, Hanna gave me a copy of an article she had written for the Ministry of Women Affairs and Child Welfare. It detailed her tumultuous experience with sexual and physical abuse that had occurred over the course of her life. Hanna was quite angry with the editors of the ministry, because they had edited out all the parts related to her lesbian identity.

> "This is not right; this is not even who I am!" she said.
> "What did Georgina think?" I asked.
> "She's pissed too."

"Where is Georgina anyway?"

"She's visiting her family in Germany."

"Why did you not join her?"

"I am still working on myself. I stopped drinking and I am finishing [high] school now. But I'm just not ready to go to Germany. I can't face her family. I don't feel good enough about myself yet to go there and be with her family. I still have a lot more work to do on myself."

\* \* \*

Kelly was known for her disarming sense of humor, and at some of the informal socials I attended she performed a convincing impression of President Nujoma, recreating his infamous call for the imprisonment and deportation of gays and lesbians. Brilliantly mocking the president's slipups in English grammar and pronunciation, Kelly had everyone in stitches.

Kelly generally wore several shirts over her pants and held her shoulders scrunched forward to appear as though she had no breasts; her shaved head finished off her look. One evening in 2002 at a *braai* (a barbecue) and dance in the courtyard outside the TRP office, Kelly and her lesbian friends Jennifer and Daphne began to dance together vigorously when American R & B artist Missy Elliott boomed through the office CD player. Although it was summer and the weather was extremely hot that evening, Kelly would not take off a single one of her many layers of clothing, repeatedly pulling down on her shirts to keep her breasts flattened so as not to disrupt the appearance of her masculine body. For Kelly, emulating a masculine body through dress and body language was an important way that she established and maintained her membership within the group.

Then, almost out of nowhere, a feminine-acting Oshivambo female appeared on the dance floor glamorously dressed with an expensive fur-trimmed full-length coat. "Where did you come from, my Ovambo princess?" Kelly asked as she swaggered up to her. The young woman, who identified as a lesbian, came from a wealthy family and was staying in the affluent district of Klein Windhoek while on study leave from an overseas university. She laughed warmly at Kelly, letting her try on the coat while they danced together. Kelly beamed with delight.

More and more people began to arrive, including the well-known local drag queen trio Destiny's Child. As the evening wore on, Kelly told me that she just loved the moffies: "They are so beautiful. God, sometimes I wish I was a moffie; they are so tall and slim like the models." Kelly joined in as Destiny's Child performed their runway model–style swagger. Everyone roared with laughter as Kelly brilliantly imitated the feminine moffie gait.

Kelly explained that although she dressed in a masculine way, she was "not really a lesbian" and was uncertain of her identity. This created much uneasiness for her.

Sometimes I just see a nice guy, I think he is cute, but the feelings I have the strongest for is woman. And I don't know how to identify myself. . . . But I feel . . . I identify myself not as a lesbian but actually as a bisexual [*looks down at the floor*]. I never tell the others [lesbians], they will have this funny attitude—okay, he's bisexual, so what is the use of staying with "her," every time a guy passes by "she" will leave. I am very young and I am turning twenty. My family is sometimes talking to me about having children, but I am saying no I am not ready for that right now [*very serious, voice falls*]. It is like a conflict process that I am going through. 'Cause sometimes I feel something for both person [men and women]. But I just get frustrated and think, "Okay, I will just be myself." That is why I like to be single all the time. It worries me too much . . . giving me these stupid headaches. Sometimes it is very confusing, I just want to kill myself.

The unity locally assumed between a lesbian identity and her sexual desires and gender identity created an uneasy fit for Kelly. Only after several months did Kelly tell me that she had once fallen in love with a guy, when she was in the Standard 9 educational level: "He's a moffie . . . but we were together for a while. At one point I thought I was pregnant with his baby." Although they had broken up for over a year, she still had strong feelings for Romeo. When he married a Dutch man in 2003 and moved to the Netherlands, Kelly was devastated. She explained that it was not uncommon for the masculine lesbians and feminine men to fall in love with each other since, as she claimed, "moffies are like beautiful women." "You get this problem, there are times we black gay people from Katutura, men and women, are sleeping together. It happens a lot, but people don't talk about it openly." The problem for Kelly was how sexual identities, as they were taught in TRP training workshops, did not always match with the sexual behaviors people practiced.

Kelly explained further: "When a butch lesbian has sex with a woman, 'he' will not allow the woman to touch her breasts or any other part of the body." When I asked why, she explained, "You are a man when you are having sex with a woman, and therefore touching the breast or [*motions to genitals*] reminds you that you are only a woman." Kelly then explained that when having sex with a moffie, "he" was allowed to penetrate the lesbian. This explanation was offered by many other masculine females I spoke to informally. When I asked again, "Why?" Kelly explained, "Because when you are with a man, you are not the real man—well, someone has to be the man!" and roared with laughter. I should note that these kinds of ambiguities were rarely discussed during sexual education and training workshops, where precise sexual identities were made to fit discrete categories.

One late Saturday afternoon in 2003, as Kelly and I sat in a shebeen she introduced me to some of her female friends, most of whom, she said, were straight. One was a girlfriend. "She is an *international* prostitute," Kelly said with excitement in her eyes. "She's not your regular streetwalker: *she is international.* She has clients who come round and pick her up in fancy cars." Her friend walked up to me dressed in a glamorous, low-cut red dress and smiled as she made the final arrangements to her hair with her fingers. Kelly introduced her and said, "Here's my girl," as she reached out to hold her by the hand. The woman sucked her lips at Kelly and grinned at me slightly to indicate that I was not supposed to know she secretly had sex with women. "Don't worry; he's a moffie like us," Kelly said. The three of us laughed. Kelly had many other girlfriends in Katutura and was not shy in saying this in front of the woman in the red dress and me. "I am like an African king," she said with a wide smile.

As Kelly's girlfriend and I talked some more, she explained that she would sometimes have sex without a condom with her European clients. "Sometimes they'll pay you a lot more without it. . . . They are safer than the men around here [in Katutura]." HIV/AIDS was something Kelly feared. She frequently expressed concern to me that she thought she might be HIV positive. "When you are drinking, you do things [have unprotected sex with men]." When I asked her if she had ever gone for an HIV test, she said, "No! I would only get tested if I get sick. If I tested positive now, I would get too stressed out and get sick faster." Like many of the masculine lesbians I had interviewed over the years, Kelly engaged in transactional sex, because she was expected to help bring in money for her household. Only after many months did she finally tell me this, as it caused her a lot of shame. Furthermore, such issues lay silent within TPR rights mobilizations. Certainly LGBT organizers were aware that this commonly occurred; there was just no "space" for it to fit within LGBT rights discourses of autonomy and self-empowerment.

In 2004 Kelly gained employment in a new textile factory. Although her wages were small and she worked long hours without compensation for overtime, she had gained some respect from her family, who previously had disapproved of her displays of masculinity, because now she was able to contribute to household expenses. At her workplace she had befriended several of the straight women and invited them to movie nights held at TRP's office. One evening, as they watched a movie with scenes depicting lesbian erotica, they sat and giggled. One said, "It is very sexy." When I asked one of the women why she liked to come to the office, she explained, "It is nice to come to such a place where it is safe for women, where you can have fun and not be bothered by men." Over the years I met other young women who did not claim a lesbian identity but still attended TRP workshops (a fact that was unknown to some of the organizers). In sum, there was a sense of camaraderie, affinity, and solidarity that women came to share around lesbian identifications and the project of self-determination enacted by women like Kelly.

When the textile industry shut down in 2008, Kelly was suddenly out of a job. Faced with limited prospects for work and with much regret, she said, "Can you see me washing clothes and cleaning homes? . . . I am too butch for that now!"

\* \* \*

Shane, who self-identified as a colored, grew up in the township of Kho-masdal and came to live in Katutura to escape his mother's disapproval of his gender identity and refusal to date boys.[3] After befriending Hanna and Kelly, he attended a few socials at TRP but was generally reluctant to attend regular membership meetings after being chastised by a staff member for his regular illicit drug consumption. When members and staff organized a special talk shop on drug and alcohol use in 2002, Shane acquiesced and agreed to attend. "I do not want anyone judging me or I'm leaving!" he sternly cautioned. During the round of introductions at the talk shop on drug and alcohol use, Shane impressed the other workshop participants when he bravely pulled out a small Mandrax tablet and passed it around for open discussion.[4]

After two months I discovered that Shane, whom I thought to be a young male, was, as TRP staff referred to him, "female transgender." But during our first interview Shane explained to me that he was "a man" *and* "a lesbian." Knowing that he had attended a couple of TRP's "sexuality lessons," I asked him if he thought of himself as transgender. He explained that he had thought of himself as a boy from a very early age, because he only hung around with other boys, played soccer with them, and was treated the same as any other boy. Further responding to my question, he adamantly said, "No! I am not a transgender. That just doesn't fit for me. I feel I am a lesbian, because I like being with other lesbians." Shane recounted how Hanna had invited him to attend a social gathering hosted by TRP: "That was the first time I saw so many lesbians together in one room [*smiles*]. That was where I learned what a lesbian was." Like Hanna and Kelly, Shane understood a lesbian identification to mean more than just sexual desire; for Shane it helped him to connect and share solidarity with a much larger community of gender-nonconforming females.

One day when I met with Shane, he showed me where a masculine woman had stabbed him in the shoulder the previous evening, "just because I wouldn't freak [have sex] with her, because I have a girlfriend!" he said with macho-like pride. As we left the office to go and talk somewhere more private, I learned that much was agitating him. "I don't have any future," he said. Shane held that he would never be able to get a job in Namibia, because he did not dress like a woman and could never wear a dress: "Employers would just take one look at me."

In the evenings I would often find Shane on the back streets near Ausspann-nplatz, where commercial sex work took place. There he socialized with a number of the female sex workers and with one in particular who was his girlfriend. It was his job to make sure she was okay when she was on the street, he told me. He expressed great concern over his girlfriend's well-being; clients frequently wanted her to have sex without condoms: "She knows she has to pull off before he goes [ejaculates]." I asked Shane if he knew that his girlfriend could still get

HIV even if she did "pull off." He said, "Yes, but you get paid a lot more to do it without a condom."

Although Shane looked after his girlfriend on the street, a more dominating male pimp managed the group of sex workers. One evening after my conversation with Shane, I looked back and watched him pleading with the pimp over something. The pimp just walked ahead of Shane, ignoring him completely while smirking at an approaching customer. It was the first time I had seen Shane's physical composure draw downward.

In my earliest interviews with Shane in 2002, he maintained that he had no sexual attractions to men, had never been with a man, and would never have sex with a man, even to satisfy his mother's desire for children. However, after several months Shane began to practice sex work alongside his girlfriend. He became pregnant and the baby was later left with his mother when he was incarcerated for stabbing a male client who refused to pay for his service.

In 2004 I spoke with Shane soon after he was released on bail while awaiting trial. Surprisingly, he seemed more optimistic than I had ever seen him. "I am finally getting my life together," he said to me. In prison he was getting daily meals, had a regular place to sleep, and had begun psychotherapeutic counseling.

In a later conversation with Shane in August 2007, he claimed to have benefited greatly from further "gender counseling" he received through PEACE after his release. Although he had ended all ties to sex work and was trying to manage his addiction to drugs and alcohol, he was concerned that he would end up working on the streets again because of his limited opportunities for employment. "I have been lucky. I don't want to get HIV. I can't be doing that with men anymore, even when I need the money. I am one hundred percent lesbian. I need to be true to myself."

\* \* \*

Initially, confrontations with heterosexism, sexual violence, HIV vulnerability, and unemployment only intensified the practices of freedom of Hanna, Kelly, and Shane. In fact, their defiant desires became vividly realized in these conflicts. Moreover, negative feedback provoked by gender dissidence, especially wearing drag, confirmed the existence of political objects that occluded the road to freedom. As these young females transgressed the boundaries of "appropriate" womanhood, they cultivated new political ground; their struggles with multiple oppressions, over time, made visible the everyday social regulations of Namibian female existence. By resisting the constraints of acceptable femininity, their defiance helped to politicize the very limits of female agency in a bodily spectacle for all to see in their lokasie. And for this reason many young women who did not identify as lesbians came to greatly admire Hanna, Kelly, and Shane for their courage to dress and act like men.

Although reasserting a lesbian identity has established important new political ground for these youths, new ethical concerns have arisen in relation to
these local identity performances. Their practices reiterate the "ideal" or "good
lesbian" as a bundle of interrelated qualities: looking masculine, having multiple
girlfriends, avoiding sex with men, and being economically and socially independent of male influence. Although these aesthetics of resistance can in some way
be traced to their imaginations of Euro-American (and sometimes cosmopolitan South African) freedoms, these global fantasies emerge in relation to *local*
struggles with male domination. In this sense the portraits of Hanna, Kelly, and
Shane offer a perspective on globalization as rooted in daily lived experience,
what Michael Burawoy (2000, 341–342; also see Wekker 2006, 223–224) refers
to as "grounded globalizations." Indeed, the ideal of lesbian self-determination
interpreted from the pages of foreign lesbian magazines and movies inspire lesbian youths to recognize, articulate, and confront everyday forms of oppression
facing all women living in Katutura. Thus, ideas of global lesbian identities take
on distinctive local meanings, values, and moral inflections.

Hardly any of the lesbian youths actually fulfill or can sustain all of these
ideals of self-determination, so the gaps play out as internal conflicts not only in
relation to the self but also toward each other, which explains why these youths
are unwilling to discuss their involvement in transactional sex during public
speaking forums. At the same time, the negative feedback provoked by masculine performances also fosters bonding and solidarities between local females,
including other working-class women, such as sex workers or textile factory
workers, who do not necessarily identify as lesbians. Furthermore, everyday performances of lesbian identities connect local masculine and feminine females to
locations beyond Namibia's borders, to more affluent fantasies of modernity and
freedom as portrayed in Missy Elliott's rap music and in Western lesbian erotica
shown during TRP movie nights.

Although the ideals of autonomy to which Hanna, Kelly, and Shane sub-
scribe are greatly disrupted by the shame they carry in having had sex with
men, their pursuit of autonomy cannot be dismissed as a form of mere escapism.
Attempting to live out their fantasies is quite productive, serving as vital ways
through which they engage with transnational queer rights protests and reimag-
ine the social, economic, and political destinies of black Namibian females. In
this way they attempt to remake themselves as "ideal citizens" as they strive to
widen their participation in public life (Castle 2008). As anthropologist Tomi
Castle describes in her ethnographic study of participants taking a citizenship
course offered by a lesbian rights organization in Brazil, becoming an "ideal citizen" is accomplished through simultaneous "capitulation and resistance" (2008,
128). Among Namibian lesbians, they appeal to dominant universalistic notions

of lesbian identities at the same time as they subvert the local boundaries of Namibian female citizenship through their everyday modes of defiance.

In Namibia enacting a masculine identity may posture female bodies more forcefully within local fields of gender power relations, but its performance also comes with immensely negative social and economic consequences (as compared to other females who are more adherent to local mores of femininity). For many of the masculine females, prospects of employment vanish, access to social status diminishes, and family relations become disrupted. How do we understand the bold and persistent pursuit of gender nonconformity under conditions of intense condemnation when transforming the appearance of the female body as a refusal to exist for the satisfaction of men's desire may attract even greater attention from men?[5] Although they transgress the boundaries of appropriate femininity by reshaping their bodies in clothing, gesture, and speech, and through practices like going after women and displaying physical violence, one is left wondering: Do their everyday attempts to remake female citizenship in some way also perpetuate hetero-masculine domination? For notions of "what makes a man" become woven into the very modes of resistance that these females enact to protest masculine domination (Bourdieu 2001, 70–71).

On the one hand, the significance of their modes of defiance here lies more in its robust and edgy appearance than in its "success" in gaining access to the dividends of masculine power. Sexual and gender defiance exemplify a very active, critical engagement with human rights ideas of liberation, generating value, authenticity, and political will as they become threaded through local histories of discrimination. Because bodily desire has come to stand as a central resource for legitimation in LGBT discourse, as discussed in the last chapter, many participants find moral salience in the sense of bodily integrity and self-knowledge they recuperate in being able to maintain authorship over their struggles with oppression.

On the other hand, statements like those made by Hanna ("I still have a lot more work to do on myself") and Shane ("I am one hundred percent lesbian. I need to be true to myself") suggest that political responsibilities are projected back onto the individual and into the personal. Rather than holding responsible governmental and institutional policies that fail to reduce male dominance in the labor market, their conflicts become internalized as problems of self-determination. Working through these conflicts in the territory of subjectivity—while creating bold self-expressions, vibrant practices of defiance, and a heightened critical awareness of gender inequalities—nevertheless confines their everyday conflicts to the marginalized status of "local identity politics," never gathering fuller recognition within the very rights discourses that give form to their resistance. Furthermore, without the support of Namibian women's groups, as I will discuss next, the political force generated through modes of lesbian self-determination, as it plays out in impoverished settings like Katutura, fails to achieve a wider political resonance with the national goal of women's equality and with the more radical reframing of gender and sexual politics in Namibia needed to address HIV vulnerability.

\* \* \*

In one of the squatter settlements in Katutura, a young woman living with HIV said to me during an interview:

> I mean, I am proud to say I am a lesbian, but then [foreigners] say, "But you have children?" That is the one thing that was hurting me the most. . . . We all have a pressure to belong because of the society, the pressure out there. Somehow there were pressures from my family to have children. There was a reason why I had to go out and sometimes [have sex with men]. I don't reject my children; they are a blessing in my life. But just the fact of how they came made me unhappy.

Explaining why they had unsafe sex with men, most lesbian youths recounted a similarly weighty sense of responsibility to their family. Their familial duties included the need to bring in a source of income, to help run the household, to care for children and sick relatives, and to participate in small income-generating projects like selling beer, washing clothing, and tending to family shebeens. During my interviews, lesbian youths claimed that the sense of obligation to have children was especially troubling for them, and these feelings often conflicted with the image they had of themselves as lesbians and as being independent from men.

Yet the fact that many Namibian lesbians were mothers lay silent in political discussion forums organized by TRP. Over many months of doing fieldwork, lesbian youths became increasingly open with me about their responsibilities as mothers in everyday township life. In Katutura I learned that being a mother accorded lesbians social status. Like other females, these youths *did* receive respect and praise in their communities for being mothers, particularly among elders who acknowledge them as becoming "real African women." Yet motherhood also conflicted with their practices of freedom. Having children was evidence that one had sex with men—a practice that sometimes threw their political membership and authenticity as a lesbian into question, as we saw in chapter 2. They also became vulnerable to HIV infection, like other females did in their lokasies.[6] Acting in concert with daily financial needs and a strong sense of familial obligation, the continual revalorization of motherhood by family members and relatives was described by the lesbian mothers I interviewed as pushing them along a path to have unprotected sex with men.

Veena Das and Renu Addlakha, in their study of disability and citizenship in postcolonial Delhi, portray the domestic sphere as "always on the verge of becoming political" as "the family confronts ways of disciplining" (2001, 512). Similarly, domestic spheres in Katutura operate as important sites where young female subjectivities are molded and where relations of obligation are patterned for young women to become dutiful daughters, income generators, and, by having children, "real African women" who bear the family's hopes for a better future.

Although the reiteration of what makes a "real African woman" suggests a timeless and archaic view of female sexuality as tied to reproduction, the prime social status accorded to motherhood (for lesbians, as well) owes much to more recent ideologies arising from the anticolonial women's movement. In fact, motherhood was a foundational ideology of the women's movement during antiapartheid uprising. Feminist writer Iina Soiri notes that when the former South African regime "threatened the lives of children in families and schools, . . . the family became then the most effective site of resistance and support which strengthened women's self-perception as 'mothers,' 'wives' and 'sisters'" (1996, 91). A "radical motherhood" developed during women's active participation in the liberation struggle, through which they "linked up the immediate concerns of daily life with the political aims of liberation. . . . [They] politicized the 'private' sphere of reproduction which was formerly considered as non- or pre-political" (93).

With the establishment of the Namibian Women's Voice (NWV) by the Council of Churches in Namibia (CCN) in 1985 (Soiri 1996, 94), and the formation of thirteen branches by 1986, maternalist ideologies garnered further political legitimacy through grassroots campaigns waged against colonial state-imposed family planning methods. The contraceptive Depo-Provera was forcibly given, and without knowledge, to black women in colonial state hospitals and mental health facilities in the early 1980s.

> Katutura Hospital, which serves the black township near Windhoek, frequently gives injections immediately after childbirth, often without the woman's knowledge or consent. . . . Even young girls 13 or 14 years old are being given Norethisterone in 200 ml dosages without parental consent. In 1984, one of the high school principals in Katutura township lined up the girls due to take matriculation and told them that they would not be entered for the exam unless they had contraceptive injections. . . .
>
> One of the leading supermarkets in Windhoek insists, as a condition of employment, that all female employees have Depo-Provera injections. (Cleaver and Wallace 1990, 52)

The NWV actively opposed this form of colonial domination and invented a unifying "traditional" pro-natalist political ethic that cut across the spectrum of women's groups that had developed at the time. In postcolonial Namibia the legacy of pro-natalist ideologies survives in the rhetoric of the SWAPO Women's

Council, constituting a form of legitimacy for women—a certain *nationness*—in being a mother.[7]

Local and national arenas concerned with HIV prevention also assume importance in postcolonial constructions of female citizenship with respect to women's obligations to the nation. Despite their acknowledged vulnerability to HIV, Namibian women have been urged to take charge of the epidemic. For example, speaking at the International Women's Day ceremony in Windhoek in 2002, First Lady Kovambo Nujoma evoked the ethical female citizen as one who must take an appropriate lead in the response against the AIDS epidemic:

> It remains imperative for *women to stay focused and seriously address the is-sues affecting them.* The majority of people infected with the deadly virus are women and recent statistics indicate the HIV/AIDS infections continue to in-crease. The effects of HIV/AIDS on the development of our country, particu-larly its impact on human resources, are already being felt. Therefore, *women should* join hands and *educate* members of our society to prevent the spread of this deadly disease. (C. Angula 2002; emphasis added)

For the last decade, ubiquitous empowerment campaigns have relentlessly tar-geted women and girls with slogans of self-determination such as "just say no," "take control," and "my future is my choice." Such discourses of sexual autonomy and individual responsibility, however, run into conflict with deeper historical and political investments in motherhood, posing a bodily dilemma for many Namibian women: How can a woman be "reproductive for the nation" and still protect the nation from HIV infection?

Interestingly, youths asserting a lesbian identity most radically put HIV-related empowerment discourses into practice by refusing (or at least attempting to refuse) to have sex with men. As one lesbian female said during an interview:

> Men are very dangerous. . . . It is more risky being with a man, I think, because men are like flies: every dress they see they want to follow. I won't know how safe I am with a man. But with my [female] partner I at least know. But this guy may be using the most expensive condom but may use a needle—and then how sure am I?

Throughout my fieldwork, lesbian youths privately spoke to me about their fear and their attempts to avoid male penetration or contact with men's bodies and semen. Such dangerous contact, referred to as a form of "pollution" (Douglas 1966), expresses a wider view of HIV vulnerability and the social bondages of Na-mibian women. Although rarely accomplished by lesbian youths, their perpetual struggle to steer the course of their bodies' destinies vividly calls attention to the wider limits of female agency in Namibia, and not just for lesbian women.

Despite the local significance of their embodied politicizations, lesbian wom-en's modes of resistance are left unappreciated and certainly unsupported within larger national political institutions that advance women's rights. The head of the Department of Women's Affairs (DWA), Netumbo Ndaitwah, who was a candidate for the SWAPO Central Committee as deputy secretary general at the time of her appointment to the DWA, publicly denounced and denied any support to the National Women's Manifesto Network, led by Sister Namibia (Geisler 2004, 132, 135–136). In addition, the SWAPO Women's Council, once a leading figure in antiapartheid uprising, also has explicitly written out "the lesbian" from the postcolonial body politic as being antithetical to their commitment to "authentic" Namibian women. When Sister Namibia released the findings from a countrywide research study on women's participation in political decision making, which briefly referred to gay and lesbian rights, Eunice Ipinge, assistant secretary of information and research for SWAPO Women's Council, announced during a press conference:

> It is unfortunate that there are some elements that would like to use gender equality as a stepping ladder to reach their own goals that have no relevance to gender. . . . [The Women's manifesto report] has no other intention but to confuse the Namibian woman and *divert them from the core concept of gender equality*. [Sister Namibia activists] will have to find another platform to address homosexuality and not within the context of gender issues. (Xoagub 1999; emphasis added)

Ipinge's distinction here between women and lesbians, which implies that lesbians do not endure the gender-related problems of other females, recognizes Namibian females only in their heterosexual role, thus delegitimating lesbian lives as they police the perimeters of female citizenship.

To conclude, the gender and sexually dissident practices of lesbian youths disturb the boundaries of ideal female citizenship and, through the conflicts their defiance ignite, make these boundaries more visible to other women living in their lokasies. Transgressive practices enable young females like Hanna, Kelly, and Shane to confront and recognize a constellation of social inequalities that more generally constrain the lives of women living in the township of Katutura. Thus, emerging lesbian subjectivities open to and join with broader yearnings for women's emancipation. At the same time, however, as the idea of women's liberation becomes heightened in the awareness of lesbian participants, the idealistic discourses of lesbian autonomy unexpectedly collude with masculine domination to undermine participants' sense of their own political agency: shame enshrouds motherhood and transactional sex in silence, eliding their experiences beneath human rights discourses that construe lesbian protestation in universalistic terms.

# 4 The Naturalization
## of Intimate Partner Violence

I am loving those straight guys—the rough ones, you know. [But] if you
ask them to put on the condom, they will give you a smack, [they'll] beat
you. But I just love them, I don't know why. It's just, it's how I feel inside.

—Tuli

THIS CHAPTER CONTINUES the story of what happens when the everyday
practices of freedom inspired by the Rainbow Project are confronted with local forms of masculine domination. TRP's empowerment strategies, which celebrate male femininities, compel youths to liberate themselves by embracing their
sexual desires and resisting the gendered terms of ideal citizenship.[1] Yet Tuli's
words of uncontrollable and unexplainable desire, above, expose an irony at play
in LGBT rights discourses that strive to free the desires of feminine males: they
inadvertently reinforce the naturalization of oppression they encounter in sexual
relationships with masculine "straight men." TRP's self-discovery programs obscure the violent ways that SWAPO's antihomosexual nationalist rhetoric con-
figures male-male sexual intimacies in gender-oppositional terms. At the same
time, the physical violence wrought by these nationalisms as they live out in the
erotic relationships between masculine and feminine males is most evident.

Postcolonial feminist scholar Anne McClintock asserts that nationalisms
usually "depend on powerful constructions of gender" (1995, 353). The debates
surrounding postcolonial gender-related legal reforms in Namibia illustrate how
nationalisms mobilize hegemonic representations of masculinity and femininity. These nationalistic constructions of gender reverberate through local gender-
power relations between males.

Independence in Namibia brought new hopes for emancipation from colonial-era laws that classified women as minors, without rights to vote or to own
or administer land without the permission of their husband (Becker 2007). Al-

though they have had a limited impact, there have been many important legal reforms that targeted gender inequality in the ten years following Namibia's independence. These include affirmative action policies to increase women's representation in local government elections, in the workforce, and in cooperative business management positions; and the House of Parliament passed a number of workplace antidiscrimination laws (Hubbard 2007). As Diane Hubbard explains, these law reforms were relatively uncontroversial. By contrast, reforms that touched more explicitly on the economic and social relationships between men and women in the domestic sphere ignited much controversy (Geisler 2004). The Married Person's Equality Act (1996) is a case in point (Becker 2007). This act granted equal rights between men and women in civil marriage and divorce with respect to the administration of property, acknowledging women's and men's equality as household heads in the management of marital assets. The tabling of the bill drew considerable opposition from male politicians (Hubbard 2007). Oppositional rhetoric employed notions of timeless African gender relations, aided and abetted by Christian ideologies, to legitimize women's subordination to men (Becker 2007). The rhetoric of "tradition" went hand in hand with assertions of "African manhood" and the "natural" right of Namibian men to rule as household heads (Hubbard 2007, 102).

The controversy surrounding the Combating of Domestic Violence Bill, which was eventually passed in 2003, also reveals the political climate that shaped postcolonial gender relations.[2] To express their opposition to the bill, male politicians deployed stereotypes of Namibian masculinities and femininities and other metaphors that invoked the vulnerability of African manhood. In 2002, during the parliamentary debates surrounding the proposed domestic violence legislation, SWAPO MP Helmut Angula expressed his opposition to the proposed legislation by employing the symbolism of "the disabled phallus":

> As a teacher of science, I know better the functioning of the body than many of you appreciate. That requirement [sex with your wife] is exactly the same as bread. If you are denied bread, you are denied food. If you are denied sex which you have been accustomed to, you will not be normal, you will be abnormal. That is why the origin of the [Combating of Domestic Violence] bill is homosexual, because they were denied the right to a partner . . . but all these have the character of creating violence.
>
> In the rural communities you find that it is not uncommon for a partner [wife] to disable the partner's phallus. . . . In other words, you find . . . that there are a host of people [men] who can wear nice shoes, drive nice cars, but they are disabled [made impotent]. They are disabled! The partner knows that the guy is disabled, let him go, where can he go? He will come back because he is disabled. It is known to the whole village. Even the *mutti* person [sender of witchcraft; original spelling] knows, "I gave the *mutti* [witchcraft] to disable the fellow." (H. Angula 2002)

Hubbard (2007, 106–10) characterizes this discussion as sparking one of the most heated debates since the Namibian parliament began. The subject of this particular speech captivated the Members of Parliament and eventually led to a lengthy pseudoscientific discussion of erectile dysfunction. The seeming absurdity of the ensuing debates, however, should not obscure the fact that the imagery of the disabled phallus constructs Namibian manhood as vulnerable to the wills of femininity instead of being vulnerable to the neoliberal economic reforms of the government, reforms that have led to astonishing increases in unemployment levels for young men.

The nationalisms that inhere in SWAPO's antihomosexual rhetoric similarly drew upon the narrative of a vulnerable masculinity. During President Sam Nujoma's reign, SWAPO's antihomosexual rhetoric deployed the dual metaphors of masculinity (to invoke notions of national protection) and of femininity (to symbolize neocolonial threats to national security). The allegory they repeatedly employed was that of the (masculine) nation that is brought to ruin by modernity (homosexuality)—a feminizing, seductive, and morally corrupting force. In 2001 this narrative of national vulnerability culminated in what came to be known as the "earring purges." Following an announcement by Nujoma that demonized homosexuals alongside criminals, a number of Special Field Forces (SFF) officers took it upon themselves to seek out and try to eliminate some of the more visible signs of "foreign corruption."

> Special Field Force members in Katutura on Monday started rounding up men wearing earrings and, in some cases, ripped them off the surprised victims' ears. They claim they were acting on an order by President Sam Nujoma to clamp down on suspected criminals and gays. . . . One of the SFF members, Victoria Pinias, who forcefully removed a stunned Stallon Shimanda's earrings at the Katutura Shopping Centre, told The Namibian the order had come from the President. "Where did you see men wearing earrings in our Oshiwambo culture. These things never happened before Independence. Why are they [men wearing earrings] only happening now after Independence?" she said. "We will order any men to take their earrings off or will use force to rip them from your ear if you don't want to comply." (Hamata 2001)[3]

Although the rounding up of young men with earrings was made on the grounds of cultural authenticity, many of the Rainbow Youth I interviewed interpreted the harassment as explicitly targeting gays. A young gay participant I interviewed recounted his experience with SFF:

> There was one day I was staying in Windhoek West. I was sitting on the corner in front of my friends' house and we were talking, and it was during that time of the hate speech and the SFF came and we were wearing those double earrings. They said, "Why should two men be wearing earrings?" A friend of mine, [the SFF officer] ripped it off, and I said, "God!" and I took off mine. They had ripped his ear because he was a gay.

The nationalist narrative of homosexuality as a feminizing and corrupting force also made its appearance in Nujoma's efforts to discredit the CoD opposition party leadership during an Africa Day rally at Okatana near Oshakati.

> [Nujoma] slammed the Congress of Democrats (CoD) leader Ben Ulenga accusing him of being gay and described CoD councilors in Oshakati as homosexuals. President Nujoma said it would be very sad to see some Africans or Namibians collaborating with those whites who wanted to re-colonize Africa or Namibia.
>
> White people, not all of them, are snakes and we have to be careful of them as they want to re-colonize us, as the Americans and the British want to do in Iraq and elsewhere. . . .
>
> Let me tell you, when Ben Ulenga was a Deputy Minister in Regional, Local Government and Housing, he came to me, asking me that he wanted long leave to study abroad. I told him that he could not get long study leave, as it is not allowed by government regulation. I therefore offered him a foreign mission post in Britain. But when he was there, he started drinking and to be useless, a gay (*eshenge*). He went to the white people to *yi ke mu ende komatako* [be taken from behind]. He then came back and formed a political party, the CoD, without a vision. (Shivute 2004)[4]

As a political tactic, the accusation of homosexuality allowed Nujoma to accomplish two rhetorical maneuvers. First, it cast the opposition party as holding affinities with Western colonial interests—as allied with the forces of globalization. Second, the mention of receptive sexual practices served as an unnatural bodily symbol, emblematic of a compromised and corrupted masculinity. Along with his supposed seduction by Western decadence, Ulenga's political integrity and legitimacy as a Namibian political party leader was thus rendered suspect. Furthermore, Nujoma's rhetoric constructed political legitimacy as achieved through disciplining one's bodily desires, thereby making connections between sexual practices and national protection. In sum, through a politics of vulgarity, Nujoma ignited national security anxieties through the metaphor of masculinity (the nation) as giving in to homosexuality (Western exploitation).

Such nationalistic anxieties over the state of Namibia's masculinity also played out in everyday township life—but with an erotic twist. Although feminine males became socially marked as a threat to cultural authenticity, their presence also became emblematic of Western decadence and excess, making them, ironically, sexually desirable to young working-class men.

This became clear to me when I started asking young feminine males in Katutura about their sexual partners. Damien, who sometimes performed in TRP-sponsored drag shows, one day responded to my question by pointing at a group of men outside a local *cuca* shop (pub), saying, "I have slept with about 90 percent of them." "Do they identify as gay or bisexual?" I asked. He said, "No, they're just men. Okay, according to TRP they're bisexuals, but they don't identify that way."

I began asking my contacts in the rainbow community about this, and almost all of the feminine males I spoke with had similar responses and gave similarly high percentages as Damien. I wondered if these were merely exaggerations. Were so many men really desiring to have sex with feminine males in such an antihomosexual climate? My time spent hanging out in township drinking establishments confirmed what feminine male youths had been telling me. Take, for example, my interview with a young unemployed man who chose to be called Fox.

> ROBERT LORWAY: So I hear that straight guys in shops and clubs like to have sex with other men.
>
> FOX: Yes . . . they are also having sex with moffies . . . it happens a lot around here [*smiles*]. Not just my age, but older men too. Moffies will suck [give oral sex] . . . they do it better than the women. Most of the men will suck my dick, but the woman, if I were to ask them that, they would be shy.
>
> RL: Do straight guys ever have sex with each other?
>
> FOX: No, we are men. . . . I would not like to be fucked! [*His tone rises sharply*]
>
> RL: Why do you like to go with moffies?
>
> FOX: Sex is safer [from HIV infection] with a moffie . . . and a woman is more dangerous, because other men have their eye on her, and she will run off with another man. The moffies make me wear condoms sometimes . . . but some of my straight friends don't, won't wear them. It is better to have sex with a moffie for a one-night stand. If you are drinking too much of that Grenadier [brand of sweet white wine], you just won't want to wear a condom.
>
> You go with them. Most of the times we are at the shebeen and the clubs. . . . The other guys just know that I am leaving to go with [moffies] from the club, because they are doing it too. My ex-girlfriend knew, but it didn't bother her.

Later in the interview I asked:

> RL: Do you want to get married in the future?
>
> FOX: To a woman or a man? I don't know; it could be either. If I get married to a woman, I will probably still have sex with men. I don't want to have any more children, though, because they are so expensive, schools fees even one hundred fifty [Namibian] dollars a year. That is a lot for me. I already have one daughter. But I don't want to have any more. Maybe it's good if I travel to the Netherlands or Germany and get married to [a man] and just stay there. In those countries they don't have a problem with gays. I would *never* get married to a man *here*, only to a woman. If I went to Europe I would get married to a man. . . . There I would have a very nice life.

For Fox, sex with women represents financial and familial obligations while sex with feminine males is conceptualized as pleasurable and "free" from responsibility and, erroneously, safer from HIV infection (also see Lorway 2006).

The way such fantasies of Western freedoms have entered the sexual desires of working-class straight men was also clearly demonstrated to me when Tuli asked a *cuca* shop owner, in the middle of the afternoon, to blast the volume on the stereo so that he could dance to the Christina Aguilera song called "Dirty." A crowd of more than twenty young straight men gathered round the eighteen-year-old and cheered him on as he jumped up on a table and spun around one of the shop's support beams in an impressive performance that rivaled any Aguilera video I have seen. At the conclusion Tuli received a handful of numbers from the young men. He then picked one masculine man to "hook up" with for sex later in the evening. The next day Tuli told me that his date forced him to have sex without a condom and then brutally beat him up when he explained that he had no extra cash to buy the man alcohol or cigarettes. Tuli later explained to me that this had happened to him on a number of occasions because of his choice in men, who were always very masculine, rough, and what he referred to as "real men."

The simultaneous attraction to and violent negation of young feminine males on the part of such masculine men played out during a TRP-sponsored drag show I attended. Here is an excerpt from a field note entry made in February 2003 that describes the ambivalent scene I witnessed:

> Tonight I attended a drag show in the township of Khomasdal with my friend Steffen, from Germany. There were about ten finalists competing for the crown. These "men" were astonishingly beautiful: the illusion was amazing. The elegant queens performed to a cheering crowd who, surprisingly, consisted mostly of straight men with their girlfriends. One young guy I had previously met at his girlfriend's braai [barbecue] approached me, looking a bit embarrassed and agitated. He said: "I like to come here because of the music, I mean . . . it's a good club. I mean, I am not into all this gay shit." When the performances began, however, his eyes could not help but be fixed on the drag queens, like everyone else. In between acts, as he became more intoxicated, he wandered behind the stage toward the dressing room where the drag queens were changing. He came out a few minutes later with a large grin. My friend Kay, who was in the show, later told me what he had been doing—he was trying to kiss and grab one of them until he was kicked out.
>
> Later in the evening when I returned from the washroom, the doormen were forcibly removing the drunken guy from the club. And as I looked at my friend Steffen, I was shocked to find his nose bloodied. Apparently, the man who had been harassing one of the drag queens had started hitting his own girlfriend in the face. When Steffen tried to intervene, he got punched, tripped, and jumped on by several other guys. Who would have thought that such a beautiful scene of parading drag queens could inspire such outbreaks of violence?

These types of violent conflicts in some way replay larger nationalistic narratives of masculinity's vulnerability to homosexuality. And TRP's public celebrations of gender nonconformity play an ironic part in this story. As signifiers of Western modernity, they intensify the ambivalent symbolic position of male femininities, unwittingly fomenting the social battlefield where Namibian manhood is continually undone through erotic desires and restored through violence.

*  *  *

With the election of the SWAPO president Hifikepunye Pohamba in 2004, and Nujoma's stepping down, opportunities for LGBT rights mobilization saw a major turning point.[5] Although Pohamba never explicitly expressed support for LGBT rights, he discontinued Nujoma's tradition of publicly vilifying homosexuals. This new policy followed on the reprimands from the new government's largest development donors, the European Union, Germany, and the United States, all of which expected improvements in Namibia's human rights record as a condition of receiving future aid.[6] This period saw the flourishing of TRP workshops on safer sex, lesbian and gay film showings, public rallies, and human rights awareness talk shops as the NGO expanded its development programs into the far corners of Namibia.[7] Small groups of young males, dressed provocatively in various degrees of drag, suddenly became extremely visible throughout the country's small towns. The formation of these groups of young feminine males stands in contrast to the beginnings of black gay activism in South Africa in the 1980s, "when black gay activists who were highly visible in anti-apartheid politics provided new role models for black gays and lesbians in South Africa" (Reid 2013, 25). Unlike South Africa, Namibia's urban locales, particularly those outside the capital city, did not possess the kind of cosmopolitan environments during the apartheid era to produce any substantial black gay bar and activist scene to emerge as it had in South Africa (see Reid 2013, 24–26). Thus, TRP's interventions in the postcolonial era should be regarded as a highly influential force in creating these communities.

As I traveled to meet with some of these groups for HIV prevention projects, three observations stood out. First, TRP's self-empowerment work fostered confidence in open displays of gender dissidence. Second, these enactments of gender dissidence heightened erotic tensions between young feminine males and local straight men. Third, sexual violence usually accompanied these erotic tensions; however, its recurrence was largely ignored in LGBT rights discourses of discrimination. Most feminine male youths became acutely aware of how to identify "antigay discrimination" and had begun to regularly report such incidents through TRP's growing outreach networks. However, when it came to their intimate sexual relationships, these youths were unable to explain, challenge, or politicize the recurring forms of sexual violence they encountered, as illustrated in Tuli's narrative at the beginning of this chapter. It is a concerning paradox I witnessed that as many of these young participants came to openly embrace and celebrate themselves as being like (other) Namibian women, they also "discovered" in themselves a sense of "powerlessness" and "helplessness" in their relationships with "real men," as though the sexual violence they experienced was a natural occurrence.

* * *

After a dizzying ride on a *kombi* (passenger van), I finally arrived at the center of the small southern Namibian town of Keetmanshoop, where I was welcomed by the Karas regional AIDS director for the Ministry of Health and Social Services. The fiery Liverpool native then whisked me away in the ministry van toward her office so that I could finish preparing a workshop for a group of young males who had previously attended TRP's sexuality and safer sex training. The group had expressed to the AIDS director that they wanted to organize an HIV awareness program after several friends had fallen sick and died from AIDS. I was invited to meet with them to provide basic information around STIs (sexually transmitted infections) and conduct a focus group to learn more about their HIV-related concerns.

Along the way to the ministry office, the director stopped at the town's graveyard, which had recently been expanded to three times its original size. Numerous fresh burial mounds mushroomed across the dusty landscape. It was a chilling reminder of the town's rising AIDS mortality. The director said that every weekend she went to at least four funerals for people who died from AIDS. "Many of them," she said, "will never get tested, and so the HIV statistics for this region don't even come close to the reality of how many people really die from AIDS."

Once I finished preparing the workshop at the ministry office, the director and I headed to an empty, run-down sports stadium to meet with "the guys," who warmly greeted us upon our arrival. Dressed in partial drag, they excitedly introduced themselves using women's names. A few wore lipstick, foundation, and mascara; one teetered in women's heels, while another was wearing a short-cropped shirt that hovered above tightly hugging women's jeans. Evert, who seemed to be the leader of the group, wore a turquoise off-the-shoulder halter top with long braids that brushed against the outline of his exposed shoulders. Together they looked like they were auditioning to be the cast of *Priscilla, Queen of the Dessert*. Later I learned they had seen this movie when TRP screened it for them following a sexual identity workshop.

After the introductions, Evert, who seemed very confident and outspoken, explained that their group frequently went about town dressed up like women. Residents were always excited to see them, he insisted. "They think we are celebrities!" He continued by saying that when the mood hits him, he likes to wear a glamorous white sundress out in public. "People just adore us," he said gleefully. Changing the tone dramatically, the somewhat older group member, Sal, cut off

Evert's enthusiasm by saying that the group travels around town together for protection. After the antihomosexual government speeches in 2001, many young effeminate males had been beaten and sexually assaulted by local police officers, relatives, and other men in their community. "We make sure to report this discrimination to friends of TRP [through our contacts] at the ministry."

As we got into the workshop discussion and arrived at the question of sexual partners, Evert admitted that he sometimes has sex for money with truck drivers and miners who pass through Keetmanshoop.[8] Sal smiled and said, "In Keetmans there are so many gay men!" The group laughed in agreement, but I was left confused because there was only a small group of them before me. After enjoying my confusion for a moment, Sal finally explained that they regularly slept with straight men. "Most of them are married or have girlfriends." These sexual partners did not identify with the identity terms disseminated by TRP. And because these straight men equated the term "gay" with the local word "moffie"—a signifier of gender nonconformity—these masculine men were able to maintain a straight identity, because their erotic desires were, nevertheless, *opposite gender* desires. My initial inability to see these other "gay men" parallels the observations of Reid in the South African township of Ermelo, where "masculine gays were an oxymoron; to be gay was to be effeminate" (2013, 49). From the perspective of the feminine males I met in Keetmanshoop, though, *any* masculine man was a potential sexual partner.

A few months later I returned to Keetmanshoop to conduct more formal ethnographic research. It was evident that young feminine males shared close social as well as sexual networks with straight men. At discos and more traditional long-arm dances, married men and those with girlfriends danced freely with the feminine males, even in the presence of their female partners, who seemed to pay little attention.[9] At the opening of a new nightclub, I spoke with some of the young straight men about their sexual relationships with feminine males. They were quite candid and repeatedly told me they liked to have sex with "the moffies" because, as one man puts it, "we can't get them pregnant or catch STIs from them." Referring to HIV infection, another man told me in a later interview, "It is safer to have sex with a moffie than a woman."[10] As reported earlier in the interview excerpt with Fox, the appeal of moffies to straight men in Keetmanshoop was their perceived freedom from social and financial obligations. One man commented: "It's expensive to get married, have a wife and a family. With moffies you don't have to worry about these things." Indeed these men conceived of same-sex practices in terms of pleasure and freedom from responsibility and familial obligation, qualities that in some way repeat SWAPO's political construction of homosexuality as a form of decadence.

When I interviewed a number of feminine males about their sexual relationships with straight men, I noted several patterns in their responses. Consistently they complained that straight men demanded anal sex from them without condoms. They explained that refusal was difficult because it usually happened while they were intoxicated, late at night after being at the club. Furthermore, if they tried to refuse the advances of straight men, they would be beaten. Some of them confided in me that they regularly experienced physical violence at the hands of these men. Although they had acquired knowledge about HIV transmission from TRP's workshops on safer sex and had become adept at reporting and standing up against discrimination, they still felt powerless to negotiate safer sex in their relationships. Sadly, most believed they had already contracted HIV but were too terrified to get tested.[11]

Knowing that many residents in Keetmanshoop struggled with poverty, I asked the young feminine males if they ever received any economic or material support from local masculine men in exchange for sex. I reasoned that transactional sexual practices would create a certain dependency that influenced their "willingness" to be with men who would coerce them into unprotected anal sex. This is a crucial part of the explanation provided in much of the literature on transactional sex in Africa (Swidler and Walkins 2007; Jewkes et al. 2006; Hallman 2004; Leclerc-Madlala 2003; Wojcicki 2002a). On the contrary, they told me that local straight men often demanded small sums of money or a beer from *them* in exchange for sex. I was puzzled, for it seemed counterintuitive: although moffies were the feminine objects of straight men's desires, the moffies were still expected to pay.[12] Moreover, masculine males would be the ones to approach the straight men, sometimes saying "*Oute i ta /gom*" (a Nama phrase for, "I want to suck you"). Sal helped to clear up my confusion. He explained that because "moffies have lots of friends at TRP" in Windhoek and got to travel to the capital city for TRP's special events, where they brushed elbows with foreigners, national entertainers, embassy directors, and even Members of Parliament, they were perceived as having greater access to economic resources. But why did this (perceived) capital not afford feminine males greater bargaining power in their sexual relationships? Evert responded to a version of this question, declaring in a matter-of-fact tone, "Well, they're men. *They* decide what happens during sex."

During interviews with other young feminine males living in Keetmanshoop, I asked why they desired sexual relationships with violent men who endangered their lives. Examples of responses I received to this question are: (1) "I don't know why I like those rough guys; I just can't help it"; and (2) "We [moffies] can't have sex with each other, because we're like sisters. I don't know why I want straight men, but [violence] is just what they do, 'cause they're real men." These iterations of uncontrollable and unexplainable desires contrasted markedly with the confident discussions of sexual identity and enactments of gender nonconformity I witnessed during interviews, focus groups, and workshops. Young feminine males appeared self-possessed in their open expression of gender defiance.

In many instances, through their association with TRP, young feminine males did in fact acquire greater access to socioeconomic resources compared to local straight men. It would seem that the road to sexual freedom opening up through TRP offered new possibilities for self-expression and social and economic mobility. Yet in intimate, sexual relationships with "real men," feminine males occupied positions of subordination and submission. For this reason the repeated retelling of narratives of powerless and uncontrollable desires led me to seriously question if the emphasis in LGBT rights discourses placed upon claiming one's desires inadvertently contributed to the naturalization of desires to be with violent men. Was their desire to be with rough men to some extent also reinforced by the very discourses of freedom that celebrated sexual and gender nonconformity? Did universalistic empowerment discourses unintentionally depoliticize the wider landscape of gender inequality from which sexual identities were being imagined? These questions recurred as I became more familiar with the daily lives of the Rainbow Youth in other parts of Namibia.

* * *

Northern Namibia holds the largest proportion of the country's population. In the late 1960s South African colonial officials designated the northern region of Ovamboland as the bantustan (homeland) for Oshivambo-speaking people, granting them a limited form of traditional self-rule. As the largest ethnic group, the Ovambo tribe came to comprise the strongest contingency in the liberation movement and today remains the most highly represented ethnic group among ruling SWAPO politicians. This tribal dominance informed the use of traditionalist language in SWAPO's antihomosexual rhetoric in the 1990s. SWAPO government officials asserted that while homosexuality may be found among tribes in central and southern Namibia, it did not exist within the traditional cultures of the north. Of all the regions of Namibia I visited, male youths identifying as gay in the northern part of the country experienced the most fear, anxiety, discrimination, and sexual violence in relation to their sexual and gender nonconformity. For instance, a young gay research assistant who helped me with interviews and translations told me a disturbing tale of his interrogation at the hands of his father. When a local journalist accidentally disclosed the young man's sexual identity by publishing his picture alongside a story about homosexuality among Oshivambo youths, his father exploded in anger. Forcing his son to strip naked, the father inspected his body to verify that he was in fact anatomically a "real man," as his father put it.

Other Oshivambo youths who displayed feminine mannerisms also encountered harassment and discrimination within their families in a similarly violent fashion, particularly from male relatives. For this reason TRP saw great strategic political significance in elevating gay and lesbian visibility in this region. In 2005

I was invited to the northern Namibian town of Oshakati to assist in the delivery of an HIV-awareness workshop led by a Danish-funded NGO that worked in close partnership with TRP. As in Keetmanshoop, all of the attendees were feminine(-acting) males who had already taken part in TRP's sexuality training workshops. To my surprise, only one of the workshop participants, Tuhafeni, identified with the Ovambo ethnic group. He wore men's clothes, seemed rather shy and nervous, and rarely spoke during the workshop. When I spoke with him during a tea break, he told me that he came from a very small village to live in Oshakati and that he would be severely punished if his community ever found out about his sexuality: "In our culture it is forbidden to be a gay. Have you heard what will happen if they find out you are an eshenge? They will take a burning stick and put it in there [your anus] so you won't ever be able to have sex again." I asked him if he knew of other Ovambo males who had same-sex sexual relationships. His mouth then widened into a large smile as he said, "Oh, they are everywhere. But they will never come to an open meeting like this!"

Another workshop participant, Hamish, who is Nama/Damara-speaking, was far more expressive than Tuhafeni. He was quite spunky, wearing a "belly shirt" and a small bright green purse over his shoulder, pressed daintily against his body with his elbow. Hamish had recently moved to the north from Windhoek to work as an attendant in a local state hospital. In bold lettering across his shirt read the phrase "Ignore Him!" which seemed to match his agitated mood. He explained during the workshop that his "Ovambo boyfriend" gave him a lot of trouble: he regularly cheated on him with other women, and when Hamish finally complained about it, his boyfriend smacked him across the face. "He never wears a condom with me, even though I ask him!" Hamish exclaimed.

After the meeting our group left the office to head to a small cuca shop for something to eat. A few of the feminine males lagged behind, and when we looked back we watched as car after car with smiling, flirtatious men inside stopped beside them. When the men rolled down their windows to chat with them, Hamish and two of the other workshop participants took out their cell phones and began busily entering the phone numbers of their admirers. When Hamish and the others rejoined our group, one of them said, "Some of those Ovambo men aren't 'real men.' They are eshenges . . . in the closet. You wouldn't believe it when you get them alone in a room; they sometimes want *you* to [penetrate] them." Most of these feminine males were suspicious of outward expressions of masculinity "in the north," where, they reasoned, the intense antihomosexual climate forced eshenges to hide their true gender identity. Thus, "real men" were proven only when masculinity was instantiated through insertive/dominant sexual practices. Hamish remarked further, with a discerning facial expression, "I only like to go with real men . . . the ones who are bisexuals." I found Hamish's statement curious, as given his previous complaint about his boyfriend's sexual relationships with women and his unwillingness to wear condoms, why did he desire his own subjugation?

* * *

It was the middle of March 2008. The children frantically crowded the public beach in Swakopmund at the coastline. Small sand pails, buckets, and plastic bags lay ready to capture the small baby sharks and other live fish that almost jumped out of the water onto the shore. Steffen, a prominent leader for the LGBT Coastal Project (an offshoot of TRP), explained, "It's just what I thought. It's a red tide."[13] A large deep-sea octopus also moved onto the shoreline, attracting a particularly large crowd of children.

Commenting on the scene as we sat and watched with amazement, Steffen said, "It's hard to believe that this beach was once only for white people. I remember not being permitted to come here as a child because I'm a colored, even though my father is white. Look, now there are mostly black people . . . but the white people, [now] they all go to the private beaches at those exclusive resorts, away from us black people."

Steffen's nostalgic mood shifted. He said he wanted to introduce me to his "Ovambo boyfriend," who lives in the black township of Kuisebmund, in the neighboring town of Walvis Bay—the center of the fishing industry, located around the only deep sea harbor on Namibia's coastline.

As we made our way through the side roads in Kuisebmund, it became clear to me that Steffen was intimately familiar with this township, although he lived in the neighboring colored township of Narraville. He continually stopped to say hello to people, mostly young, straight black men he had previously dated, and a few masculine lesbians, who were members of the local TRP chapter, and their families. Finally we arrived at his boyfriend's place, located among a number of concrete block houses displaying numerous small SWAPO flags—a reminder to us that Independence Day was coming soon. "Those are mostly Ovambos flying those flags," Steffen said. "SWAPO provides incentives for them to relocate here from Ovamboland, to increase their constituents in this region."

Stopping in front of a mauve-colored house, a rather tall and lanky young fellow who appeared to be in about his early twenties came running out the door, excited to greet Steffen. Our small group agreed to head to what Steffen told me is "the former black beach," now renamed Independence Beach.

While Steffen talked with some of his friends, his boyfriend started telling me about how he could never come out about his sexuality to his family living up north, because "Ovambos are not supposed to be gays [*laughs*]. You must have heard what will happen. They'll stick a burning rod up your ass to punish you." I nodded.

Our conversation was interrupted, however, when Petrus, a young HIV counselor working in Walvis Bay, appeared and sat down next to us on the sand. I had already met Petrus a few years ago at a sexual identity training workshop organized by Steffen and other TRP members near Kuisebmund. According to Petrus, that was when he first began to accept his gender and sexual difference. Petrus proudly pointed to his boyfriend, who was splashing about in the water. Steffen soon rushed in to join him.

"He is so straight-looking, isn't he?" Petrus said, referring to his boyfriend. "He's from Katutura and he visits me every weekend. The only problem is that he drinks all my money away, and then he *really* can get violent." Petrus said this in a laughing tone.

I ask, "Why do you keep inviting him back if he treats you like that?"

"He is just so masculine and straight, you know. I can't help myself. Just look at him. That's just my type, I guess."

Later that evening Steffen received an alarming call from Petrus. We rushed to Petrus's home and found shards of smashed bottles littering the floor of his apartment, Petrus was standing there with cuts on his face, looking battered. His boyfriend had beaten him quite badly this time and had forced him to have sex without a condom—"again," Petrus said to me. Nevertheless, Petrus invited his boyfriend back again to stay with him the following weekend.

\* \* \*

For the gay community in the Windhoek urban area, 2005 was an exciting year: it saw the establishment of the first official gay club, known as Ekuta, in the heart of the commercial district.[14] An "out," white, South African gay man owned and operated Ekuta, yet only a few local gay whites ever frequented the club. However, the club did attract a diverse crowd of black men and women from the surrounding townships of Katutura and Khomasdal. TRP sponsored several parties and special events at Ekuta, making it a celebrated space for LGBT Namibians. Although the club stayed open for only a few months, I witnessed several interesting events there. Groups of masculine men began frequenting the place, looking to pick up local gays.

One evening, at a private party organized by TRP, a group of feminine males sitting around a table at Ekuta began to cheer when their grinning friend Maurice arrived with a beautiful, muscular "straight boyfriend," as they called him, on his arm. Commenting on Maurice's trophy-like display of the local athlete, one of the feminine males at our table blurted out, "Maurice is so lucky that he can afford him." And indeed Maurice was economically independent. By working for a tourism company, he managed to escape the high rate of unemployment and low-paying jobs that plagued the majority of people living in Katutura.

In the capital city of Windhoek, a new community of socially and economically mobile black gay men was beginning to establish its public presence.[15] They frequently dated expatriates (see chapter 5) with whom they have traveled to South Africa and Europe to sample a more cosmopolitan gay life. Some have had their educations paid for by wealthier white men. Many worked in banking, hospitality, tourism, and in NGOs, particularly those related to sexual health, and their incomes made them the breadwinners in their families. Together with their wealthier expatriate boyfriends, they threw lively parties in the affluent suburbs of Windhoek and invited poorer straight black men who became the boyfriends of both the white elite and local blacks who could afford their company.

The new group of upwardly mobile, black gay men seemed to be empowered and independent in every way. They were out about their sexual desires and gender nonconformity, having attended many TRP workshops. They were "fabulously dressed" in the latest fashions and were able to attract their pick of sought-after masculine men. Yet during private conversations and interviews many described their struggles with beatings, coerced anal sex, and other forms of abuse at the hands of the masculine men they dated. Several of these feminine gay men discussed the damage they experienced to their anus through forceful penetration, which in their description sounded unambiguously like rape. Others received black eyes and other bodily bruises. During one interview with a young feminine male, when the subject of sexual violence arose, he said, "I don't know why. Maybe I'm crazy or something, but I really love those 'homo thugs' [rough guys]." In another interview, Ron, a young bank teller, explains the violence he regularly encountered:

> I have a "straight" boyfriend in [Katutura]. He is very aggressive, very violent. I told him I don't like to be fucked all the time and I said, "Sometimes I must do it [penetrate you]," and he got so worked up at the club. He was beating me with brooms and champagne glasses. He would not go fifty-fifty. Sometimes straight guys, they won't want to use the condom and you say no and you get a smack on the face. . . . When he hits me, I think he loves me. I know that he loves me.

Economically disadvantaged feminine males living in Katutura echoed this kind of narrative. Herman, for example, left his small village up north to come to Windhoek "to be myself," which, he claimed, TRP had helped him to achieve. He worked in an NGO as a cleaner, making barely enough to support himself when I first met him. His low wages did allow him, however, to buy enough materials to build a small, one-room makeshift home in Katutura, consisting of wiring, wooden beams, paneling, and steel-sheet roofing. One day Herman came home to find his boyfriend having sex with a woman at his place. Feeling devastated, he told his boyfriend to leave because their relationship had to end. His boyfriend then destroyed his home by setting it on fire. Herman knew, of course, that he had little recourse: the police would never open a case file involving a same-sex relationship and with his home not legally registered as a residence, like many abodes in Katutura.

A few days later a group of us helped Herman to rebuild his home. In the course of our reconstruction, he began to talk about how he had given his boy-friend money, fed him, and bought him alcohol even though he could hardly af-ford to support himself. Herman then admitted that his boyfriend had regularly abused him physically and sexually and explained that he had stayed with him for so long because he desired "a man who is physically strong and powerful. I don't want to be with someone who is weak . . . like a woman." A year or so passed, and in 2007 I returned to Herman's place only to find that his home had been destroyed again, this time by his new boyfriend, a local boxer, who had bro-ken in to steal some of Herman's possessions.

\* \* \*

The foregoing vignettes demonstrate how the gendered antagonism that re-sides at the heart of antihomosexual, nationalistic rhetoric plays out in the sexual relationships between masculine and feminine male subjects. The sudden and more pronounced appearance of male femininities throughout Namibia fuels the conflicts in masculinity experienced by working-class "straight men," conflicts that are partly tied to "the erosion of jobs in an increasingly competitive global market" and the "increased feelings of insecurity . . . for men who have been brought up to play the role of 'provider'" (Becker 2000, 56; also see Morrell 1998). On the one hand, they enjoy sexual pleasures with feminine males—pleasures that are imagined as forms of Western decadence free from sexually transmit-ted diseases and familial obligations, and that furnish access to monetary and material resources. On the other hand, these same men also rush to defend the vulnerability of masculinity (the nation) by violently negating moffies (the for-eign threat). In the absence of any real legal protective mechanisms for gay men, "straight men" become licensed to exert physical force over them, and thus, in effect, assume a defining role of the state's agency.

In characterizing the ironic desires of feminine males, I would tend to avoid the suggestions of "masochism" and "learned helplessness" that are often associ-ated with the battered wife syndrome (Walker 1979). Instead, I consider the ex-pression of these ironic desires, in part, as the unexpected side effects of the col-lision between TRP's techniques for enhancing self-awareness and postcolonial nationalisms that essentialize the "natural" and immutable right of "real men" to rule. For feminine males the fallout from these collisions replays in the territory of subjectivity rather than through practices of freedom that reach outwardly in making critical associations with more pervasive forms of gender inequality that are commonly experienced by Namibian women.

Highlighting idioms of uncontrollable and unexplainable desires illuminates how feminine males seem to subject themselves to sexual violence. According to Alan Sinfield, one of the reasons "power differentials are remarkably persistent in gay fantasies and in the stories of gayness that circulate, is that *it is sexy...* despite or because of its bond with oppression" (2004, 1–2; emphasis added). These words do draw our attention to the ways oppressive power inequalities can form the ground of the erotic and suggest the important emotional stakes for these feminine youths in cultivating their own sense of erotic freedom, living out and imagining scenarios of subjugation as well as empowerment (33, 58). However, Sinfield's line of thinking does not help us to understand why, within the context of a human rights and sexual health intervention, such life-threatening forms of violence (whether desired or not) remain unpoliticized by these budding activists as well as the organizers who guide and encourage their mobilizations. The primary concern here lies more with issues of political awareness: gender-based inequalities of power in male-male sexual relationships remain on the periphery of TRP's interventions, even at a moment in history when an acute awareness of intimate partner and domestic violence (suffered by women) pervades southern Africa.

TRP's empowerment programs guide feminine males to embrace the truth of their inner desires as the path toward liberation. And as individuals become embroiled in reflecting upon the nature of their being, experiences of gender inequality become submerged beneath the universalistic project of "freedom," at times resurfacing as unexplainable and uncontrollable desires for "real men"— their "natural" sexual counterpart. By grounding political resistance in universalistic notions of selfhood, then, TRP discourses inadvertently depoliticize the way prevailing gender-power inequalities refract through male-male sexual relationships. Therefore, while TRP programs are particularly effective in ushering in confident femininities, at the same time they overlook important political opportunities. Moreover, these well-intentioned programs inadvertently contribute to the naturalization of violence between intimate partners as male participants are guided to more fully "discover" themselves as subjects of femininity.

Of course this is not to suggest that TRP interventions are the all-encompassing and determining force behind the violence that feminine youths encounter, for such violence likely would occur between masculine and feminine males even in the absence of TRP's intervention. In a study by Graeme Reid (2013, 50–51), one of his feminine male informants describes the kind of domestic violence he encountered in his relationship with his boyfriend as though it were part of the more routinized experience of domestic violence in the township. Here the normalization of domestic violence occurred without the kind of intense convergence of transnational attention received under the Rainbow Project. The point made, however, is that TRP programs, which inspired open public displays of gender dissidence in the quest for LGBT rights, did aggravate existing social fault lines, and they did so without any strategies that might compel a reflection on the political implications of the oppressions these youths encounter in their intimate relationships.

# 5  Thinking through
## the Foreigner Fetish

Important tensions may arise when places that have been
imagined at a distance must become lived spaces.

—Akhil Gupta and James Ferguson, *Culture, Power, Place*

In late 2007 TRP's new health officer and I completed an HIV-related training workshop with gay and lesbian community researchers. The group decided we would all go to Windhoek's only sex shop, located in a predominantly
white neighborhood, to see what safer-sex resources were available beyond the
free condoms provided by the Ministry of Health and Social Services. The females were particularly eager to find out if the shop carried any dental dams or
products specifically designed for lesbians. The health officer and I were standing outside, recapping the success of the training, when three of the community
researchers exited the store with annoyed faces. "That [shop] owner is racist,"
Hanna blurted out. "They don't want too many of *us* in there at the same time."
The health officer, a well-educated Damara man, rushed inside and in his usual
tactful tone tried to reason with the owner and ease his anxieties by explaining
the educational purpose of our visit. As I walked in and approached the counter
where the health officer stood face-to-face with the owner, I overheard the owner
saying, "I don't want *one of them* stealing something from my shop." I then joined
the argument.

As the three of us continued to argue, one of the community researchers,
who thought he had unearthed yet more evidence of racism, approached the
owner's counter after having perused the gay magazine shelves and exclaimed,
"You don't even carry *Black Inches* or *Latin Inches* [gay porn magazines depicting
men of color] here!" The owner smirked at us and said, "Yes, we do, but it is always the first to sell out with our customers, mostly the foreigners. We can hardly
keep them on the shelf." The irony here left the community researcher speechless,

with his eyes widening. In the shop, black people were delegitimated as potential consumers of sexual erotica while, at the same time, images of their bodies, as highly prized and fetishized objects, were swiftly consumed by a mostly white and foreigner clientele.[1]

In this chapter I highlight the subjectivities of black gay youths in relation to the inequalities they encountered in their relationships with foreigners and local elites, most of whom were white. Through their re-attendance at TRP's workshops, the Rainbow Youth invest considerable energy in liberating themselves and realizing their practices of freedom. To accomplish this, they not only ground themselves in notions of traditional culture, as we saw in chapter 2, but they also orient themselves toward a "global gay peoplehood" (Kapac 1998), which creates a view of their own communities as a natural part of human diversity. This orientation profoundly transformed how the Rainbow Youth were able to value and legitimate themselves in local contexts and in relation to the nation state.

The identity work of the Rainbow Youth also granted access to new global streams of resources and, particularly for males, to emotional, practical, and financial opportunities in the sexual intimacies they come to share with foreigners. Over time, however, the youths I interviewed on various occasions came to realize that the journey toward "freeing" their desires often plays into other forms of subjugation. This is not unlike the community researcher above who, after his training in sexual health, was excited to explore gay erotica in the white neighborhood. When he actually arrived at the shop, he was troubled to learn of his social exclusion and the exploited position of his body in this transnational economy of desires.[2]

In particular the lived experiences of three self-identified gay men, Romeo, Travis, and Winston, can help us to understand how these social inequalities take shape. From the time I first met these young men, and over the course of a number of years, I heard repeated stories about the racialized conflicts they endured and how their struggles pivoted on the commodification of black bodies. Before turning our focus to these youths, I have provided two short field note excerpts to contextualize the wider global economic milieu of Namibia's tourism industry, which produces representations of Namibian culture and ethnicity that are intended to appeal to the desires of foreigners. This discussion is a necessary detour in the story of the Rainbow Project, because the tourism industry more generally capitalizes on and conditions the unequal relations between black and white bodies in Namibia.

## Sketch 1: "Nearly Naked San"

The owner of an American tourism company based in Windhoek approached me in a local pub. She asked, "So have you seen the bushmen yet?" I hesitantly responded, "Well, I'm working with various San communities (a less pejorative name for the communities she was referring to) at a local university center." She shook her head and said, "No, no—the *real* bushmen, who still hunt with bows and arrows and live out in the bush. You know, the nearly naked ones." My first thought was that if she had actually spoken with some of the San (*Ju//houansi*) men and women I worked with about their lives, she would have quickly learned that such indigeneity was usually performed as a way to bring in revenue to their impoverished communities at game reserves. Then I wondered if perhaps she already knew about this staging of indigeneity. Knowing or unknowing, she reminded me that the nearly naked "bushmen" certainly do *exist* as a prized commodity within Namibia's booming tourism industry, both for visiting tourists and for the production of San community livelihood.

### Sketch 2: "Hunting Women"

A visiting professor of anthropology and her student, both African Americans, invited me to join them earlier one afternoon for a tour of Windhoek. Although not particularly fond of assuming the role of a tourist, I agreed to join the tour in order so that I could have more time to socialize with them. The hired driver soon arrived at the small university center in Eros (a residential area in Windhoek), where we were staying for the week. And so we began our tour. We traveled around the parliament buildings, passing the prominent Dutch Reform church, the Equestrian Statue, and other landmarks from the colonial past as the guide recited factual tidbits about apartheid and the struggle for liberation.

Midway through the tour the Afrikaner driver became flustered while delivering her script, bringing her recitation sputtering to a halt. After an awkward moment of silence, she asked, "Is it okay for me to say 'black people'? Normally I am used to giving tours to, ah, Europeans, mostly Germans." By "Europeans" she was, of course, referring to white tourists. It would seem that our being of color muddled the typical relation between tourists, local white tour operators, and the production of historical blurbs used to capture the struggle of black Namibians. As her script continued to wane, we initiated a different conversation with her by asking about her experiences of working with her typical clients—"Europeans," as she put it. She explained that she encountered two recurring problems. She was troubled when clients asked her to take them on a tour of the township of Katutura, a place that seemed remarkable to them only because it displayed intense poverty, greatly contrasting with Windhoek's more affluent districts. Then she began to speak at length about the "troupes of German men" who frequently traveled to Namibia to hunt "big game" at the privately owned game farms. She had been asked by such groups on more than one occasion, and much to her dismay, to "take us to the black women [for sex]." In a disgusted tone she continued, "They come here to hunt our animals and our women."

Tourism is the fastest-growing economic sector in Namibia, which is highly prized for the foreign exchange revenues it generates and its potential to finance national infrastructure and projects that promote further economic development. The direct and indirect impact of tourism accounts for 17.7 percent of total employment and 16 percent of the country's gross domestic product (Eita and ve Jordaan 2007). The thriving nature of this industry is also reflected in Namibia's more than eighty-five official tour and safari companies located in Windhoek. There are also plentiful small, unofficial, independent safari companies based in Windhoek.

With respect to marketing, Namibia is not promoted as a destination for "sex tourism"—at least not explicitly. It happens more tacitly at a symbolic representational level through the colonial-like narratives mobilized in advertising. Scanning the most frequently visited tourism websites, it is clear how Namibia is marketed: as possessing a "pristine," picturesque landscape, teeming with abundant and exotic wildlife at the many private game reserves and national parks, such as the famous Etosha Pans. Tourism companies also boast of Namibia's striking displays of cultural diversity among indigenous people, "still" living in "traditional" cultural settings, particularly those in the north. Bare-breasted Himba women, stained with rancid butterfat and brilliant red ochre and "scented with the aromatic resin of the Omuzumba shrub,"[3] perhaps best exemplify how tourism marketing commodifies Namibia's "exoticism." These advertising photos depict Himba women, like the "nearly naked San" described earlier, as melding with a naturalistic portrait of Namibia's landscape. Selling this imaginary of Namibia's "untamed" exoticism is what excites the German hunters described above, for it offers them the opportunity to seek out and realize colonial fantasies of "conquering" nature, which includes local black women. The cooption of bodies that are "closer to nature" in the marketing schemes of tourism companies produces ethnicity as a consumable cultural product (Comaroff and Comaroff 2009), the "benefits" of which are available to indigenous people as well as local tourism companies.

The commodification of black bodies also inheres in emerging forms of gay tourism in Namibia, a point Jacqui Alexander makes explicit in reference to the growth of global gay tourism outside of the West. Alexander analyzes the production of gay consumer identities, assumed to be white and male, in Western travel guides produced by the International Gay Travel Association: "Travel guides comprise one of gay tourism's primary ideological anchors . . . in which Third World gay men get positioned as the objects of sexual consumption rather than as agents of sexual exchange" (Alexander 2006, 79; also see Puar 2002 and Manalansan 2003, 85). These words resonate with the stories told to me by the Rainbow Youth and the way their bodies were commonly viewed within local networks of gay expats and white elites in Windhoek.

One evening I sat among a group of German researchers at the Warehouse Lounge, a common hangout where local urbanites and expats went to enjoy live performances of African popular music. Jan, whose wealthy family owned a local game farm that served mostly European tourists, initiated a conversation with me on my research, having heard about it from a TRP board member. At first he seemed quite nervous as he brought up the topic of my research. Jan told me that as a white Afrikaner, it was particularly difficult to be "out," because his community was small, tightly knit, and "very Christian." As the evening wore on, Jan certainly became less inhibited and began to explain how he faced numerous problems with "those black guys" with whom he had sexual relationships: "One guy even came to my workplace trying to get one hundred rand out of me." I asked where he generally met local black men and he said, "Usually at [a certain five-star hotel], in the lounge." He went on to explain, grinning from ear to ear, that tourists staying at this hotel could "order their 'boy' or 'girl' for the weekend with their booking if they want." I then asked if he ever had relationships with men in the Afrikaner community. He said he preferred to have sex with black men: "They just give themselves to you so freely during sex; it's almost like they are animals."

At Windhoek's five-star hotel lobbies, nightclubs, and bars where local black women sell sex to visiting male foreigners and local elites, both black and white, there can also be found a growing number of young black men who sell sex to more affluent gays as a way to make a living or to supplement their incomes. Gay youths repeatedly spoke to me about their encounters with the racial objectification of their bodies in their sexual relationships with foreigners. However, in order to more fully understand the forms of domination at play in these financially uneven relationships, one must go beyond notions of racial commodification and globalization as a unidirectional process. One must also critically examine the local expansion of transnational resources that become available to the Rainbow Youth: emergent systems of cultural value, solidarities, and new routes for mobility within the reconfigurations of their social networks. In other words, in order to understand how global capitalism operates to shape inequalities within the sexual relationships of local gay youths with foreigners and local elites, we must take fuller stock of the multidirectional exchanges occurring within these expansions and, with regard to male youths, the articulations with their practices of freedom.

It was my first "movie night" with TRP staff and the young members. I had not yet begun any formal interviewing and had been given only brief introductions to the members by TRP staff. A good-size crowd of about forty people, including Hanna, Shane, Kelly, Louami, and Travis, was ready to screen two movies: *Simon & Me*, a story about the lives and political work of South African gay and lesbian activists Simon Nikoli and Bev Palesa Ditsie, and *It's My Life*, which chronicles the rise of the Treatment Action Campaign (TAC) led by Zackie Achmat, which eventually forced the South African government to adopt a program of universal antiretroviral access.

The young man I was seated next to, Romeo, introduced himself by saying, "So you are a Canadian. I had a boyfriend from Peru once who was studying his masters and another boyfriend from Germany. I mostly like to have foreign boy-friends [*pauses*]. I don't know why; I just love them the most."

"So you meet a lot of foreigners here in Windhoek?" I asked.

"Yes, everyone in the world knows what our president says about gays and lesbians. Many foreigners like you have come to our office because of the hate speeches." I nodded, and he continued, saying, "I heard about your research on HIV and AIDS. I have many friends who have died of AIDS, but nobody talks about it in the family. It's like it doesn't exist or something."

We chatted further about the research, and Romeo eagerly asked to partici-pate in my study. I told him that I first wanted to conduct a pre-interview to fa-miliarize him with the sensitive issues that the interview raises. This would also give him time to decide if he really wanted to participate, I explained. Romeo asked me to meet him on his day off at the entrance of the mall beneath a five-star hotel known as the Kalahari Sands at 5:00 PM.

By the time Romeo arrived on the appointed day, it was already after 7:00 PM and quite dark. He suggested we head to a nearby restaurant known as the Spur. On the way we passed Town Square, where he called out to a friend hang-ing around in a dark corner. After we finished chatting, Romeo explained that his friend is "a bisexual and a hustler" who sells sex to gay foreigners.

We then entered the restaurant, a rather garish sight with images of Ameri-can cowboys and Indians plastered throughout the space, set in a ranch-themed decor. Romeo seemed to know all the waiters and told me that mostly moffies worked there.

One of the waiters seated us next to a young man whom Romeo instantly rec-ognized. The man had several gold chains around his neck, a long sports jersey, a baseball cap worn sideways, and baggy jeans. A gold star filling flashed in our direction when he smiled. "He's a bisexual and has lots of European boyfriends. He's a real player," Romeo said with delight. He then jumped up from the table and began busily moving about the room, going from table to table as though he were hosting a fabulous dinner party at his home and checking up on his guests. As he talked with friends, he periodically pointed back at me as people giggled.

What I found most interesting about the scene Romeo created was the di-verse network of people with whom he was interacting. In addition to the young wait staff and the male sex worker, Romeo spoke with a government minister he had met during a TRP event; two West African businessmen, whose cell phone numbers he now entered into his phone; two Afrikaner lawyers; and a small group of young female students from the local polytechnic, one of whom was a relative. By the end of the evening his socializing had left little chance for us to discuss the research in any depth, but after quickly examining some of the ques-tions I had jotted down for him, he agreed to do the interview, insisting that I meet him at his home in Damara Lokasie next time.

A week later we met again on a Saturday afternoon. It was Romeo's day off from working as a bellboy at an upscale hotel. He took me around his neighborhood from home to home, introducing me to moffies and their families as well as numerous small groups of young men whom he identified as bisexuals. I found it odd that they didn't seem to mind when Romeo openly identified their sexuality. From what I could observe, the bisexual men were distinguishable from other men only by their recognizably more Western-style hip-hop attire and their consumption of sweet white wine and brandy. Romeo eventually explained to me that through his contact at TRP he was able to connect these guys with foreigners who were interested in having sex with black men: "Sometimes I help them out. It's difficult to make money these days, so I try to hook them up with foreigners, you know."

At the first home we visited, Romeo gave a small sum of money to the senior woman who heads the household in exchange for two large tumblers of Tafel lager beer, which the woman sold from the kitchen refrigerator. He shared one of the beers with the woman's adult son and girlfriend. At the next home, Romeo shared the second beer with the family, who in turn gave him a small sum of money. He then used this money to buy beer at the next home of a relative, who went around the back of the house to the small shebeen for more Tafel lager. Romeo again shared the beer, received money at the next stop, and continued this pattern until at the end he had more money than he started with, had enjoyed at least four large bottles of Tafel lager, and had socialized with friends and relatives at more than fifteen homes.

Finally we arrived back at Romeo's home but decided to postpone the interview, given that we had both consumed too much beer. Romeo suggested we should eat something. He asked me for some money and I explained that I had only a 20 Namibian dollar note left, part of which I would need for my taxi ride home. Nevertheless, he took the money from my hand and called out to a young man next door, who grabbed the money and took off. A few minutes later the young guy returned with a can of soup and some concert tickets, but without any change. I asked Romeo if I could get some change back, enough to take a taxi. He said confidently, "Don't worry; you'll get *all* your money back soon." Then there was a knock at the door. Five young guys whom Romeo had previously introduced to me as "bisexuals" asked permission to hang out at his place to drink a bottle of brandy they had just purchased. Romeo agreed and they also bought some of the tickets from him.

Over the next few hours I was stunned to witness the dizzying number of exchanges of food, cash, alcohol, and drugs (including Mandrax and *dagga,* or marijuana) accompanied by a continuous flow of people in and out of the house. Money, goods, and people appeared, disappeared, and reappeared from one moment to the next. And by the end of the evening Romeo was very pleased with himself when he was able to present me with 20 Namibian dollars from the large pile of funds he had accumulated. In fact, he had accumulated more than he had "invested." He also gave me a small gift: a professionally produced photo of himself with his smiling face resting on his clenched fist. "I like to give this to all my friends who are foreigners," he said.

Although we never got to conduct the interview that evening, I instantly became fascinated with the intensity of exchanges. Another evening I counted fourteen exchanges in two hours at Romeo's home. *How can anyone keep track of what they owe to others?* I wondered. But eventually I learned the principles of economic life in Damara Lokasie: "losing track" was what sustained these exchanges. Because one could never keep track, one always felt obligated to others (Godelier 1999). This sense of obligation, however, while holding together and reaffirming social ties, often led to fights when extravagant items were displayed.

One day Romeo was walking down the street in Damara Lokasie with his new silk boxer shorts visible over the waist of his jeans. They had been a recent gift from a wealthy British boyfriend he had met through his association with TRP. Several people came up to him and began arguing with him. He explained to me later that if you had anything luxurious, like his new boxers, you were assumed to be stealing and were not contributing what you owed to the community.

A week later I finally conducted my first of many interviews with Romeo, who recounted how he had lost both of his parents at a young age and was left with the responsibility of running the household. On weekends he looked after his sisters' children in addition to holding down a part-time job at the hotel. This job, he said, did not pay much—money was always a struggle. He wanted very much to sell the house and take a PR course at the local polytechnic, but, he insisted, although the house was a huge burden, he needed to keep it for his nieces and nephews, because "it's the family house!"

Romeo first attended a TRP social gathering when Travis invited him to the office's open house held during Human Rights Week in 2000. He reminisced about how excited he felt: "To see all of those people like me, it was so amazing! And there was this dance at Club Thriller with foreigners and professional people; there was this transgender lesbian running it [the club]. It was like we all came there . . . together we would fight against what the president was saying. It was a true rainbow [of diversity] that night."

At least once a week Romeo would try to drop by TRP's office when he had time off. Like many of the members, he loved reading the American, European, and South African gay current affairs magazines. He told me that he most loved the pictures of Gay Pride parades and festivities in other countries, once commenting that "someday we must celebrate like that in Namibia."

At one of TRP's earliest socials, Romeo met his first foreign boyfriend, a Dutch businessman working in Windhoek. "Being with him helped give me the confidence to get work at the hotel. Well, he actually helped me get that job by introducing me to the right people." After a few months, Romeo's boyfriend left him for a "black guy." Romeo described the "other man":

> He's straighter than me. He's a bisexual. I guess he [the Dutch businessman] likes it rough [*laughs*]. But you know, working at the hotel, there are so many gay foreigners I can meet and I get their numbers. . . . Being gay, you know, I get a lot of good tips working there.
>
> I have also been with some of those bisexual guys, in Katutura, you know the straight ones, but they just don't understand why it's important being *out* and *coming out.* You know, they would never go to a TRP meeting or do marches or anything like that. They also expect money from us, because they know we have international friends like you. They just want to take from us.

Soon after his relationship with the Dutch businessman ended, Romeo met a wealthy black restaurant owner originally from North Africa.

> We were dating for two years. He [the restaurant owner] was older than me. He was very possessive. If I was dancing in the club or chatting with another guy too long, he would smash me in the face. The problem was we are always drinking too much together.

During one interview Romeo explained that he was trying hard to get out of this relationship, not only because of the physical violence but also because his new boyfriend "won't let me wear condoms. At first I didn't know you could get it [HIV] from a man down there [gestures toward anal region]." But when Romeo's close friend, whom his boyfriend had also slept with, had tested positive, he said, "I then abstained from [anal] sex and my partner and I only do oral sex." Violence erupted around this refusal, Romeo confided, and eventually he ended the relationship.

A few months passed and Romeo text-messaged me. I returned the call and he sounded eager to meet and share some good news with me. When we met he told me he was going to the Netherlands to marry his new boyfriend. He said he was finally getting his life together and had even decided to quit drinking, a condition imposed by his new boyfriend. He insisted that the man was now treating him very well. "I am so nervous to meet his family, though," he said.

Romeo left Namibia shortly thereafter and permitted his younger sister to move into the family house with her children. After his departure a swirl of rumors began. Some said that Romeo had made up the entire story of his marriage and that he had actually just gone to the United Kingdom for a vacation with one of his foreign boyfriends. Several gay youths who worked as airline attendants said they had spotted Romeo roaming the streets in London, where he was working as a "rent boy" (a male sex worker).

What became clear, however, was that Romeo's departure marked the opening up of a new, vital flow of goods. A year later, when I bumped into Romeo in Katutura on my way to visit Hanna, he invited me to see the changes he had made to the family home. From the outside the small, concrete-block house looked relatively the same, except now it was freshly painted. But inside, the worn linoleum flooring had been replaced with expensive ceramic tiling, on which new furniture was displayed. Sitting on the new couches was a group of young men watching movies on an enormous plasma-screen television hanging on the newly replastered wall. Not only did the stream of resources that Romeo discovered along the road to sexual freedom provide for material accumulation and personal mobility, but it also allowed him to divert much of it back to his community to reaffirm local social ties and fulfill obligations to his community. One day in early 2008, however, Romeo said, in a heavy tone of regret, "You know, I have a lot more money now, but I feel I don't belong anywhere now. Not here, and definitely not in Europe—they don't respect us black people in those countries."

\* \* \*

Romeo's statement "it's important being *out* and *coming out*" highlights his awareness of the socioeconomic benefits garnered through his practices of freedom. "Coming out" certainly opens up new possibilities for mobility. Unlike some of his bisexual friends in Katutura, who often depend on him to find foreign sexual partners, being "out" affords Romeo more independence, in the form of direct entrée into expatriate circles that form at TRP's social and political forums. He also receives cash tips from gay foreigners at the hotel where he works, as a product of his visibility. His decision to come out and participate in TRP mobilizations has led to the expansion and diversification of his social network—one that extends outside his social class and beyond Namibia's borders. Furthermore, this network expansion has indeed translated into new flows of financial capital.

Although his display of extravagant items at times creates conflicts with local people in Katutura, Romeo eventually invests what he accumulates abroad into the family house, an investment that helps to reaffirm local ties to family and friends. With the financial acumen that allows him to accumulate more than he contributes to during local transactions, Romeo is able to mediate transnational flows of resources to his gain in his sexual relationships with foreigners. The way he acts upon these flows of resources in many ways counters ideas of globalization as a unidirectional homogenizing force, the notion of which has rightly come under criticism in anthropological studies of sexuality (see, for example,

Boellstorff 2005; Dave 2012; Gaudio 2009; Manalansan 2003; Wekker 2006). However, over the years Romeo has begun to express his ambivalence toward his participation in these transnational economic arrangements as he grows aware of how the denigration of black people accompany some of the accumulations he derives from his practice of being "out."

The two ethnographic sketches that follow describe a similar emotional passage over time—from excitement and optimism to regret and disappointment—as Travis and Winston come to an awareness of the exploited and racialized position of their bodies in their relationships with foreigners.

\* \* \*

On August 14, 2001, Travis took the stage at the Warehouse Lounge after the performance of a rousing jazz standard sung by local artist Sharon van Roi. The eighteen-year-old sat at the table as the technician adjusted the mike for him to speak. Travis nodded knowingly. This special occasion, a gay and lesbian poetry reading and storytelling session, drew together a diverse crowd of antiapartheid activists; national politicians, including CoD MP Rosa Namises; European embassy representatives; NGO workers; artists; local and foreign journalists; and many young people from Katutura Township. Travis began to tell his story before the crowd with a confidence that seemed well beyond his years. Understandably, as a Damara speaker he struggled with some of his English pronunciations, but when his testimonial of discrimination came to the queer phrases "in the closet," "homophobia," and "coming out," he could not have sounded more articulate. His personal account drew tremendous applause from the crowd because it was so important that a black Namibian was willing to speak out against the president.

Next, three stunningly tall and slender black drag queens around sixteen or seventeen years of age danced a lip-synced performance to the tune of "I'm a Survivor," a popular American song by female R & B trio Destiny's Child. Concluding the poetry and testimonial readings, TRP's director, Ian Swartz, delivered an impassioned political speech in which he brought together "human rights for LGBT people" and "the legalization of prostitution" in the same breath—*An interesting bridging of political discourses,* I thought.

Travis and his friend Isaiah then introduced me to two young black men who were in the company of a considerably older, white European man. Later Travis commented with a mischievous grin that the white man "owned" the two black teens: "He clothes them, feeds them, and sleeps with them." That night I met numerous interracial couples who could be similarly characterized in terms of financial disparity and age difference. In the name of sexual freedom, various relationships between young black men and considerably older and wealthier white men regularly formed and were visible at TRP's social and political events.

For Travis it would take some time before he realized that his entanglement in this expanding network of unequal power relationships would lead to his own undoing.

A year later when I interviewed Travis, I noticed that he had become more confident in speaking English. His hair was now painstakingly straightened to emulate particular European styles he had viewed in TRP's magazine collection. By this time he had given a number of interviews to the local and foreign press and had recited his testimonial at various human rights forums and celebrations. Lately sporting the most fashionable attire, he was beginning to be criticized by fellow TRP members for dressing "beyond his means." One fellow member even disparaged him to his friends by calling him a "coconut" (someone who is black on the outside and white on the inside) and a "puppet" (under the control of white people).

During a meeting we had at a library to compose his employment resume, Travis brought along his photo album and showed me some pictures of former boyfriends. The first, taken when Travis was sixteen, was a fifty-year-old Roman Catholic priest. Next, he showed me a picture of a local man—"He's a *boer*" [Afrikaans word for white farmer, used here in a derogatory way]—who was his boyfriend for several months. He went on to show me other pictures of boyfriends, all of whom were similar in two respects: they were white, and they were considerably older than Travis. He explained that he desired white men and liked foreigners in particular because "they know how to treat you right and take care of you. The black guys just want to take from you; they are so dependent."

Several months later Travis seemed upset. He had caught his current partner in bed with someone else—"another black guy," he exclaimed. And it was someone who had been a longtime friend. Travis said he no longer wanted to date white men, even though they had money. He declared one day, "I would rather be poor!" But it was particularly difficult for Travis to find work because he had come out so publicly about his sexuality during Nujoma's hate speeches. He pleaded, "Who would hire me now?" He was quite angry with his ex-boyfriend for having treated him like a "common street prostitute." Although he liked that his former partner had money, took him to dinner, and bought him gifts, Travis was "with him for love," he explained adamantly. For this reason Travis had been faithful to his partner. After two months into the relationship, Travis told me, he had trusted his partner enough to have unprotected anal sex: "I always practice safer sex, but sometimes you trust your partner and you are faithful but the other person is not. They are faithful in front of you. I left that relationship because I became so scared of HIV."

Travis was greatly concerned about getting HIV, and it was certainly close to home for him. Two of his sisters had already tested positive and now were sick and dying with AIDS. One day he showed me the official papers documenting the fact that he had been approved for the adoption of a sister's newborn HIV-positive baby, proudly bearing the new responsibility. Leaving his boyfriend, therefore, was a difficult decision to make because of the financial difficulties he experienced. As I got to know Travis over the course of a year, he told me that occasionally he had sex for money with foreigners he met at local discos. "It was exciting to be wanted like that," he said. "It makes you feel attractive and good about yourself."

One day a World Bank representative came to TRP's office to speak about the organization's development programs supporting LGBT people in different regions of Africa. I was invited to talk to him about HIV research, and Travis was invited to provide "the local perspective" on LGBT discrimination in Namibia. The representative, an American in his late fifties, introduced himself as gay and HIV positive. Throughout the meeting he continually made suggestive glances at Travis and directed a few joking sexual comments toward him. Travis beamed with delight. By the end of the meeting the two had arranged a date.

That weekend Travis showed up at the popular disco La de Das with the World Bank representative. He approached me with a smile as he said, "I'm his 'chaperone' for the weekend. I'll be 'accompanying' him at the Kalahari Sands [Hotel]." He then nervously began to fire detailed questions about HIV transmission at me, such as "Now, if I just shaved my chest and got semen on it, can I get HIV?" and "How long is it, again, after I brush my teeth before I can have oral sex?"

The following week the word had spread throughout TRP and Katutura: "Travis 'screwed' the World Bank." *How ironic,* I thought. But during our next conversation, Travis repeatedly said he was not a prostitute, because he did not do it all the time, and what he was really looking for was "love that was lasting."

A year later I asked twenty-year-old Travis how he imagined his life in ten years. He said, "Living in a big house with my partner from Germany or the Netherlands or maybe somewhere else—you know I love the European men, the fair ones, I just can't help it—and I see myself working in the news media somehow, probably as a news broadcaster or reporter or owning my own business. Something like that." By 2005 part of his vision seemed to be materializing. He was raising his sister's child while living with a German man in an affluent district of Windhoek and working part-time at an NGO that did a great deal of work with the local news media. But because he did not have an advanced formal education, he was not getting paid very much. He regularly complained of his problems with his boyfriend, whom he felt didn't respect him, and so Travis eventually left him. "I hated feeling so dependent!" he told me.

By 2007 Travis was unemployed again and hoping to go back to school. In our last interview, in 2008, he expressed an outpouring of regret. He said he was too young to have come out "so openly" when he was in his teens and he felt used by TRP. "I really didn't get what I hoped for."

\* \* \*

When I first met nineteen-year-old Winston in 2002, his appearance was striking. He wore bright purple eye shadow and matching lipstick and nail polish. Donning a leopard print cowboy hat, he looked as though he had just stepped out of a Madonna video. Winston, who self-identified as Ovambo, came to live in Katutura to get away from what he described as intense homophobia that broke out in his village near Oshakati, northern Namibia, during SWAPO's antihomosexual pronouncements. As related in chapter 2, Winston's father had beaten him and had him committed to a mental institution when he came out. He was also raped by a family friend. When Winston moved to Katutura, fleeing the mental institution, TRP assisted him in finding a place to live and supported his application for legal aid to press charges against his uncle's friend who had sexually assaulted him. During public forums, Winston commonly delivered his testimonial of "coming out in Ovamboland" with surprising humor. Once, during a meeting with a member from ILGHRC, Winston began delivering his testimonial by saying, "The president is wrong that there are no gays and lesbians in Namibia, because I am Ovambo and a gay—a gay eshenge. If the president wants to deport me to Europe, I am happy to go there, but he must pay for my flight!" The crowd could not contain its laughter and applause.

Through his association with TRP and his attendance at political rallies and other public events, Winston's social and sexual networks rapidly expanded to include a number of expats working in Windhoek as well as visiting tourists. As I came to know him well, he mentioned that he had used cocaine on several occasions and that two wealthy gay foreigners living in Windhoek supplied him with the drug. He had a regular sexual relationship with one of them, whom he referred to as his boyfriend. He also mentioned that he had occasionally had sex with "butch lesbians," as he called them. "They sometimes would fight over me when I am at the shebeen," he added with a loud laugh.

Winston maintained that most of the time he practiced safer sex with both men and women. His knowledge of HIV transmission, like that of most youths, was excellent. However, it was difficult sometimes to practice safer sex because of drugs and "how they make you feel." He explained during an interview in 2002:

Dagga [marijuana] and cocaine make you want to do things. . . . Cocaine is very expensive. Sometimes you get it from your partner, usually the rich gay people, especially the white[s]. Some of my friends work on the street. The rich people will take you home and they will give you cocaine, and then you give it to your friends to try.

Then Winston paused and began to glow as he described his feelings about white men:

> I love to date white men. I think that there is never a white man that is not cute. I was involved with a man from the USA. I was involved with him for two years. He was a priest. I was finishing my Standard ten. I was fifteen years old. [In 1997 through 1999] I was staying with him at the mission. He liked to have sex. He used to preach in the church, and after, when he returned, we would have our sex.

With laughter, Winston added, "When the nuns came around, he pretended to be very holy."

Toward the end of 2003, after his father died, Winston reconnected with his mother up north and provided her with some information pamphlets on sexual identity supplied by TRP. He explained to me that this information greatly helped. His mother told him she still loves him but asked him to stop wearing the cowboy hat and lipstick, saying it made him "look like one of the prostitutes," he told me. He was extremely happy after this reconciliation. Winston stopped wearing the hat, but he continued to wear some lipstick and eye shadow and eyeliner, although it was much more subdued.

When I returned to Namibia in 2004, I reconnected with Winston at a small nightclub off Independence Avenue owned by a gay man from the Netherlands. Winston was no longer wearing partial drag or makeup. Instead he was wearing a tank top and baseball hat. One of the masculine lesbians who was a close friend of his commented, "He thinks that he is bisexual now.... He is dressing like a man." Winston smiled at me and jokingly said, "I am good at pretending to be the man."

He was now dating two different foreigners, one who was forty-five and another who was fifty-six. They were white businessmen who were "women," Winston explained, because he penetrated them during sex. "Now I am dressed like a man, but sometimes, if there is a [drag] competition, I will do it still [dress up like a woman]. But they [my boyfriends] don't know about it." Winston recounted how he met his boyfriends in Windhoek:

> When I came to the club I was dressed like a man. I was putting the [jersey] hood on my head, I looked very nice, I was very sexy.... When I came home the people were making fun: "Oh, you look like an Angolan man." I was looking so fantastic that day.
>
> [The club owner] had to call the security to come because two girls were fighting over me and everyone in the club was laughing: "Oh, how cute—the two girls are fighting for the gay man." Two beautiful girls . . . one was a colored, the other was Angolan. And one of my friends there who was gay said, "Oh, are you a straight man now?"
>
> I was down the other side [of the club] when he saw me. He said he liked me and said he liked the way I dressed. He wanted to go for coffee, and I went

to see his house in [an affluent district in Windhoek]. And he was showing me blue movies, and he told me he liked me and wanted me to be his lover, and I said okay. He didn't do the sex [penetration]; he was just sucking on me and I came in his mouth. When we went back to the club, we enjoyed drinks and then he gave me fifty dollars. Then he said he was going back home. Now we have been seeing each other for a while and he wants me to fuck him all the time.

With my other boyfriend . . . he is from Europe but he lives here now. He owns a business, and he was telling me what [sexual practices] he liked and disliked, and I told him what I like. And then he wanted me to go to his office and he showed me some pictures and asked if I wanted something to drink. I went back to see his house. He was also showing me the movies. Then he asked if I wanted to spend the weekend at his place. I had to phone home to tell my friends that I was staying with him. I tell you, he was so mean to me, but the next Saturday he came to see me, and I don't know if he was testing me or was trying to see if he could trust me. . . . He said I must count the money for the business and then we were taking it to the bank. And *then* he was liking me so much after that—"How have you been? You are so cute!" But I don't steal! I don't know why he tested me like that! But then we were running around in Windhoek and he wanted me to stay with him, but the other one wanted me to stay with him also, so I have a choice now. I love them both; one is fifty-six and [the other is] forty-five. I don't know if I must take the old one or take the "young" one [*laughs loudly*].

I wear condoms with both boyfriends all the time, because I am like a boy with them [the one who penetrates] . . . they are my girlfriends. I never sleep with them without a condom. But the last time I was with the one from [an affluent district of Windhoek] . . . he was not wanting to do it with a condom. . . . He gave me a tough, tough, tough time about not wearing a condom—Oh, shit! The first time I wore it, the second time he wanted me to use the condom, but the third time he didn't want to use it. . . . But he had given me six hundred dollars the last time I went to the north [to visit my mother].

Winston returned from the north, where he had visited with his family. His father had since passed away, and the rest of his family had begun to accept that he slept with men. By 2005 Winston had begun nursing studies at the university. He proudly wore his white nurse's lab coat to display his soon-to-be professional identity, but this was short-lived, as university officials discovered that he had forged his high school transcripts. Nevertheless, he continued to wear his lab coat around Windhoek for some time.

One afternoon in 2005 Winston phoned me to meet up with him for an interview in Zoo Park, located in the commercial district, just off of Independence Avenue. I arrived twenty minutes later, and as soon as I turned the recorder on, he began to speak without my posing any questions. He was unsettled that day.

Three weekends ago these three gays, all of them were these Germans. I was liking them so much at first because they asked me to go with them to Swakopmund [a popular European tourism destination], and they let me stay with them in this really amazing place with them. They were looking so cute, all of them. Robert, you won't believe it, they were wanting to have sex with me, all of them at the same time [*laughs nervously*]. It was fun, but [*pauses*], they wanted to film me. I was not feeling comfortable, and they were pressuring me into it. So I did it. It was feeling nice, but after [*pauses*]. . . . now I am feeling like they were not respecting me. I mean they didn't even call me, and I just saw them now—they are back in Windhoek with these different black guys.

* * *

The power dynamics and inequalities that Romeo, Travis, and Winston confronted in their relationships with wealthier sexual partners certainly relate to the high rates of unemployment that occur along the historical fault lines of entrenched racial inequality. As in most African countries, the distribution of wealth in Namibia is marked by enormous disparities. Structural inequalities, grounded in the history of colonial apartheid, are sustained and exacerbated through the government's implementation of neoliberal economic policies that favor foreign investment over the interests of working-class Namibians. Sustained poverty is compounded by Namibia's lack of minimum wage regulations and inadequate access to higher education. Only 8 percent of the employed population and less than 2 percent of the unemployed population have completed any form of tertiary education (Central Bureau of Statistics 2005, 40–42).

However, an understanding of how unequal power relations take hold in their lives cannot be entirely distilled to the unidirectional effects of global market forces or the implicit and explicit commodifications of race that inhere in Namibia's tourism industry. To move beyond facile notions of the commodification of black bodies, it is necessary to consider how the field of identity politics, stimulated by TRP's intervention, gives rise to what I call "foreigner fetish narratives"—that is, idioms of uncontrollable love of foreigners repeated by impoverished gay people of color (Lorway 2008b). These idioms of desire were exemplified when Romeo said, "I mostly like to have foreign boyfriends. I don't know why; I just love them the most"; when Travis reminded me, "You know I love the European men, the fair ones, I just can't help it"; and when Winston exclaimed, "I love to date white men. I think that there is never a white man that is not cute." These foreigner fetish narratives recurred among male (and some female) youths and persisted throughout much of my fieldwork, raising significant questions about how postcolonial regimes of power and knowledge in Namibia pattern the relations between local and foreign subjects at the crossroads between LGBT rights and global gay tourism.

Thinking through the foreigner fetish also disrupts popular attitudes I encountered within expatriate communities working in Namibia's sexual health development sector. My participation within these networks as a Western HIV researcher enabled me to witness how impoverished Namibian's articulations of "uncontrollable love" are commonly interpreted and received by gay foreigners—as bizarre, compulsive, excessive, and seemingly pathological projections of erotic interest in them. These local narratives are generally regarded with bemusement or irritation by foreigners and become dismissed as the incidental psychological effects of poverty. This became particularly clear to me when a leading HIV/AIDS policy maker told me he had received *so* much attention from local black men that he could never date "one of them. They only love you because you are a foreigner . . . and I don't have enough money to keep one." In addition to constructing a demeaning stereotype, this dismissive perspective also overlooks the considerable energy the Rainbow Youth invest in revaluing themselves in relation to the universalistic project of LGBT rights. Under the banner of freedom, these youths generally expected that the foreigners they entered into relationships with would understand, respect, and appreciate the identity work they had accomplished, unlike the local "bisexual men" in their community did. In other words, when Travis said in the early years of the TRP's intervention, *"they* [foreigners] know how to treat you right," he was referring not only to material currencies but also to exchanges that value forms of selfhood.

Over the years of interviewing these young males, it became clear that their practices of freedom, although opening up new streams of resources in their expanding sociosexual networks, in fact became entangled in competing systems of desire that moved to commodify their bodies. For most of the gay youths I spoke with, it took a number of years of struggle before the exploitative side of this economic arrangement more fully registered. I would argue that the way TRP constituted subjectivity as a political territory inadvertently inhibited this realization.

Let me review the pathways through which youths like Romeo, Travis, and Winston arrived at these unequal economic arrangements: The first is through the way selfhood is reoriented in relation to the universalistic project of freedom. Public forums, social events, spotlights, and exuberant applause create "safe spaces" and transnational contact zones that *appear* on the surface to transcend class, race, and nationhood. Moreover, the sudden presence of more affluent foreigners in close proximity to the Rainbow Youth gives emancipation a certain *tangibility, imminence,* and, thus, *intensity* for local people. Second, during TRP training, desire takes center stage as LGBT rights discourses compel social actors to reflect upon the value and authenticity of their self in relation to what it means to be a "traditional," "modern," and "sexually liberated" person. This "freeing" of the self opens up perceptual routes to grasp global cultural flows, engaging and forming subjectivities as they stretch perceptions of solidarity beyond the borders of Namibia. For instance, Tuli, who struggled greatly with poverty, told me in one of our earliest conversations, "I read about a gay man in a magazine.... When I read the article I thought it was about my life." When he later showed me the article, I was somewhat surprised to see that the illustration accompanying the article depicted a noticeably wealthy gay character from the United Kingdom standing in front of his London-based townhouse with a two-car garage and luxury car. Tuli did *not*, however, comment on the affluence represented in the article to which he referred. What was noteworthy for him was the gay character's internal struggle for self-knowledge, which the article's author referred to in terms of "coming out."

Therefore, as new ways of being and belonging are "discovered" in universalistic frames of human rights, local reappraisals of selfhood quietly embed an affluent aesthetic, one that hinders recognition of class inequalities and its historical grounding in racism. In this way an intimate and highly effective form of hegemony is at work here, where class disparity—the unacknowledged lack—is "misrecognized" (Bourdieu 1990, 140–141) as originating from the body in uncontrollable desires for foreigners. Thus, the recent mobilization of Namibian gay and lesbian subjectivities and local idioms of desire for gay foreigners, articulated in terms of unexplainable and uncontrollable desires, reveals a particular movement of power that aligns with the government's neoliberal economic practices that operate to attract foreign capital to the detriment of working-class Namibians.

Interfacing with international LGBT networks, TRP has emerged as a protected yet porous zone that fosters the rapid cultural diffusion of global discourses, images, values, practices, and people (Appadurai 1996; Altman 2002). TRP's resource center provides young members with a rich source of international gay and lesbian cultural materials (magazines from Germany, the United Kingdom, the United States, and South Africa; videos about Stonewall; books on how to come out to your parents; HIV/AIDS safer-sex materials published in Germany, the Netherlands, and the United States; and International Gay and Lesbian Human Rights Commission documents). Movie nights feature films such as *Bent; When Night Is Falling; Torch Song Trilogy; Pricilla, Queen of the Desert;* and *Stonewall* as well as South African queer movies such as *Simon and Me* and *It's My Life*. Although many of the Rainbow Youth claimed during interviews that they had neither heard of the terms "gay" or "lesbian" nor knew what they meant before their introduction to the Rainbow Project, they were well versed in global queer pop culture by the time I had begun my ethnographic endeavors in 2001. When I first met them, they commonly asked if I had seen *To Wong Fu (Thanks for Everything, Julie Newmar)* and the British version of *Queer as Folk*. They not only regularly accessed TRP's queer cultural resources, but they also referred to them in their everyday conversations with one another.

Over time, through their association with TRP networks, members eventually began to contribute to the circulating streams of global queer culture. Their life stories and testimonials headlined news media broadcasts, press releases, letters to the editor of the *Namibian,* international magazine articles, Internet blogs, foreign documentaries, and scholarly research projects.[4] Some of the young members received sponsorships to attend the Gay Games in Australia (2002) and the World Out Games in Montreal (2006), where they delivered their testimonials of discrimination before an eager international audience.[5] TRP staff and young volunteers also kept records of interviews they gave to local and international journalists, human rights representatives, and foreign researchers. In this way TRP's office served as an important accumulation and connectivity point where youths disseminated their narratives across transnational communication channels and viewed representations of their community reflected in pictures and in print, linking local conflicts with the struggles of gays and lesbians worldwide.

Despite their active participation in the global streaming of local experiences, universal LGBT rights discourses tend to place Western gay people and nations at the *center* of sexual liberational achievement. For this reason, narratives of wanting to migrate from Namibia often accompany foreigner fetish narratives. As one nineteen-year-old gay man from Katutura repeated on several occasions: "I would love to have a Dutch boyfriend. I would love to live there—it is very gay positive. I heard you can be openly gay and even get married there." Therefore, the *locations* where youths imagine greater freedoms to reside—in Western liberal democratic nations—significantly mediate their practices of freedom. As ruling government officials continually vilify homosexuality across the African continent, local political salvation has come to be located beyond Namibia's borders—allowing Western notions of personhood to occupy prominent symbolic ground. This movement of power is strongly implicated in the way "economic mobility" and "sexual freedom" have become paradoxically interwoven in youths' perceptions and in their longings, fantasies, and anticipations of the future.

To my surprise, when asked how they envisioned their lives in ten years, many of the young male youths responded much like Travis did: as owning a "big house"; being highly successful in their work lives; and, for some, living with their boyfriends in northern Europe. Earlier in the LGBT movement, lesbian youths also had similarly broad visions and fantasies of social and economic emancipation. In 2002 Roxy, who lived in one of the poorest locations of Katutura, told me about her painful struggle with her family over her unwillingness to date boys. She then described how she pictured her life with her partner in the future: "I see myself as married, having *our* baby with *my* partner in *our* home in Holland. We even thought about buying someone's sperm [her emphasis]."

Here I raise the following questions: As global ideas and images of "freedom" translate into local idioms that express hopes for the future and distress over experiences of discrimination, does the idea of "sexual liberation" misleadingly promise these impoverished men and women with an (inevitable) path to financial prosperity? And does the seeming impossibility of achieving such emancipation create an unbridgeable gap in subjectivity for many youths like Travis and Roxy?

What I learned from speaking with the Rainbow Youth is that the desires and fantasies produced within this (economic) gap do not simply well up from a sense of longing that demands fulfillment. Instead what I have tried to show in this chapter, and throughout this book, is a form of lacking that is "created, planned and organized in and through social production" (Deleuze and Guattari 1983, 28). This means that desire can be conceptualized as embodied in and through social practices—generated in everyday speech events, public forums, testimonials; in email pen pal letters to foreigners; in interviews with press, international development representatives, and journalists; and by researchers and anthropologists like me: "desire is verbalized, and verbalization becomes the occasion for desire" (Butler 1987, 220).

As Namibian same-sex desires and genders are reconstituted within a global frame, the freeing of sexuality disguises the many new conflicts that enter the body of lived experience. The recurring scene of foreign fetishism thus displays the *effect* of a form of power that has impinged on people's bodies and their pleasures (Foucault 1978). One of the few ways the (affluent) aesthetic of gay and lesbian liberation has been made achievable is in sexual relationships with foreigners. In other words, relationships with foreigners have become both the imagined and real grounds not only for escaping poverty and oppression but also for uncovering, liberating, and valuing the self. With so much at stake, unsafe sex with foreigners often becomes worth the risk.

# Conclusion

## Post-Structural Violence

Aꜰᴛᴇʀ ᴍᴀɴʏ ʟᴏɴɢ hours, our HIV/AIDS awareness committee finished painting the walls of TRP's offices in preparation for a safer-sex poster exhibition. As some of us began crumpling up the newspapers that served as a drop cloth, from the corner of my eye I watched a heated argument spark between Hanna and a feminine male named Melvin. Hanna accused Melvin of sexually coercing a young gay friend of hers at a safer-sex educational weekend organized by the Rainbow Project and me a few weeks previously. Melvin adamantly denied it.

Despite our best attempts to settle the argument, it continued to escalate, especially when Melvin placed his hands on Hanna's shoulders. We all knew that this physical contact would further set off Hanna, who had endured intense physical and sexual abuse at the hands of men beginning when she was a child. As more members of the working group became drawn into the dispute, a barrage of insults flew, such as "At least *my* mother didn't die of AIDS," "Your aunt is a prostitute and has a sugar daddy," "You only have Standard six," "Ovambos are dirty," and "Damaras don't have real culture." The hurling of such deeply cutting insults culminated in physical violence between six of the members. The eventual casualties included a bloodied lip, a broken tooth, a slashed-open knee, and other bodily bruises.

Beyond the physical injuries, what unsettled me most were the embodied forms the violence took during the episode. The previously proud composure of the masculine lesbians noticeably drew downward while the posture of the three feminine males inflated. Earlier that day I saw these same feminine males ask "the men" (Hanna and some of the other masculine lesbians) to move the office's furniture in preparation for the painting, indicating with gestures that they were physically too delicate to accomplish the task themselves; Hanna and her masculine friends were more than happy to demonstrate their strength. Now, however, the vibrant physical presence of these females diminished. They appeared vulnerable and tentative, similar to what I had witnessed among other young women in Katutura when they encountered violence from men. As for the dainty, feminine-acting males, they appeared to drop all traces of effeminacy before my eyes, transforming into violent and aggressive men.

The episode reached an abrupt denouement when Hanna noticed two "non-members" of TRP lurking about outside the office. She insisted that both young men, *botsosos* (criminals) she called them, wanted to rob TRP. One of them asked if he could enter the center, even though it was well after hours. Hanna instantly shouted, "*Nie* [no], man . . . you can't come in," and then crouched down and began to draw an imaginary outline around the front of the office door with her hand while repeating, "This is LGBT safe space. You are not allowed in here." One of the men began ridiculing Hanna and the other masculine lesbians, saying, "Why are *you* dressing like men?" He then called us all "moffies" with great disdain and hurled a large, empty beer bottle at one of the newly painted walls inside the center, sending fragments flying, just missing a few of us. In the midst of all this commotion, Hanna, with almost manic devotion, repeated her mantra: "This is LGBT safe space."

As portrayed in this scene and throughout the book, the idealism of LGBT rights continually collides with participants' everyday struggles with social inequality. Initially the conflicts they encountered in these collisions intensified their political resolution to achieve liberation. However, over the course of years the continual undoing of participants' practices of freedom eventually began to wear thin, and what began as committed resolve fell into deep frustration and disappointment.

I now return to the scene from which this story began, where Hanna and her friends' expressions of deep disenfranchisement culminated in Tuli's exclamation, "Most of us do not need our rights to be fought for. Right now we need to be socially and economically emancipated!" These provocative words echo many of the conflicts that erupted, time and time again, among the young Namibians I came to know who grappled with the visions of freedom that were stimulated by LGBT rights discourses. While TRP's programs venerate "diversity" and "plurality," they exclude recognition of the diverse material grounds that constitute human intimacies and indeed fail to politicize the social effects of capitalism.[1] Casting their own universalities, like other rights discourses, the Rainbow Project not only overlooked but even contributed to the naturalization of the social struggles of impoverished sexual minorities. And despite the many stirrings in political consciousness that universalistic ideologies stimulated on the ground, the force and very possibility of an organic leadership that could mobilize more extensive solidarities well beyond communities of "sexual minorities" dissipated as quickly as it forms. Herein lies the mode of violence I have sought to illustrate, one that fires up political imaginations, even to radical extents, and then severs and sets adrift *real* political possibilities in the wake of its aftermath as enthusiasm vanishes and disillusionment sets in. This post-structural violence, which takes hold of political aspirations and imaginations, is the effect of the dispersion of democratic ideologies and state power that fragments political possibilities and depoliticizes politics (Mbembe 2005; Comaroff and Comaroff 2005, 129).

Social movements and collective political struggles are perhaps always founded upon impossible utopias, but what is important to note in the practices of freedom described in this book is how the very discourses that condition and heighten political awareness also occlude wider and more enduring projects of social and political emancipation. The diffusion of neoliberal democratic ideologies through various interventions into "African sexuality" *internalizes* the fallout of the "sex wars" that continue to wreak havoc across the continent's contemporary political landscape: the threat of HIV and AIDS; the dangers of "sugar daddy" relationships; the prevalence of rape (of infants, lesbians, and other women); survival and transactional sex among impoverished women; and homosexuality as an imported, neocolonial cultural practice. Movements to free southern Africans from these life-and-death perils through the vehicle of democratic pluralism *recaptures and sorts the very political energies it "liberates."* Thus, desire is *resourced* in the dissemination of democratic ideologies, simultaneously opening up and restraining the body while enlisting emergent identity politics into larger neoliberal economic regimes that route new systems of value into the very recesses of subjectivity. More to the point, Tuli's political aspirations were cut short not by the intentions or inaction of TRP developers per se but by the limits of universalistic rights discourse, by their very design, and by their articulations with postcolonial governmentalities.

Attempts to forge legitimacy for Namibian sexual minorities through appeals to "culture" and "indigeneity" in the invention of "traditional homosexuality," as we saw in chapter 2, inadvertently abets the dispersion of political power exercised in SWAPO's rhetoric of African sexuality. Sexuality has become a vital instrument of both SWAPO and the transnational response in the reconstruction of a traditionalist body politic "in which people enjoy (or are denied) entitlements by virtue of putatively primordial characteristics" (Comaroff and Comaroff 1997, 127). Working in tandem with the state, the plays of strategic essentialism staged by TRP and its allies are therefore also implicated in the postcolonial remaking of a "traditional authority" that is historically traceable to complex responses to colonialism and that works to the detriment of a deracialized, detribalized, and decolonized democratization (Mamdani 1996).

Sexuality as a technology of citizenship displays its effectiveness in how it reaches into the very being of citizens, compelling them, in their quest for political legitimacy, to wrestle with their place(s) of belonging within tribe, race, the nation-state, and "universal humanity." Borrowing Michel Foucault's words, sexuality is "an especially dense transfer point" in the circulation of liberal democratic ideas (1978, 103). But in the case of LGBT rights in postcolonial Namibia, ideas of individual and collective liberty have taken hold in the most unexpected of places: in impoverished townships where everyday decision making and individual "choice" are greatly restricted by the exigencies of survival and social suffering. Sexual identities, coming out narratives, and other technologies of the self, for the most part, do provide the keys for youths to "unlock the meaning of contemporary power relations" (Mansfield 2000, 116) and the multiple oppressions that surround their community. They also allow them to make associations between intimate bodily practices, such as penetration and safer-sex negotiations, and larger notions of political democracy ("going fifty-fifty"), facilitated by TRP's global communication channels that transmit and receive representations of their struggles within Western liberal democratic frames. But the transnational power relations that initially opened the self to "the global" in some sense are forgotten as the sacrifices of coming out to family, community, and nation also open up new conflicts and inequalities at the level of subjectivity: (1) foreigner fetish narratives exemplify how elevated self-awareness, while still rooted in archaic notions of "the traditional," unknowingly feed practices of freedom into the wider commodification of African bodies; (2) the complex daily navigations between autonomy and subjugation of young females engaged with lesbian identities fail to bring their social struggles into wider resonance with the women's movement, because the very discursive framing of their struggles does not permit "space" to forge a politics that considers motherhood, "family pressure," and transactional sex alongside liberal notions of self-determination and bodily integrity; and (3) feminine males, who are compelled to view their struggles through identities that are decontextualized from historically embedded gender-power relations, celebrate their self-discovery and gender nonconformity without being able to liberate themselves from sexual violence at the hands of "real men."

In sum, the way sexuality as an intervention technology harnesses desire as an *ethical substance* masks the relation between circulations of liberal democratic ideologies and movements of global capitalism that reproduce and intensify a constellation of social inequalities. Unlike anticolonial resistance that once employed the unifying language of external oppression (a discourse repeated in SWAPO's xenophobic maneuvers to consolidate its political base), the postcolonial conflicts I have highlighted replay themselves internally, at the level of the body, at times resurfacing as idioms of unknowable and uncontrollable desires, which tend *not* to lend themselves to wider politicization, but rather, over time, to a descent into nihilism.

\* \* \*

The dialectical tale I have told of conflict in the pursuit of freedom reveals a history of the body as a resource of creative insight and ambiguity, of connectivity and displacement, of morality and shame, of consciousness and uncertainty, of knowledge and mystification, and of liberation and subjugation. And like all such tales, it cannot not pretend to reach any definitive conclusion. Regarding the peculiar idioms of desire on which I have focused as pre-political discourses may offer glimmers of what is yet to come: the possibility of mobilizing the exploding identity politics throughout Africa in ways that bring pluralistic politics into more radical reckoning with the exploitative effects of global capitalism. What is perhaps more certain, though, is how sexuality has ever more tightly enmeshed the body in the making of antimodern modernities in postcolonial Namibia.

# Notes

## Prologue

1. Based in Windhoek, Sister Namibia has been funded by the Royal Netherlands Embassy, the Dutch development foundation known as Hivos, Germany's Heinrich Böll Foundation, and Oxfam Canada.

2. The HIV/AIDS research capacity–building project involved the Universities of Namibia, Toronto, and Columbia University (sponsored by the Fogarty Foundation, Columbia University Department of Public Health). I began my preliminary doctoral fieldwork during this seven-week period in June and July, 2001. This project was led by anthropologists Richard B. Lee and Ida Susser.

3. At the time I began my fieldwork, in 2001, I could find only one published peer-reviewed article discussing HIV sexual risk taking between males in Africa: Niels Teunis's (2001) study of men who have sex with men in Dakar, Senegal. For this reason my earliest published work was devoted to issues related to HIV vulnerability. See Lorway 2006; 2007; 2008b; and 2009.

4. In the early 1900s the "Main Location," where black people were forced to live under the apartheid regime, had expanded to such a degree that "whites and nonwhites [were brought] into closer proximity" (Pendleton 1993, 15). The Windhoek municipality in the late 1940s sought to keep the black population at the Main Location close to the Windhoek city core (to be able to work for the white elite), but also wanted to keep them far enough away to abate settlers' anxieties over social safety. Such anxieties stemmed from the increase in health problems that the black communities were experiencing as a result of forced overcrowding and unequal access to health care resources (Emmett 1999, 304). In the 1940s, to satisfy colonial desires for security, a new location was built outside walking distance from Windhoek's business and commercial center. In the 1950s the residents from the Main Location were forced to move to this new location. After a violent shooting aimed at silencing protest, the new location was renamed with the Herero word "Katutura," which means "the place where we do not want to stay" (Pendleton 1993, 18–20).

5. This multisited fieldwork approach traced the practices of social actors across contrasting settings to expose the malleable and contingent quality of cultural phenomenon (Marcus 1995). Following the "movements of a particular group of initial subjects" (Marcus 1995, 106) allowed me to witness how social actors navigated enactments of sexual and gender defiance across a complex and shifting urban terrain marked by multiple languages, economic statuses, ages, and ethnicities.

6. These sites were also epidemiologically significant in relation to HIV transmission, because extensive sexual-network hubs form here. For this reason my ethnographer fieldwork often overlapped with HIV prevention activities for which I provided technical assistance. I also conducted HIV prevention research on a voluntary basis for the local branch office of the Danish development association, Danida; for the Windhoek and Oshakati (northern Namibia) offices of the University Centre for Studies in Namibia (TUCSIN); and for the Karas Regional Ministry of Health.

7. For this reason, I tend to agree with Tom Boellstorff's (2005, 11) thinking on sexuality and gender, which sees the two concepts as more mutually constituting than analytically distinct, as Rubin (1984) asserts.

8. For a more in-depth etymological examination of the word "moffie," see Gevisser and Cameron (1995, xiii).

9. During a few TRP workshops I attended in Windhoek, a South African facilitator referred to a couple of the participants as "non-op transgenders" to signify the reality that for most youths in the region who felt their physical anatomy did not match with their gender identity, sex reassignment surgery was not financially possible. Interestingly, this category in some way paralleled South Africa's Alteration of Sex Description and Sex Status Act 49, which was passed in May 2003 in South Africa. The act allows intersex and transgender people to have their gender legally changed without surgery, which previously was prohibited by legislation introduced in 1992 (Currier 2012, 41–42).

10. Bisexual behavior was also practiced between effeminate gays and masculine lesbians.

11. In 2007 an "I" standing for "intersexual" was added to the acronym "LGBT" after a young person with ambiguous genitalia, who was experiencing discrimination in his community, received a referral to TRP's services by a family member.

12. The largest donors of ODA to Namibia are the European Union, Germany, and the United States. Other important donors include Finland, France, Sweden, China, the Netherlands, Japan, and Luxembourg. Grants from these donors have helped to reduce Namibia's need to borrow from international money-lending institutions like the World Bank and the IMF. ODA to Namibia increased from 2.8 percent of the GDP in 2001–2002 to 7.8 percent in 2006–2007. The ODA increase in 2006–2007 stemmed from new sources of funding such as the Global Fund, Global Environmental Facility (GEF), the President's Emergency Programme for AIDS Relief (PEPFAR), and the Millennium Challenge Account (African Development Bank 2009, 11).

## Introduction

1. All participant names in this book are pseudonyms.

2. This community center was established by the Rössing Uranium Mining Company as part of its attempt toward social responsibility. Its mandate has been to support a broad spectrum of community development activities, including education, health, poverty alleviation, innovation, the environment, and enterprise development. This center was the meeting hall of preference for the Rainbow Youth because it was within walking distance for people living in Katutura.

3. The term "colored" is an accepted ethnic-identity term used to refer to communities of people who are lighter skinned or of mixed racial heritage.

4. On July 24, 1995, the organizers of the Zimbabwean International Book Fair received a letter from the Zimbabwean government requesting the withdrawal of materials to be presented by the NGO called Gays and Lesbians of Zimbabwe (GALZ). At that time GALZ had provided social support for a small group of members who were primarily white, and the book fair offered a way to raise their public profile. (Keith Goddard, the late director of GLAZ, provided this information in a discussion I had with him on March 12, 2003.) International Book Fair participants, who included Namibian scholars, openly protested the Zimbabwean government interdiction in a plethora of statements released to the international news media. Zimbabwean president Robert Mugabe, however, did not let such public outcry prevent him

from opening the book fair in August and placing homosexuality at the center of his speech: "If we accept homosexuality as a right, as is argued by the association of sodomists and sexual perverts, what moral fiber shall our society ever have to deny organized drug addicts, or even those given to bestiality, the rights they might claim and allege they possess under the rubric of individual freedom and human rights, including the freedom of the Press to write, publish and publicize their literature" (IGLHRC 2003, 14–15).

In 1998 the Namibian minister of home affairs, Jerry Ekandjo, attempted to have antihomosexuality legislation drafted. Although unsuccessful in his attempts, Ekandjo later publicly announced to police graduates that the "constitution does not guarantee rights for gays and lesbians" and that they must combat "all such unnatural acts including murder" (*Namibian* 2000).

5. Mark Gevisser and Edwin Cameron's *Defiant Desire* (1995) is perhaps one of the most significant anthologies devoted to the subject of non-normative African sexualities and genders. It was published before Mugabe's infamous antihomosexual remarks.

6. In trying to understand the sexual development and attachments of children, Talavera (2002) poses questions such as "Could there be an Oedipus complex?" and "Could there be an Electra complex?" in relation to the "father-mother-child triangle" and particular sleeping arrangements.

7. The question that Talavera poses nevertheless speaks to much longer debates in anthropology pertaining to the self. See, for example, Sökefeld (1999, 417–448).

8. Also see Ann Laura Stoler (1995, 7) for an ample critique of *The History of Sexuality* by Foucault as missing how practices that racialized bodies in the colonies contributed to the production of European bourgeois sexuality in the eighteenth and nineteenth centuries. Donald L. Donham, in his study of male-male sexuality in Soweto, aptly points to the difficulty of using Foucault in postcolonial contexts: "The . . . limitation of Foucault's work on sexuality stems from his over-reliance on the texts of medical specialists to infer the categories and commitments of ordinary people" (1998, 17).

9. My thinking here owes much to the rich body of social scientific literature on citizenship (e.g., Isin 2008, and Plummer 2003). This field of inquiry has increasingly departed from the traditional notion of citizenship as a "natural" legal status bestowed upon rights-bearing individuals, those who belong to the nation-state according to their birthright (Marshall 1950). As many social scientists rightly insist, the issue of who belongs to the nation-state is certainly no straightforward matter (Alexander 1994).

10. For example, to attract foreign business, the government lifted a number of tariffs such as harbor docking fees for the now defunct textile company Ramatex, the surplus of which could have otherwise gone into improving health and social welfare services. Although this action did generate jobs, for the most part factory workers received low wages and were not paid for overtime.

11. Tom Boellstorff (2009, 355) offers an interesting and helpful distinction between confessions and testimonials.

12. Foucault (1997) challenges this conceptualization, asserting that the very idea of the "liberated authentic self" is itself always socially constituted through antecedent relations of power. By regarding knowledge produced on the self as a kind of resource rather than as something that can be uncovered, I similarly unsettle the idea that when one is free from various forms of social oppression—such as gender inequality, racism, and heterosexism—then an "authentic self," an entity that exists prior to structure, will have its true expression.

13. Mark Hunter (2010, 130) develops an interesting discussion about the details of this musical refrain as it pertains to gender and rights in South Africa.

## 1. The Instrumentality of Sex

1. For additional accounts of male-male sexual relationships in mining compounds in South Africa, see Harries (1994), Moodie and Ndastshe (1994), and Niehaus (2002).

2. Many of the elders, particularly the grandparents of the Rainbow Youth, made similar comments that tied the seeming plenitude and visibility of moffies to national liberation.

3. I performed the first sorting and listing of archival materials gathered from the personal archives of Stephen Scholtz. The 336 newspaper articles and editorial letters on homosexuality came from the following Namibian newspapers: the *Namibian, New Era, Die Republikein,* the *Windhoek Observer, Allgemeine Zeitung,* the *Namibian Weekender,* and the *Windhoek Advertiser.*

4. Throughout this book I refer to and emphasize the importance of the *Namibian* to LGBT mobilizations for three reasons. For one, this newspaper has kept close track of the debates regarding homosexuality among political leaders in Namibia since the early 1990s. Second, this newspaper has been widely distributed throughout Namibia and was kept at a fixed and affordable cost of two Namibian dollars (equal to thirty-six cents US during my fieldwork period). Third, and most important, most of my research participants and their families read this newspaper and mentioned its reports in their daily conversations. The editor in chief of the *Namibian,* Gwen Lister, is a well-known former antiapartheid journalist who continues to maintain a critical stance in covering government politics. The *New Era* newspaper, however, is subsidized by the government and tends to run articles that promote SWAPO's political agendas. In 1995, when the hate speeches began in Namibia, *New Era* ran a series of hate speeches from SWAPO MPs Helmut Angula and Hadino Hishongwa. The *Namibian* openly criticized *New Era* for running such hate speeches. The ensuing debate between newspaper editors culminated with the government withdrawing all advertising support for the *Namibian* and placed an official ban on it for government employees who were previously provided with the newspaper free of cost. In an interview with a lesbian reporter working for *Die Republikein,* I was told that the owners of the Afrikaner newspaper were "very conservative and homophobic" and therefore tended not to cover the issues related to homosexuality with as much detail as the *Namibian.*

5. After the election of President Hifikepunye Pohamba in 2004, the hate speeches died down considerably until 2005, when Deputy Minister of Home Affairs Mushelenga asserted that homosexuals were responsible for the AIDS epidemic in Namibia. This set off another explosion of public controversy, culminating in the TRP's call for the deputy minister's resignation. Although few antihomosexual outbursts occurred after this incident, the stigmatizing association between homosexuality and AIDS, which had not existed in Namibia as it had in the West (as discussed in Lorway 2006), became deeply imprinted in public memory. I was called upon by TRP to provide a research-based statement to condemn the remarks on the ground of the advancement of sexual health in Namibia. This statement was included in TRP's September 8, 2005, press release titled "TRP's Response to Anti-Sexual Minorities Statement by SWAPO MP Theopolina Mushelenga" (TRP 2005). The document can be retrieved on the IGLHRC website (http://www.iglhrc.org/content/namibia-african-ngos-respond-statement-namibian-deputy-minister-gays-and-lesbians-betraying).

6. HIV seroprevalence refers to the proportion of individuals in a population that have the virus in their blood serum.

7. At the World Summit on Sustainable Development in Johannesburg, Nujoma made the following statement during an interview with BBC News: "The British and the Europeans, after you colonized us, you gave us nothing. In the G8 in Canada you decided that the only

government that is worth to be given development aid from the G8 countries is a country that would have political good governance, human rights. To you human rights this includes homosexualism, lesbianism" (Amupadhi 2002b).

8. It was not until 1927 that laws were passed to forbid sexual contact between black and white people. Such "illicit carnal knowledge" was defined as occurring only between men and women. These miscegenation laws were cited under the Immorality Act, Act No. 5 of 1927 (Union of South Africa).

9. Legal scholar and Africanist Oliver Phillips (1997, 479), provides more recent examples, between 1966 and 1994, in which white men were tried for sodomy and unnatural offenses in higher jurisdictions than black men, who were tried in lower courts and received less attention in the criminal justice system.

10. This description bears similarity to the rules of "mine marriage" in Zimbabwe that prohibited anal penetration, the transgression of which resulted in harsh punishment (Moodie and Ndatshe 1994, 128; Epprecht 2004, 61).

11. Epprecht (2004) also notes disputes over money in Zimbabwean sodomy cases during the same period.

12. Excerpts from *Rex de Kroon versus Dwasbasam* No. 949 and *Standato* No. 2522 (sodomy trial transcripts), Lüderitz, May 20, 1927.

13. Although some marriage accommodations were introduced in 1925, women were *not* afforded any legal rights of protection or independence within these hostels, even if they were married (see Government Notice 26/1925, *Sanitation and Housing,* dated 17/1/1925). Although black women's morality was continually monitored and placed under question, it would seem that their well-being was neglected in this government notice.

14. See "Report on the Native of South West Africa and Their Treatment by Germany" (Union of South Africa 1918).

15. Excerpt from *Rex de Kroon versus Wilhelm Leichert* (sentencing hearing), Windhoek, April 28, 1924.

16. Excerpt from *King versus Hermann Schneidenberger* (sodomy trial transcripts), Grootfontein, September 22, 1920.

17. Legal distinction was also made between men and women in the Immorality Act of 1927, according to subtle differences in legal language. Men (black or white) were accused of "illicit carnal intercourse" if they had sex with females outside their race; women (black or white) were accused when they *permitted* males outside their race to have sex with them.

18. This is a point that both Phillips (1997) and Epprecht (2004, 105–106) raise.

19. Excerpts from *Rex de Kroon versus Petrus,* Lüderitz, June 1923.

20. For example, SWAPO unleashed virulent antihomosexual rhetoric in 2002 and 2003 shortly after the media exposed the financial crises faced by two important parastatals, Air Namibia and NamPower, and when the resulting layoffs sparked public outrage against SWAPO.

## 2. Subjectivity as a Political Territory

1. This is an issue Douglas Torr and I also discussed on March 23, 2003.

2. The notion that same-sex practices are less stigmatized among Damara youths is also supported by Khaxas and Wieringa's findings of Damara women in same-sex relationships who "live their lives more openly than woman of other communities in Namibia" (2005, 123).

3. LAC is funded by the Ford Foundation.

4. In fact, they formed their own "over 30s social group," which held monthly meetings. At one of the gatherings I attended, they spoke disparagingly of the youths at TRP, referring to them as the "Damara kindergarten."

5. I translated this workshop from Afrikaans, with some assistance from Frank Fielding. In addition to gender, the Afrikaans word *geslag* carries the denotations of sex, race, and ethnicity.

6. In this example we see the sociopolitical process that Vincanne Adams and Stacy Leigh Pigg refer to as "the mutual constitution of scientific knowledge and political will" (2005, 24).

7. According to Rudi Bleys, Kurt Falk "corroborated [Hirschfield's] model of innate homosexuality." This was evidenced by Falk's distinction between real or "true inverts" and incidental or "pseudo" homosexuality (Bleys 1995, 221–222).

8. This portrayal of female African sexuality as excessive is consistent with nineteenth-century scientific representations that constructed the African female body as drenched in sexuality. For a further discussion of this scientific preoccupation, see Sander Gilman's *Difference and Pathology* (1985, 76–108).

9. This magazine serves as one of the few sources of gay and lesbian current affairs and is circulated widely within NGO networks throughout Namibia and beyond.

10. An ekola is a musical instrument made from glued-together hollow calabashes, which resonate when the overlaid palm rib notches are rubbed.

11. However, the contemporary Oshivambo word "eshenge" held similar meaning to what Falk maintained in his research in the early twentieth century. He asserted that *ovashengi* was a form of "inborn" homosexuality (Bleys 1995, 221). This continuity suggests a more sustained moral-political investment in marking out forms of gender and sexual difference in this region of Namibia, related to the orchestration of "traditional rule" by the colonial state.

12. Also see Donham's (1998) discussion of how the emergence of modern male-male sexualities as same-gender relationships signified a transformation in South African sex/gender systems. He claims that this occurrence was tied to the internationally mediated process of liberation.

13. Here I am referring to one of the more popular AIDS awareness campaigns in southern Africa, "ABC: Abstain, Be faithful, Condomize."

14. Helping me to understand the way that desire is *practiced* among the Rainbow Youth is Max Weber's *The Sociology of Religion* and his ideas pertaining to the "different roads to salvation" that come through ritualistic devotion (1963, 151). By viewing the intensification of sexual desire as a form of ethics, however, I question Weber's modernist and cultural evolutionary frame in which he conceives of "more evolved" religions as moving to eliminate sexuality, "the sexual orgy," from religious ceremony (238–239). My discussion of desire as ethics challenges Weber's notion of asceticism, in which he asserts: "rational, ascetic alertness, self-control, and methodical planning of life *are seriously threatened by the peculiar irrationality of the sexual act,* which is ultimately and uniquely *unsusceptible to rational organization*" (238; emphasis added). By contrast, I regard sexual desire, in the case of my participants' practices, not as undoing rationality but as providing the very ethical grounds for governing one's life.

15. How African women become vulnerable to HIV infection through "transactional sex" has received significant attention from academics and policy makers. By 2004 local multimedia campaigns in Namibia began to portray the danger of "sugar daddy" relationships on billboards, posters, and in small television spots. Today such relationships are commonly referred to in daily discussions of sexual politics in the townships. But only more recently these relationships have become associated with African lesbians in the emerging HIV prevention discourse on WSW or "women-who-have-sex-with-women." In 2007 the Dutch humanitarian foundation Schorer expanded its global health development program known as the Prevention Initiative for Sexual Minorities (PRISM) to include Botswana, Zimbabwe, Namibia, and South

Africa. I was involved in the development of the community-based methodology for Namibia's needs assessment sponsored by Schorer. At a planning workshop with TRP, two Schorer representatives defined lesbians and WSW as "closeted women in heterosexual settings," in order to identify them as a vulnerable group that needed to be targeted for the needs assessment. Representatives from the Netherlands and various African sexual minority rights organizations concluded that because of economic dependence and stigma, WSW frequently came to be in unwanted heterosexual relationships.

16. Unlike North American drag performers, who generally tuck or strap down their genitals to emulate a female body, many of the drag queens in Katutura and Khomasdal left their genitals bulging during their performances. This show of gender-sexual ambiguity created considerable humor and enjoyment for the audience.

17. This latter point follows on Mark Johnson's somewhat parallel discussion of how same-sex sexual identities and practices "unfurl across . . . national boundaries and borders" in the Philippines (1998, 209). See also Boellstorff's (2005, 211) sophisticated discussion of the geographic dispersions of same-sex sexual subjectivities in Indonesia.

## 3. Remaking Female Citizenship

1. At the time I conducted my research, Namibia held one of the highest Gini coefficients in the world. The Gini coefficient is a measure of inequality in terms of wage distribution; however, it should be noted that this economic indicator has not been measured for every country.

2. I am most grateful to Peter Geschiere for reminding me of this point.

3. The former colonial regime segregated Windhoek's outlying townships along the similar ethnic/racial lines they used to divide the "traditional homelands" or "bantustans." While Katutura was designated as a "black township," Khomasdal was defined as the "colored township" for lighter-skinned people of "interracial" descent.

4. This drug, which contains high levels of methaqualone, was originally used as a legal sleeping tablet. Now, as a recreational drug, Mandrax is frequently smoked with cannabis.

5. This contradiction recalls Bourdieu's (2001) notion of a "being perceived."

6. Elsewhere I have written about how regional human rights discourses commonly attribute sex between African lesbians and men to "corrective rape" or other overt forms of sexual violence (Lorway 2010).

7. In postcolonial Namibia the legacy of pro-natalist ideologies survives in the rhetoric of the SWAPO Women's Council and, as a result, abortion continues to be illegal and unsupported by major factions of the women's movement in Namibia.

## 4. The Naturalization of Intimate Partner Violence

1. Separating my focus between masculine females and feminine males is not intended to reinforce a problematic male-female dichotomy that ignores calls by feminists and queer theorists to think beyond biological reifications of sex. It certainly would be possible to discuss how intersecting notions of femininity and masculinity shape participants' practices of the self, regardless of local assignments of anatomical sex. Nevertheless, my approach aims to more clearly illuminate how LGBT rights discourses create different conflicts as well as possibilities for pursing ideas of freedom as they attach to anatomical notions of sex.

2. Regarded as a highly progressive law, the *Combating of Rape Act 8 of 2000* moves away from notions of consent that often place the victim "on trial"; instead, it covers a range of coercive sexual acts in an effort to be more protective of the rape survivor (Hubbard 2007, 104).

Heated parliamentary debates surrounding this law reform, however, pivoted on the question of marital rape and men's "right" to have sex with their wives. Some parliamentarians "doubted that rape could occur within marriage" (105). Opposition expressed toward the passing of the *Combatting of Domestic Violence Act 4 of 2003* built on this idea of "the denial of sex" as a violation of men's sexual rights.

3. According to Max Hamata, SFF commander Sacharia Asheela reprimanded the SFF officers by saying, "I told you not to assault or touch anybody. Who told you to take these men's earrings? . . . It should not be repeated again." In a later press release, Asheela said the SFF operations complied with the president's order "to help fight crime and let our citizens walk freely without fear of criminals . . . not to take off people's earrings" (Hamata 2001). Dr. Ndeutala Angolo, special aide to the president, maintained in a press statement that she was unaware of any presidential order to remove men's earrings. Legal Assistance Centre director Clement Daniels said he thought the SFF members' behavior was triggered by Nujoma's recent calls to arrest gays and lesbians. "What kind of interpretation do you expect from illiterate Special Field Force members?" he said.

4. Namibian social justice activist Henrietta Rispel explained to me that this announcement was made shortly before the SWAPO presidential candidate election in 2004 to discourage Hidipo Hamutenya, a well-liked SWAPO minister, from joining the CoD party. It should also be noted the CoD MP, Rosa Namises, has been one of the most vocal and politically active female MPs to have spoken out against SWAPO's homophobic rhetoric and to have challenged SWAPO's resistance to the domestic violence bill when it was first tabled. Having met Rosa Namises at several events sponsored by Sister Namibia, I have also learned directly that she publicly supports Sister Namibia's political platforms.

5. However, local suspicions of Nujoma as Pohamba's puppeteer abounded.

6. Although the election of Pohamba did see a marked decrease in political hate speeches made by Pohamba, according to a press release from the Namibia's National Society for Human Rights (NSHR), former president Sam Nujoma referred to the NSHR director Phil ya Nangolo as a homosexual at the Mandume Primary School in Katutura East Constituency on Saturday, July 29, 2006.

7. Ashley Currier (2012, 126) also documents the introduction of TRP's video project, which screened various Western films such as *Priscilla, Queen of the Desert* in rural towns, asking the participants to relate the film's subject matter to their own lives.

8. Keetmanshoop is a vibrant hub for South African truck drivers and other foreign national migrant laborers.

9. One evening, after Sal finished taking the lead in a "Nama-style" long-arm dance with a woman, he smoothly shifted to being led by a married man who, in front of his wife, asked him to dance.

10. The notion that it was safer to have sex with moffies changed drastically in 2005, when Deputy Minister of Home Affairs Mushelenga spoke in the north during a Hero's Day celebration, a commemoration ceremony for soldiers who died fighting for liberation. Mushelenga publicly declared that gays were responsible for the HIV epidemic in Namibia. There were two media versions that were constructed out of this statement: the *Namibian* claimed that "the AIDS epidemic started in gay communities and spread to Namibia," while the Afrikaans newspaper *die Republikein* reported Mushelenga as having said that "gay Namibians were responsible for spreading HIV within the country."

11. This reluctance to get tested is by no means peculiar to feminine males in Namibia.

12. This practice complicates the picture of gender power dynamics drawn by Wojcicki (2002b) in her discussion of women's susceptibility to violence and powerlessness to negotiate safer sex when accepting a drink from a man, having "drank his money."

13. For more on the red tide, see "2. Namibia: Oyster Farmers Fight Red Tide (The Namibian, New Era)" Farm Radio Weekly, April 28, 2008, http://weekly.farmradio.org/2008/04/28/2-namibia-oyster-farmers-fight-red-tide-the-namibian-new-era. This rare occurrence takes place only when a warm ocean current breeds red-colored algae, which rapidly fills the water with toxins. Choking the oxygen from the water, the toxins force fish and other aquatic life to surface, gasping for air and washing in with the tide.

14. There were, of course, many smaller shebeens and clubs known to welcome gays and lesbians (such as Casablanca, Club Thriller, Sparks, and Club Remix) at different times. In 2008, the club Donna Bella was regarded as Windhoek's main gay club; however, most of the participants in my interviews considered it to be a "club for whites" and tended not to frequent it, except during special TRP events.

15. The emergence of sexual life I describe in this section somewhat parallels Vinh-Kim Nguyen's description of "sexual modernity" in Abidjan (2005, 248). However, "homosocial" culture in Katutura Township during the 1970s and 1980s took shape around the social networks in bachelor compounds. There was not the same kind of cosmopolitan culture around which homosocialities formed.

## 5. Thinking through the Foreigner Fetish

1. Field notes, November 2007.

2. This example bears some similarity with Frantz Fanon's portrayal of a young black Antillean schoolboy who, he maintains, misidentified with colonial cultural origins by "believing he was French" and adopting a "white man's attitude. But he is a Negro. That he will learn once he goes to Europe; when he hears 'negroes' mentioned he will recognize that the word includes himself" (1967, 147–148). However, unlike Fanon, I do not regard this case as a solidifying form of cultural imperialism or neocolonialism, what Fanon has referred to as "the formation and crystallization of an attitude and a way of thinking and seeing that are essentially [Western]" (148), for gay research participants' understandings of eroticism were very much mediated by local forms of knowledge, even though they shared a sense of solidarity with global gay and lesbian communities.

3. "Namibia," Umfulana, http://www.umfulana.com/namibia/country-people/regions/himba/625.

4. I am grateful to Stephen Scholtz for showing me these materials in his personal archival collection.

5. I learned this in a discussion with Carol Millward, former office administrator of the Rainbow Project of Namibia, September 2007.

## Conclusion

1. I have found the following passage particularly helpful for understanding the contradictions I was observing in my everyday ethnographic work: "Postmodern politics definitely has the merit that it 'repoliticizes' a series of domains previously considered 'apolitical' or 'private'; the fact remains that it does not repoliticize capitalism, because the very notion and form of the 'political' within which it operates is grounded in the depoliticization of the economy. If we are to play the postmodern game of plurality of political subjectivizations, it is formally necessary that we do not ask certain questions (about how to subvert capitalism as such, about the constitutive limits of political democracy and/or the democratic state as such)" (Žižek 2000, 99–100).

# Bibliography

Achmat, Zackie. 1993. "'Apostles of Civilised Vice': 'Immoral Practices' and 'Unnatural Vice' in South African Prisons and Compounds, 1890–1920." *Social Dynamics* 19 (2): 92–110.

Adams, Vincanne, and Stacey Leigh Pigg, eds. 2005. "Introduction: The Moral Object of Sex." In *Sex in Development: Science, Development, and Sexuality in Global Perspective*, 1–38. Durham, N.C.: Duke University Press.

African Development Bank. 2009. Namibia: Country Strategy Report (2009–2013). http://www.afdb.org/fileadmin/uploads/afdb/Documents/Project-and-Operations/Namibia-CSP-OPs%20COM%206.pdf.

Alexander, M. Jacqui. 1994. "Not Just (Any) Body Can Be a Citizen: The Politics of Law, Sexuality and Postcoloniality in Trinidad and Tobago and the Bahamas." *Feminist Review* 48 (1): 5–23.

———. 2006. *Pedagogies of Crossing: Meditations on Feminism, Sexual Politics, Memory, and the Sacred.* Durham, N.C.: Duke University Press.

Altman, Dennis. 2002. *Global Sex.* Chicago: University of Chicago Press.

Amupadhi, T. 2002a. "'You Can Keep Your Aid,' Nujoma Tells West." *Namibian,* September 3. Available at http://www.namibian.com.na/archive19982004/2002/August/news/02805D4E9F.html?highlight=nujoma+you+can+keep+your+aid.

———. 2002b. "Nujoma Makes Headlines across Globe." *Namibian,* September 4. Available at http://www.namibian.com.na/archive19982004/2002/September/national/0280AB8382.html?highlight=nujoma+makes+headlines+across+the+globe.

Angula, Conrad. 2002. "Women Most Affected by HIV-AIDS—First Lady." *Namibian,* March 11. Available at http://www.namibian.com.na/archive19982004/2002/March/news/024A2A909E.html?highlight=first+lady+womens+day+aids.

Angula, Helmut. 2002. *Parliamentary Session Transcript: Speech Expressed in Opposition to Proposed Domestic Violence Bill.* Windhoek: Parliamentary Library, October 30.

Anonymous. 1995. "Sister Roars Back on Gay Rights." *Namibian,* October 10, 3.

Antze, Paul, and Michael Lambek, eds. 1996. "Introduction: Forecasting Memory." In *Tense Past: Cultural Essays in Trauma and Memory,* xi–xxxviii. New York: Routledge.

Appadurai, Arjun. 1996. *Modernity at Large: Cultural Dimensions of Globalization.* Minneapolis: University of Minnesota Press.

———. 2001. "Grassroots Globalization and the Research Imagination." In *Globalization,* 1–21. Durham, N.C.: Duke University Press.

Awondo, Patrick, Peter Geschiere, and Graeme Reid. 2012. "Homophobic Africa? Toward a More Nuanced View." *African Studies Review* 55 (03): 145–168.

Becker, Heike. 2000. "'Becoming Men': Masculine Identities among Young Men in Two Namibian Locations." *Development Update* 3 (2): 54–70.

———. 2007. "Making Tradition: A Historical Perspective on Gender in Namibia." In *Unravelling Taboos,* edited by Suzanne LaFont and Dianne Hubbard, 22–38. Windhoek: Legal Assistance Centre.

Bleys, Rudi. 1995. *The Geography of Perversion: Male-Male Sexual Behavior outside the West and the Ethnographic Imagination, 1750–1918.* New York: New York University Press.

Boellstorff, Tom. 2005. *The Gay Archipelago: Sexuality and Nation in Indonesia.* Princeton, N.J.: Princeton University Press.

——. 2009. "Nuri's Testimony: HIV/AIDS in Indonesia and Bare Knowledge." *American Ethnologist* 36 (2): 351–363.

Bourdieu, Pierre. 1990. *The Logic of Practice.* Cambridge, U.K.: Polity Press.

——. 2001. *Masculine Domination.* Stanford, Calif.: Stanford University Press.

Burawoy, Michael, ed. 2000. *Global Ethnography: Forces, Connections, and Imaginations in a Postmodern World.* Berkeley: University of California Press.

Butler, Judith. 1987. *Subjects of Desire: Hegelian Reflections in Twentieth-Century France.* New York: Routledge.

Cage, Ken. 2003. "From Moffietaal to Gayle: The Evolution of a South African Gay Argot." Paper presented at the *International Association for the Study of Sexuality, Culture, and Society,* Johannesburg (Sex and Secrecy Conference), June 22–25.

Cameron, Deborah, and Don Kulick. 2003. *Language and Sexuality.* Cambridge, U.K.: Cambridge University Press.

Castle, Tomi. 2008. "Sexual Citizenship: Articulating Citizenship, Identity, and the Pursuit of the Good Life in Urban Brazil." *Political and Legal Anthropology Review* 31 (1): 118–133.

Central Bureau of Statistics. 2005. *2001 Population and Housing Census: Basic Analysis and Highlights.* Windhoek: National Planning Commission, Republic of Namibia.

Cleaver, Tessa, and Marion Wallace. 1990. *Namibia Women in War.* London: Zed Books.

Comaroff, John L., and Jean Comaroff. 1997. "Postcolonial Politics and Discourses of Democracy in Southern Africa: An Anthropological Reflection on African Political Modernities." *Journal of Anthropological Research* 53 (2): 123–146.

——, eds. 2001. "Millennial Capitalism: First Thoughts on a Second Coming." In *Millennial Capitalism and the Culture of Neoliberalism,*1–56. Durham, N.C.: Duke University Press.

——. 2005. "Naturing the Nation: Aliens, Apocalypse, and the Postcolonial State." In *Sovereign Bodies: Citizens, Migrants, and States in the Postcolonial World,* edited by Thomas Blom Hansen and Finn Stepputat, 120–147. Princeton, N.J.: Princeton University Press.

——. 2009. *Ethnicity, Inc.* Chicago: University of Chicago Press.

Cruikshank, Barbara. 1999. *The Will to Empower: Democratic Citizens and Other Subjects.* Ithaca, N.Y.: Cornell University Press.

Currier, Ashley. 2010. "Political Homophobia in Postcolonial Namibia." *Gender & Society* 24 (1): 110–129.

——. 2012. *Out in Africa: LGBT Organizing in Namibia and South Africa.* Minneapolis: University of Minnesota Press.

Das, Veena, and Renu Addlakha. 2001. "Disability and Domestic Citizenship: Voice, Gender, and the Making of the Subject." *Public Culture* 13 (3): 511–531.

Dave, Naisargi. 2012. *Queer Activism in India: A Story in the Anthropology of Ethics.* Durham, N.C.: Duke University Press.

Dean, Mitchell. 1999. *Governmentality: Power and Rule in Modern Society.* London: Sage.

Deleuze, Gilles, and Felix Guattari. 1983. *Anti-Oedipus: Capitalism and Schizophrenia.* Minneapolis: University of Minnesota Press.

Donham, Donald L. 1998. "Freeing South Africa: The 'Modernization' of Male-Male Sexuality in Soweto." *Cultural Anthropology* 13 (1): 3–21.

Douglas, Mary. 1966. *Purity and Danger: An Analysis of Pollution and Taboo.* New York: Routledge.

Dunton, Chris, and Mai Palmberg. 1996. *Human Rights and Homosexuality in Southern Africa.* Copenhagen: Freemuse.

Eita, J. H., and ve Jordaan, A. C. (2007). "Estimating the Tourism Potential in Namibia." *MPRA Paper,* No. 5788.

Emmett, Tony. 1999. *Popular Resistance and the Roots of Nationalism in Namibia (1915–1966).* Basel, Switzerland: P. Schlettwein.

Epprecht, Marc. 1998. "Good God Almighty, what's this!': Homosexual 'Crime' in Early Colonial Zimbabwe." In Murray and Roscoe, *Boy-Wives and Female Husbands,* 197–221.

———. 2004. *Hungochani: The History of a Dissident Sexuality in Southern Africa.* Montreal: McGill-Queen's University Press.

Falk, Kurt. 1998. "Homosexuality among the Natives of Southwest Africa." Translated by Bradley Rose and Will Roscoe. First published 1925–1926. Reprinted in Murray and Roscoe, *Boy-Wives and Female Husbands.*

Fanon, Frantz. 1967. *Black Skin, White Mask.* New York: Grove Press.

Farmer, Paul. 1996. "On Suffering and Structural Violence: A View from Below." *Daedalus* 125 (1): 261–283.

Ferguson, James. 2006. *Global Shadows: Africa in the Neoliberal World Order.* Durham, N.C.: Duke University Press.

Foucault, Michel. 1978. *The History of Sexuality: An Introduction,* vol. 1. New York: Vintage.

———. 1997. *Foucault's Ethics: Subjectivity and Truth. Essential Works of Foucault, 1954–1984,* vol. 1. New York: New Press.

Gaudio, Rudolf Pell. 2009. *Allah Made Us: Sexual Outlaws in an Islamic African City.* Hoboken, N.J.: Wiley-Blackwell.

Geisler, Gisela G. 2004. *Women and the Remaking of Politics in Southern Africa: Negotiating Autonomy, Incorporation, and Representation.* Uppsala, Sweden: Nordic Africa Institute.

Gevisser, Mark, and Edwin Cameron, eds. 1995. *Defiant Desire: Gay and Lesbian Lives in South Africa.* New York: Routledge.

Gilman, Sander. 1985. *Difference and Pathology Stereotypes of Sexuality, Race, and Madness.* Ithaca, N.Y.: Cornell University Press.

Godelier, Maurice. 1999. *The Enigma of the Gift.* Chicago: University of Chicago Press.

Goering, Laurie. 2004. "Africa's Gays Persecuted as Cause of Ills." *Chicago Tribune,* June 9. Available at http://www.glapn.org/sodomylaws/world/wonews027.htm.

Goldstein, Donna. 2001. "Microenterprise Training Programs, Neo-Liberal Common Sense, and the Discourses of Self-Esteem." In *The New Poverty Studies: The Ethnography of Politics, Policy and Impoverished People in the United States,* edited by Judith Goode and Jeff Maskovsky, 236–272. New York: New York University Press.

Gordon, Colin. 1991. "Governmental Rationality: An Introduction." In *The Foucault Effect: Studies in Governmentality,* edited by Graham Burchell, Colin Gordon, and Peter Miller, 1–51. Hemel Hampstead, England: Harvester Wheatsheaf.

Hallman, K. 2004. *Socioeconomic Disadvantage and Unsafe Sexual Behaviors among Young Women and Men in South Africa.* New York: Population Council. (Policy Research Division Working Paper No. 190.) Available at http://www.popcouncil.org/pdfs/wp/190.pdf.

Hamata, Max. 2001. "SFF Launches Earring 'Purge.'" *Namibian,* May 2.

Hancox, Toni. 2000. *Constitutional and Human Rights Unit Annual Report.* Windhoek: Legal Assistance Centre.

Harries, Patrick. 1994. *Work, Culture, and Identity: Migrant Laborers in Mozambique and South Africa, c. 1860–1910.* Portsmouth, N.H.: Heinemann.

Hilgers, Mathieu. 2012. "The Historicity of the Neoliberal State." *Social Anthropology* 20 (1): 80–94.

Hiltunen, Maija, 1993. *Good Magic in Ovambo.* Transactions 33/The Finnish Anthropological Society. Helsinki, Finland: Suomen Antropologinen Seura.

Hoad, Neville. 2007. *African Intimacies: Race, Homosexuality, and Globalization.* Minneapolis: University of Minnesota Press.

Hubbard, Dianne. 2007. "Gender and Sexuality: The Law Reform Landscape." In *Unravelling Taboos,* edited by Suzanne LaFont and Dianne Hubbard, 99–128. Windhoek: Legal Assistance Centre.

Hunter, Mark. 2010. *Love in the Time of AIDS: Inequality, Gender, and Rights in South Africa.* Bloomington: Indiana University Press.

Iipinge, Eunice, and Debbie LeBeau. 2005. *Beyond Inequalities: Women in Namibia.* Windhoek: University of Namibia.

International Gay and Lesbian Human Rights Commission (IGLHRC). 2003. *More Than a Name: State-Sponsored Homophobia and Its Consequences in Southern Africa.* New York: IGLHRC.

Isaacks, Madelene, and Ruth Morgan. 2005. "'I Don't Force My Feelings for Other Women, My Feelings Force Me': Same-Sex Sexuality amongst Ovambo Women in Namibia." In Morgan and Wieringa, *Tommy Boys,* 77–120.

Isin, Engin F., ed. 2008. *Recasting the Social in Citizenship.* Toronto: University of Toronto Press.

Jauch, Herbert. 2002. "From Liberation Struggle to Social Partnership? The Challenge of Change for the Namibian Labor Movement." In *Namibia, Society, and Sociology,* edited by V. Winterfeldt, T. Fox, and P. Mufane, 27–37. Windhoek: University of Namibia.

———. 2007. "Between Politics and the Shop Floor: Which Way for Namibia's Labour Movement?" In *Transitions in Namibia: Which Changes for Whom?,* edited by Henning Melber, 50–64. Stockholm: Nordiska Afrikainstitutet.

Jauch, Herbert, Lucy Edwards, and Braam Cupido. 2009. *A Rich Country with Poor People: Inequality in Namibia.* Windhoek: Labour Resource and Research Institute.

———. 2011. "Inequality in Namibia." In *Tearing Us Apart: Inequalities in Southern Africa,* edited by H. Jauch and D. Muchena. 181–255. Johannesburg: Open Society for Southern Arica.

Jewkes, R., K. Dunkleb, M. P. Koss, J. B. Levin, M. Nduna, et al. 2006. "Rape Perpetration by Young, Rural South African Men: Prevalence, Patterns, and Risk Factors." *Social Science & Medicine* 63 (11): 2949–2961.

Johnson, M. 1998. "Global Desirings and Translocal Loves: Transgendering and Same Sex Sexuality in the Southern Philippines." *American Ethnologist* 25 (4): 695–711.

Kapac, Jack. 1998. "Culture/Community/Race: Chinese Gay Men and the Politics of Identity." *Anthropologica* 40 (2): 169–181.

Katjavivi, Peter, Per Frostin, and Kaire Mbuende. 1989. *Church and Liberation in Namibia.* London: Pluto Press.

Khaxas, Elizabeth, and Saskia Wieringa. 2005. "'I Am a Pet Goat, I Will Not Be Slaughtered': Female Masculinity and Femme Strength amongst the Damara in Namibia." In Morgan and Wieringa, *Tommy Boys,* 123–196.

Kinsey, A. C., W. B. Pomeroy, and C. E. Martin. 1948. *Sexual Behavior in the Human Male.* Philadelphia: Saunders.

Kirby, Percival Robson. 1942. "A Secret Musical Instrument: The Ekola of the Ovakuanyama of Ovamboland." *South African Journal of Science* 38: 345–351.

Klerck, Gilton. 2008. "Industrial Relations in Namibia since Independence: Between Neoliberalism and Neo-corporatism?" *Employee Relations* 30 (4): 355–371.

Laclau, Ernesto. 1996. *Emancipation(s).* New York: Verso.

Leclerc-Madlala, S. 2003. "Transactional Sex and the Pursuit of Modernity." *Social Dynamics* 29 (2): 213–233. Available at http://www.healthdev.org/eforums/Editor/assets /acceleratingprevention/Transactional_sex_and_the_pursuit_of_modernity.pdf.

Lorway, Robert. 2006. "Dispelling 'Heterosexual African AIDS' in Namibia: Same-Sex Sexuality in the Township of Katutura." *Culture, Health, and Sexuality* 8 (5): 435–449.

———. 2007. "Breaking a Public Health Silence: HIV Risk and Male-Male Sexual Practices in the Windhoek Urban Area." In *Unravelling Taboos: Gender and Sexuality in Namibia,* edited by Suzanne LaFont and Dianne Hubbard, 276–295.Windhoek: Legal Assistance Centre.

———. 2008a. "Defiant Desire in Namibia: Female Sexual–Gender Transgression and the Making of Political Being." *American Ethnologist* 35 (1): 20–33.

———. 2008b. "'Where Can I Be Deported?' Thinking through the 'Foreigner Fetish' in Namibia." *Medical Anthropology* 27 (1): 70–97.

———. 2009. "Beyond the New Geography of Dissident Gender-Sexual Identity Categories: Masculinities, Homosexualities, and Intimate Partner Violence in Namibia." In *The Fourth Wave: An Assault on Women. Gender, Culture, and HIV in the 21st Century,* edited by Vinh-Kim Nguyen and Jennifer F. Klot, 347–363. New York: Social Science Research Council–UNESCO volume.

Lurie, Peter, Percy C. Hintzen, and Robert A. Lowe. 2004. "Socioeconomic Obstacles to HIV Prevention and Treatment in Developing Countries: The Role of the International Monetary Fund and the World Bank." In *HIV/AIDS in Africa: Beyond Epidemiology,* edited by Ezekiel Kalipeni, Susan Craddock, Joseph R. Oppong, and Jayati Ghosh, 204–212. Malden, Mass.: Blackwell.

Maletsky, Christof. 2001. "Madness 'On the Loose,' Says Nujoma." *Namibian,* April 23, 1.

Mamdani, Mahmood. 1996. *Citizen and Subject: Contemporary Africa and the Legacy of Late Colonialism.* Princeton, N.J.: Princeton University Press.

Manalansan IV, Martin F. 2003.*Global Divas: Filipino Gay Men in the Diaspora.* Durham, N.C.: Duke University Press.

Mansfield, Nick. 2000. *Subjectivity: Theories of the Self from Freud to Haraway.* New York: New York University Press.

Marcus, George. 1995. "Ethnography in/of the World System: The Emergence of Multi-Sited Ethnography." *Annual Review of Anthropology* 24: 95–117.

Marshall, Thomas Humphrey. 1950. *Citizenship and Social Class and Other Essays.* Cambridge, U.K.: Cambridge University Press.

Mbembe, Achille. 2001. *On the Postcolony.* Berkeley: University of California Press.

———. 2005. "Sovereignty as a Form of Expenditure." In *Sovereign Bodies: Citizens, Migrants, and States in the Postcolonial World,* edited by Thomas Blom Hansen and Finn Stepputat, 148–166. Princeton, N.J.: Princeton University Press.

McElhinny, Bonnie. 2001. "Language, Sexuality, and Political Economy." In *Language and Sexuality: Contesting Meaning in Theory and Practice,* edited by Kathryn Campbell-Kibler, Robert J. Podesva, Sarah J. Roberts, and Andrew Wong, 111–134. Stanford, Calif.: CSLI Publications.

McClintock, Anne. 1995. *Imperial Leather: Race, Gender, and Sexuality in the Colonial Contest.* New York: Routledge.

McLean, Hugh, and Linda Ngcobo. 1995. "Abangibhamayo bathi ngimnandi (Those who fuck me say I'm tasty): Gay Sexuality in Reef Townships." In *Defiant Desire: Gay and Lesbian Lives in South Africa,* edited by Mark Gevisser and Edwin Cameron, 158–185. New York: Routledge.

Melber, Henning. 2003. "Limits to Liberation: An Introduction to Namibia's Postcolonial Political Culture." In *Reexamining Liberation in Namibia: Political Culture since Independence,* 9–24. Uppsala: Nordiska Afrikainstitutet.

Menges, Werner. 2001. "Rights Group Fears Effects of President's Statements." *Namibian,* April 6, 5.

Ministry of Health and Social Services (MoHSS). 2009. *Report of the 2008 National HIV Sentinel Survey.* Windhoek, Namibia.

Moodie, Dunbar T., and Vivienne Ndatshe. 1994. *Going for Gold: Men, Mines, and Migration.* Berkeley: University of California Press.

Moore, Henrietta. 2007. *The Subject of Anthropology: Symbolism and Psychoanalysis.* Cambridge, Mass.: Polity Press.

Morgan, Ruth, and Saskia Wieringa. 2005. *Tommy Boys, Lesbian Men, and Ancestral Wives.* Johannesburg: Jacana Media.

Morrell, Robert. 1998. "Of Boys and Men: Masculinity and Gender in Southern African Studies." *Journal of Southern African Studies* 24 (4): 605–630.

Murray, Stephen O., and Will Roscoe, eds. 1998. *Boy-Wives and Female Husbands: Studies in African Homosexualities.* New York: Palgrave.

Mwilima, Fred. 1995. "Homosexuality Is Like Cancer or the AIDS Scourge." *New Era*, October 5–11: 2.

*Namibian.* 2000. "Jerry in New Anti-Gay Rant." *Namibian*, October 2.

Nathanael, Keshii Pelao. 2002. *A Journey to Exile: The Story of a Namibian Freedom Fighter.* Aberystwyth, U.K.: Sosiumi Press.

Nguyen, Vinh-Kim. 2005. "Uses and Pleasures: Sexual Modernity, HIV/AIDS, and Confessional Technologies in a West African Metropolis." In *Sex in Development: Science, Sexuality, and Morality in Global Perspective,* edited by Vincanne Adams and Stacy Leigh Pigg, 245–267. Durham, N.C.: Duke University Press.

———. 2010. *The Republic of Therapy: Triage and Sovereignty in West Africa's Time of AIDS.* Durham, N.C.: Duke University Press.

Niehaus, Isak A. 2002. "Renegotiating Masculinity in the South African Lowveld: Narratives of Male-Male Sex in Labor Compounds and in Prisons." *African Studies* 61 (1): 77–97.

O'Neill, Craig, and Kathleen Ritter. 1992. *Coming Out Within: Stages of Spiritual Awakening for Lesbians and Gay Men.* New York: HarperCollins.

Østreng, Dorte. 1997. *Domestic Workers' Daily Lives in Post-apartheid Namibia.* Windhoek: Namibian Economic Policy Research Unit.

Palmberg, Mai. 1998. "Emerging Visibility of Gays and Lesbians in Southern Africa: Contrasting Contexts." In *The Global Emergence of Gay and Lesbian Politics: National Imprints of a Worldwide Movement,* edited by Barry D. Adam, Jan Willem Duyvendak, and André Krouwel, 266–292. Philadelphia: Temple University Press.

Parker, Richard G. 2001. "Sexuality, Culture, and Power in HIV/AIDS Research." *Annual Review of Anthropology* (30): 163–179.

Pendleton, Wade. 1993. *Katutura: A Place Where We Stay.* Western Cape, South Africa: Gamsberg Macmillan.

Phillips, Oliver. 1997. "Zimbabwean Law and the Production of a White Man's Disease." *Social & Legal Studies* 6 (4): 471–491.

Plummer, Ken. 2003. *Intimate Citizenship: Private Decisions and Public Dialogues.* Seattle: University of Washington Press.

Posel, Deborah. 2005. "Sex, Death, and the Fate of the Nation: Reflections on the Politicization of Sexuality in Post-Apartheid South Africa." *Africa-London-International-African-Institute* 75 (2): 125–153.

Puar, Jasbir. 2002. "Circuits of Queer Mobility: Tourism, Travel, and Globalization." *GLQ: A Journal of Lesbian and Gay Studies* 8 (1–2): 101–137.

Rainbow Project, The. 2003. Namibia's Rainbow Project Votes for Change. Interview with the Press (Behind the Mask). September 17. Available at http://www.gmax.co.za/look/09/17-MASKnamibia.html

———. 2005. TRP's Response to Anti-sexual Minorities Statement by SWAPO MP Theopo-lina Mushelenga. September 8. Available at http://www.iglhrc.org/content/namibia-african-ngos-respond-statement-namibian-deputy-minister-gays-and-lesbians-betraying.

Ranger, Terence O., and Eric J. Hobsbawm, eds. 1983. *The Invention of Tradition.* Cambridge, U.K.: Cambridge University Press.

Reid, Graeme. 2013. *How to Be a Real Gay: Gay Identities in Small-Town South Africa.* Scotts-ville, South Africa: University of KwaZulu-Natal Press.

Rose, N. 1999. *Powers of Freedom: Reframing Political Thought.* New York: Cambridge University Press.

Rubin, Gayle. 1984. "Thinking Sex: Notes for a Radical Theory of the Politics of Sexuality." In *Pleasure and Danger: Exploring Female Sexuality,* edited by Carol S. Vance, 267–319. London: Routledge and Kegan Paul.

Schoepf, Brooke G. 2001. "International AIDS Research in Anthropology: Taking a Critical Perspective on the Crisis." *Annual Review of Anthropology* (30): 335–361.

Shivute, Oswald. 2001. "Round Up-Gays, Urges Nujoma." *Namibian.* April 2.

———. 2004. "Nujoma Attacks Whites, Neo-Colonialists, CoD." *Namibian May 26.*

Sinfield, Alan. 2004. *On Sexuality and Power.* New York: Columbia University Press.

Sister Namibia. 2000–2001. *LGBT Week 2000: Reaffirming Who We Are.* Windhoek: Sister Namibia.

———. 2001 (April-May). *Litmus for Human Rights.* Windhoek: Sister Namibia.

Soiri, Iina. 1996. *The Radical Motherhood: Namibian Women's Independence Struggle.* Phila-delphia: Coronet Books.

Sökefeld, Martin. 1999. "Debating Self, Identity, and Culture in Anthropology." *Current Anthropology* 40 (4): 417–448.

Spivak, Guyatri. 1990. *Post-Colonial Critic.* London: Routledge.

Spurlin, William. 2001. "Broadening Postcolonial Studies/Decolonizing Queer Studies." In *Postcolonial, Queer: Theoretical Intersections,* edited by John C. Hawley, 185–205. New York: SUNY Press.

Stoler, Ann Laura. 1995. *Race and the Education of Desire: Foucault's History of Sexuality and the Colonial Order of Things.* Durham, N.C.: Duke University Press.

SWAPO (Office of the Secretary for Information and Publicity). 1997. *Press Release* (Official Stance on Homosexuality). January 28.

Swidler, A., and S. C. Walkins. 2007. "Ties of Dependence: AIDS and Transactional Sex in Malawi." *Studies in Family Planning* 38 (3): 147–162.

Talavera, Philippe. 2002. *Challenging the Namibian Perception of Sexuality: A Case Study of Ovahimba and Ovaherero Models in Kune North in an HIV/AIDS Context.* Windhoek: Gamsberg Macmillan.

Teunis, Niels. 2001. "Same-Sex Sexuality in Africa: A Case Study from Senegal." *AIDS and Behavior* 5 (2): 173–182.

Vaughan, Megan. 1991. *Curing Their Ills: Colonial Power and African Illness.* Stanford, Calif.: Stanford University Press.

Vigne, Randolph. 1987. "SWAPO of Namibia: A Movement in Exile." *Third World Quarterly* 9 (1): 85–107.

Walker, L. E. 1979. *The Battered Woman.* New York: Harper and Row.

Wallace, Marion. 2002. *Health, Power, and Politics in Windhoek.* Basel, Switzerland: P. Sch-lettwein.

Wax, Emily. 2005. "Namibia Chips Away at African Taboos on Homosexuality." *Washington Post,* October 24. Available at http://www.washingtonpost.com/wp-dyn/content/article/2005/10/23/AR2005102301163.html.

Weber, Max. 1963. *The Sociology of Religion*. Translated by Ephraim Fischoff. Boston: Beacon Press.

Wekker, Gloria. 2006. *The Politics of Passion: Women's Sexual Culture in the Afro-Surinamese Diaspora*. New York: Columbia University Press.

Wojcicki, J. M. 2002a. "Commercial Sex Work or Ukuphanda? Sex for Money Exchange in Soweto and Hammanskraal Area, South Africa." *Culture, Medicine, and Psychiatry* 26: 339–370.

———. 2002b. "'She drank his money': Survival Sex and the Problem of Violence in Taverns in Gauteng Province, South Africa." *Medical Anthropology Quarterly* 16 (3): 267–293.

Xoagub, Francis. 1999. "SWC Unleashes Salvo at Women's Manifesto." *Namibian*, October 7.

Žižek, Slavoj. 2000. "Class Struggle or Postmodernism? Yes, Please!" In *Contingency, Hegemony, Universality: Contemporary Dialogues on the Left*, edited by Judith P. Butler, Ernest Laclau, and Slavoj Žižek, 90–135. New York: Verso Books.

## Primary Archival Documents Cited

Act No. 5 of 1927; Section 1–7: to prohibit illicit intercourse between European and Natives and other Acts in Relation thereto. (Windhoek Parliamentary Library) Government Notice 26/1925 dated 17/1/1925: *Sanitation and Housing*. (National Archives of Namibia, Windhoek).

Great Britain. Union of South Africa. "Report on the Natives of South-West Africa and Their Treatment by Germany." Prepared in the Administrator's Office, Windhoek, South West Africa, January 1918. Available at http://www.lac.org.na/projects/lead/Pdf /nativesSWA_germans.pdf.

Labour Act 1992. Dated March 13, 1992. Government Gazette: April 8, 1992, No. 388. Available at http://www.superiorcourts.org.na/high/docs/LabAct1992.pdf.

Union of South Africa. Immorality Act, Act No. 5 of 1927. http://www.disa.ukzn.ac.za/index .php?option=com_displaydc&recordID=leg19270327.028.020.005.

### *Archives of the Magistrate of Luderitz (LLU)*

LLU 1/1/7: 311. Crime of Sodomy. *Rex de Kroon versus Dwasbsam No. 949 and Standato No. 2522*. May 20, 1927. National Archives of Namibia, Windhoek.

LLU 1/1/5: 111. Crime of Sodomy. *Rex de Kroon versus Petrus*. Lüderitz. June 1923. National Archives of Namibia, Windhoek.

### *Supreme Court Windhoek (SCW)*

SCW 1/1/16: 10 Crime of Sodomy. *Rex de Kroon versus Wilhelm Leichert*. April 28, 1924. National Archives of Namibia, Windhoek.

SCW 1/1/2. Crime of Sodomy and Assault. *King versus Hermann Schneidenberger* (sodomy trial). Grootfontein. September 22, 1920. National Archives of Namibia, Windhoek.

# Index

ROBERT LORWAY is Assistant Professor of Community Health Sciences at the University of Manitoba where he holds a New Investigator Award from the Canadian Institutes of Health Research.